Bravery
in
Battle

Bravery in Battle

Stories from the Front Line

DAVID ESHEL

ARMS AND
ARMOUR

Arms and Armour Press
An Imprint of the Cassell Group
Wellington House, 125 Strand, London WC2R 0BB

Distributed in the USA by Sterling Publishing Co.
Inc., 387 Park Avenue South, New York,
NY 10016-8810.

British Library Cataloguing-in-Publication Data:
a catalogue record for this book is available from
the British Library

ISBN 1-85409-338-X

Designed and edited by DAG Publications Ltd.
Designed by David Gibbons; layout by Anthony A.
Evans; edited by Gerald Napier; indexed by John
Gilbert; printed and bound in Great Britain by
Creative Print and Design (Wales), Ebbw Vale.

CONTENTS

CONTENTS

THE CONQUEST OF FEAR

'I saw the thing coming at me. It looked like a wobbling, wavering ball of fire. Suddenly, as I ducked into the commander's turret, there was a terrific bang. The tank stopped in its tracks and I lost my balance, cracking my head against the optics. Everything went bright red. The turret front became a searing hot mixture of molten steel. As if in a dream I heard the loader, Danny, yelling at me through the intercom. As I pulled myself up, my arm touched the red hot steel and I smelt my own flesh burn! Before the pain set in, nausea hit me; then I must have fainted. But not for long – I wanted to get out of that blazing steel coffin! Pulling wildly at the straps of my tanker's helmet, unable to find the control box to disconnect the radio plug, I pushed myself up through the loader's hatch – just in time to watch his legs disappear from view. I looked down and saw the gunner's position in a complete shambles, the gunner lying prone backwards with his eyes open wide – he must have died instantly. There was not a moment to lose if I was to live! With my last bit of strength I pulled myself out of the hatch and fell gasping onto the engine deck.

'Nearby I saw the war going on. Harman's tank was blazing only twenty metres away and, on the hilltop, another Patton tank had just been hit, some of the crew bailing out as it exploded in a ball of fire. I watched this scene as detached as if I was watching a war movie, as if it did not concern me – then something hot rudely woke me from my daydream. I was on fire myself! I rolled down from the blazing engine deck onto the ground below, soft sand welcoming me as I frantically tried to unzip my overalls with my good arm, scooping sand onto the painful spots on my body. The overall was in shreds – mostly burned away. The pain increased; it was almost unbearable now. Suddenly the earth erupted as the tank's ammunition exploded; the turret flew off, leaving a large fireball where it had been. I was shocked, frozen with fear, but then I tried to crawl away from that ghastly scene, repeating to myself loudly: "I am strong and I am going to survive. I must live!" I remembered that half of our company was in support on the hill way back and tried to get my bearings to crawl in the right direction. The last thing that I remember is someone calling my name. I tried to answer – my head became heavy and the world turned black....'

This vivid description by a young Israeli tank commander who survived his terrible ordeal gives some idea of what tank fighting is about. There is no glamour, not much heroics, but lots of blood, sweat (literally) and toil in fighting from a tank hull enclosed by cold steel which can become burning hot within seconds – a death trap for those huddled in its cramped interior, surrounded by lethal ammunition which could explode within seconds, burning all in its way. It needs a lot of courage to enter into such a vehicle and perform one's duty in combat.

Fear is common to all in time of war. It is there all the time; before going into action it is a nagging feeling that follows you around everywhere you go, and most soldiers, regardless of their rank, have such feelings at one time or another. It is the conquest of that fear that is the real heroism. Once in action, you are too busy to worry about your feelings; you act instinctively as you are trained. When the shooting starts, adrenalin is released into your blood stream, filling you with energy. If you are a commander you are responsible for your men and this responsibility drives any personal feelings away. If you are an ordinary fighting man, the fellowship factor takes over, and this is the reason why so many fighting men sacrifice their own lives to rescue their comrades under fire.

There is a difference between soldiers on the ground and in the air. Since man began to fly, the fear of death has haunted every airman. Fear is the inevitable companion of the flyer. It never leaves him, from mission briefing until his return to mother earth. But it is the conquest of that fear that sets the flying man apart from other mortals. Those on the ground are usually surrounded by others, normally with their commanders in sight, or at least in the vicinity, for guidance. The action is prolonged – it can last for hours, days, or even weeks. The noise of battle, the suffocation, the dust and the constant fatigue dull the senses, so that fear is just one more reason for misery. Moreover, the long periods of monotonous training and the seemingly endless waiting about actually make soldiers long for combat so that they get it over with. The release of tension is like the uncoiling of a spring.

In the air, though, men are on their own. They have no leader close by; once in action, it is every man for himself. Worse, the airman is thrown into battle abruptly; he leaves clean, orderly surroundings at his air base and, after a relatively short time, he suddenly faces death – in a barrage of fire, often over a hostile locale with inhabitants who would have no mercy if his plane was hit and he managed to eject. The terrors of a dogfight, where violent death lurks everywhere, or the slower agony of a bomber crew twisting and turning to escape attacking fighters, are difficult for the layman to imagine. If he survives that particular mission, the airman goes home, only to face death once again the next day, or the day after that.

Men grow old quickly in battle. Even if they still appear young and vigorous, in their glamorous uniforms and sporting the coveted wings or medals, you see the true story if you look into their tortured eyes. Young men living through combat find it extremely hard to readjust to normality, even if they do survive their long and hazardous ordeals. Some never do. Their experiences haunt them until they die.

The stories that follow in this book describe human courage far beyond the call of duty. These are deeds of dedication and bravery which no cynic can debunk or erase. I hope that this book will serve as a small tribute to those who died – and to those who lived to tell their tale.

CHAPTER ONE

OMDURMAN: CHARGING THE KHALIFA

At the end of the nineteenth century, a major focus of British interest was Egypt, with particular emphasis on the River Nile. Britain's strategic goal here was to safeguard her lifeline to the Empire: the newly built Suez Canal. One hotly disputed issue was the headwaters of the Nile, a river which, since time immemorial, has guaranteed survival to the millions of people living along its banks, mainly Egyptians and Sudanese, who, without its resources, could not exist.

The towns of Khartoum and Omdurman are situated at the confluence of the Blue and White Niles and were thus of primary interest to the world powers at that time. In 1884 General Charles Gordon was sent to Khartoum with orders to evacuate the army and civilians from the country threatened to be overwhelmed by the revolt led by Mohammed Ahmad, the Mahdi, a fanatical Moslem and self-styled 'Messiah'. Gordon was already famous for his daring exploits as a young officer in the Chinese wars and later for his achievements in the Sudan where in the 1870s he had been given the task of suppressing the notorious slave trade and re-establishing some law and order throughout the lands. Gordon arrived at Khartoum to face an impossible situation. A vast army, led by the Mahdi, a genius at desert warfare, soon had Khartoum besieged. Gordon's courageous stand and his dramatic death at the hands of the dervishes who stormed his palace one fateful morning in

January 1885 has become a symbol in military history for great courage combined with political stupidity. But the man had become a legend and the word 'Khartoum' a symbolic thorn in the flesh to every Briton so that, when a few years later, a dispute broke out between Britain and France over the control of the Upper Nile, the Sudan became an emotional issue as well as a strategic one.

Since the death of Gordon, the dervishes totally controlled the Sudan; the Mahdi himself was dead but his successor, the Khalifa Abdulla, kept his domain in a tight grip. An ambitious man, his aspirations reached towards Abyssinia and even Egypt, and the British grew extremely concerned. Something had to be done, and quickly. The man chosen to lead the new expedition into the Sudan, in 1896, was an extraordinary officer, perfectly suited for the job – Major General Sir Herbert Kitchener, Sirdar (commander) of the British trained and led Egyptian Army. A former Royal Engineer, he had already gained a great reputation as a military organiser. Both feared and admired, thorough, dispassionate and of a machine-like efficiency, Kitchener was the very man to avenge Gordon (also a former Royal Engineer), and was determined to do so.

The reconquest of the Sudan would not be easy, however. The harsh desert conditions presented a challenge to Kitchener's army, but he left nothing to chance. The expedition was painstakingly planned and well directed. Supply being the chief problem, Kitchener built a military railway through some thousand kilometres of arid desert land, so that it took nearly two years for Kitchener's force to reach the outskirts of Khartoum. During the methodical expedition, some sharp battles were fought, one at Hafir on 19 September 1896 and another at Atbara Fort on 8 April 1898 against furious opposition; nevertheless, these vital points were captured and the slow, steady progress went on.

Meanwhile the Khalifa concentrated his efforts on the defence of Khartoum and Omdurman, which he was certain were Kitchener's true objectives. He had a force of over 40,000 including a highly effective and well-armed force of riflemen, and Baggara horsemen. The Khalifa's forces outnumbered Kitchener's nearly threefold – but it would be modern military machinery and not weight of numbers that would decide the battle for Khartoum.

The total strength of the British Expeditionary Force amounted to 8,000 British and 17,000 Egyptian soldiers, with 44 guns, 20 Maxim machine guns, 36 ship-mounted guns and 24 machine guns mounted on river boats. The Hiram Maxim machine gun was an American invention.

Here on the Nile it made its battle debut, and it proved an extremely lethal weapon. Here, too, the British fought for the first time in Africa in khaki, a welcome change from the combat dress which, although colourful, had proved uncomfortable and made them easy marks for their enemies. Another improvement was the Magazine Lee Metford service rifle, using smokeless ammunition, which did away once and for all with the old problem of smoke after each volley. Also present was a flotilla of modern gunboats which had moved up the river parallel with the advancing forces and was now coming within range of the objective, where its lethal, highly accurate guns could be brought into play.

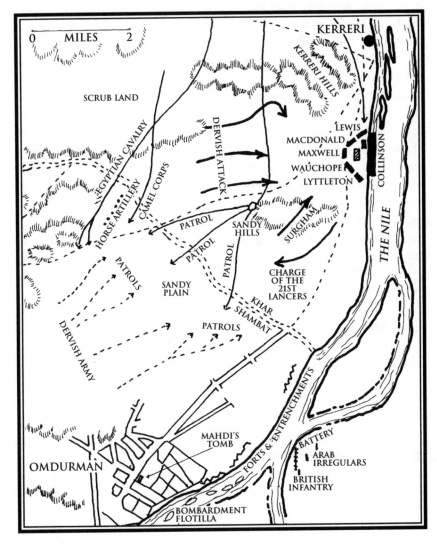

What the dervish troops lacked, however, in modern weapons they made up for with motivation and courage. And the Khalifa was still very much in control, despite the reverses he had suffered from Kitchener's forces as they advanced along the Nile. Still, British Intelligence, under the command of the brilliant Major Reginald Wingate, who had painstakingly constructed an effective network of agents throughout the dervish-ruled Sudan, estimated that the Khalifa stood little chance against Kitchener's modern weapons.

The Khalifa did not agree: totally unversed in modern military thinking, he thought that if he fought the British at Omdurman, backed by his own base, he would have the upper hand, since Kitchener's supply lines would be stretched to the limit. But the British general had already thought of that and not until he had built his railhead as far as Berber did he accept the Khalifa's challenge. By this time, two years after he had begun his dogged advance, Kitchener had at his disposal twice the strength and material with which he had started.

Nothing like the Battle of Omdurman will ever be fought again. It was the last in a long line of spectacular campaigns where the sight of colourful uniforms, the fluttering of banners, the sensation of great masses on a battlefield as whole armies marched against each other, all stirred the blood both of combatant and observer. The introduction of weapons of mass destruction has changed all that. Soldiers search for, and are only too glad to find, some cover from the monstrous machines. But, here on the banks of the Nile, one of the last old-fashioned cavalry charges could be seen horses and men galloping in close order, while infantry and spearmen stood erect to face the onslaught, protected only by courage.

The battle that was about to unfold took place on a featureless plain, bare of cover except for some shallow depressions. Some four kilometres due south-west lay a rocky jebel (mount), rising some 80 metres above the desert, which dominated the ground half the way to Omdurman. At a similar distance, but north-west of the river, were the Kerreri Hills, a horn-shaped feature six kilometres wide and running from east to west. Omdurman itself, facing Khartoum on the other side of the Nile, was no more than an array of dilapidated mud houses, but it also housed two extremely important strategic features: it was the headquarters of the Khalifa; from here he had conducted his reign of terror throughout the dervish Empire. The second feature was no less important: here lay the Mahdi's last resting place – a dome shaped tomb which stood out for miles around and, in consequence, became a focal point for the British guns.

To the south of the British position, about two kilometres towards Khartoum, the expeditionary force established a defensive cordon, or zariba, protected by rows of thorn bushes and backing on the west bank of the Nile. On the night of 31 August a great thunderstorm raged through the desert – the sky was lit with great blue flashes of lightning and the crescendo of thunder roared above the heads of the men and their animals. The storm lasted until dawn and torrents of water turned the shallow troughs into seas of mud. But with the dawn the skies cleared and the troops watching up on the Kerreri Hills could see the white dome of the Mahdi's tomb rising above the blurred horizon.

The 21st Lancers, in the British advance guard, were nearest to the river and, as they crested the hills, they could see the white boats of the British flotilla, commanded by Commander Colin Keppel RN, slowly wending their way upstream. Soon the boats began to blast the Khalifa's defences, using 5-inch howitzers which had been landed on the right bank, with the tomb as a ranging mark. The shells crashed into the city, sending the dervishes scattering for cover. The firing was so accurate that some of the shells actually blasted the Mahdi's tomb itself, causing great clouds of dust to rise from the squalid mud houses which surrounded it. Scores of people were seen streaming into the streets, awakened from sleep, while dervish leaders galloped along the narrow alleys, trying to rally their men, while shells exploded at their heels.

Later, while the rest of the Expeditionary Force was organising in the zariba near the village of El Egeiga which sat close to the river, the 21st Lancers and the Khedival squadrons advanced across an open sandy plain towards Jebel Surgham, the dominating black rock which stood six kilometres from Omdurman. All seemed quiet up front, although a long black line, dotted with white spots, could be seen. At first the officers, peering through their binoculars, thought it looked like a zariba of thorn bushes in the distance, but suddenly the line moved forward. It was the enemy, and it was advancing fast, with many horsemen riding on the flanks in front of the black line of foot soldiers. Several British lancers dismounted and engaged at long range with their carbines, at which several of the horsemen were seen to fall. But the enemy kept on coming, and by just before noon the Khalifa's army had advanced to within four kilometres of Jebel Surgham, watched by the British cavalry and the camel corps which withdrew slowly before the moving mass.

The rest of the British and Egyptian infantry had now debouched from the Kerreri Hills and had taken up defensive positions with their backs to the river, where Keppel's gunboats were still firing. A great battle seemed imminent but on this day – 1 September – there was to be no battle. The dervish army halted, fired off their rifles, more for display than use, and then settled down for the night. As darkness came down, both sides camped in the zaribas. No one was in any doubt, however, that the following day would see a crucial battle.

During the night Keppel's gunboats swept the approaches of the British zariba with their searchlights, lighting up the area to thwart dervish attacks, but there were none. But the Khalifa had not been idle. His spies and night patrols had been busy all night, probing the British camp and its environs, and reported back that large scale troop movements were taking place. So sure was the Khalifa of his ability to beat his opponents that, after rallying his men, he decided to attack immediately, in full daylight. He was completely oblivious of the new firepower which his men would have to face. It was a fateful decision, and one that would cost him dear....

The bugles rang out over the British camp long before dawn and the great army rose to face battle on 2 September 1898 – the decisive day in the Battle of Omdurman. Before daylight the British and Egyptian forces were already manoeuvring into battle order to await the Khalifa's expected attack. After initially reconnoitring to the south-west, nine squadrons of Egyptian cavalry, commanded by Colonel Broadwood, and eight companies of the Egyptian Camel Corps under Major Tudway, supported by the Horse Artillery field batteries, trotted out to deploy near the Kerreri Hills, enticing a proportion of the enemy to follow.

A few kilometres to the south, Jebel Surgham, that black brooding hill, could now be seen by all as the morning mist rose from the desert. The rolling plain which led to Omdurman also became slowly visible, but no movement could be seen, except for the white boats of Keppel's flotilla sailing gracefully along the shimmering, silvery waters.

The 21st Lancers, the most junior cavalry regiment of the British force, commanded by Brevet Colonel R. M. Martin, were deployed in probing patrols toward Jebel Surgham. Serving as a young subaltern in the regiment (he had been attached at his own request, from the 4th Hussars) was Lieutenant Winston Churchill who would later describe, in his own incomparable words, the vivid sensation of battle as he lived through it – one of the best eyewitness descriptions of battle ever recorded. Churchill was given the honour by his commander, Major Finn, of leading his troop to reconnoitre the peak. He was just climbing up to the crest when the morning mist lifted, presenting a breathtaking scene to the young lieutenant. As he reined in his horse, he saw an enormous human wave advancing below, coming straight for his position. Thousands upon thousands of them – howling, screaming, and waving their banners. A frantic exchange of heliograph signals resulted in Churchill and his troops being ordered to withdraw – but to remain in contact with the enemy. Under the crackle of musketry they rode down the slope, with the vanguard of the dervishes in hot pursuit, a mere 150 metres away, but the cavalry made it to the safety of the zariba by the skin of their teeth, giving protection to the left flank, close to the river bank.

On a vantage point, General Kitchener was on horseback, the British Union flag flying proudly alongside the banner of Egypt. The general was ready for battle. At last, the time had come to avenge General Gordon; it was for this that he and his great army had come all this long journey under such difficult conditions. The great moment had come.

Now the British in the zariba began to hear the distant sounds of war drums as the Khalifa deployed his army for battle. They streamed out into the desert morning, led by the Khalifa himself – a massive array which spanned more than five kilometres. Some 60,000 men, many of them on horseback, began to swing around Jebel Surgham in a wide sweep. Suddenly, the whole hillside to the south was covered with long lines of men, their blades glittering in the morning sun. Enemy in sight! The call went round the British line at once. An officer patrol hurried off to report to the general, who received the message with his customary grave serenity, and sent his orderlies out to the troops with their orders.

The Khalifa's great black flag could be seen in the midst of a throng of mounted sheikhs and standard bearers. The mullahs intoned chants to inspire their men with a killing frenzy. Then, at about 200 metres, the British line opened up withering rifle fire. The leading ranks of the dervishes were shot away, bodies piling up where they fell. But they kept coming from behind. Each time a banner bearer fell, another came along to pick up the sacred flag from the dead man and raise it high again. The British fired until their rifles and machine gun barrels became too hot to handle; some colder ones were passed from behind to replace them until they cooled. The dervish attack lasted for over two hours until, totally exhausted, their line finally broke and the survivors withdrew, dragging their wounded with them. As the guns fell silent, the battlefield was littered with over ten thousand of the dervish dead. Only the terrifying moaning of the wounded writhing in pain could be heard. But the battle for Omdurman was not over yet; more, and worse, was to come on that fateful day.

On the Kerreri Hills, the cavalry and Camel Corps watched as another part of the Khalifa's army, 20,000 strong, advanced towards them in the plain below. Sparkling in the sun were thousands of glittering spearpoints and sword blades. They were in grave danger of being cut off and Broadwood decided to withdraw back to the zariba. They succeeded, but only after gunfire from the Horse Artillery and two of Keppel's gunboats had driven off the enemy with great loss.

General Kitchener now decided to advance on Omdurman, ten kilometres to the south. He was convinced that the Khalifa's army was already beaten. But the dervish leader still had some 30,000 men hidden behind some rocky hills. The battle for Omdurman would certainly be no picnic. The plan was for Jebel Surgham to be taken first so as to secure the advance. After conferring with Colonel Martin, Kitchener ordered the 21st Lancers to advance and secure the position on the Jebel, pending the main attack on Omdurman. Within two minutes the regiment was riding out; many of the dervish warriors were seen streaming back to their stronghold, and victory seemed within the grasp of the British forces. But the 21st Lancers were in for a big surprise....

As they advanced over the hill, the vanguard, some sixteen strong, stumbled upon what they thought was a small force of dervishes, dismounted, hiding in a shallow creek. But it turned out to be part of a strong force of about 700, still ready to fight. The patrol commander sent word to the colonel, and Martin decided to attack immediately, telling his trumpeter to sound the charge. As the sixteen Lancers were swinging into battle line, the first volley of musket fire crashed into them. Several men were hit and fell from their horses. But the regiment now rode into battle, banners flying proudly as the long line of horses spanned the hill. Yelling at the top of their lungs, the Lancers went into a gallop, going straight for the crouching dervishes...

Suddenly, as they entered the shallow depression, there appeared a mass of men, twelve deep, extending almost the length of the regimental front. Horses and men crashed into each other with terrifying force – the momentum of the cavalry charge carried some of the lancers straight through the dervish line and up to the far side of the slope. Within two minutes some 120 horses and 70 men lay on the ground, cut to pieces, shuddering in the throes of death. dervishes ran around, cutting and stabbing at everything that still moved. But the situation changed when, reaching positions up the slope of the hill, the lancers dismounted and opened up with rifle fire to relieve their trapped comrades fighting for their lives down below. The dervish attack faltered and the survivors withdrew in the direction of the Khalifa's black banner still waving at the top of the hill.

The Victoria Cross was awarded to three members of the 21st Lancers for their conspicuous acts of bravery that day on Jebel Surgham. Captain Paul Kenna saw his comrade, Major Crole-Wyndham riding in the mêlée when a dervish shot his horse from under him by actually pressing the muzzle of his rifle to the horse before firing. The major fell into the midst of a surging, stabbing mob of dervishes when, like some miracle, Captain Kenna appeared and lifted the major on to his own horse. While the major fired around him, the two rode to safety. But once the major was safe, Kenna turned around and went down into the mob again to help another brother officer, Lieutenant Montmorency, who was also surrounded by blood hungry dervishes.

Private Thomas Byrne, himself badly wounded by several sword strokes, went back and rescued Lieutenant Molyneux, his troop leader, who stood alone fighting the mob, totally cut off from his men. Byrne rode straight into the mass and, even though wounded again, took his officer into his saddle.

Lieutenant Nesham had an even more harrowing experience when a dervish scrambled uphill and seized his bridle. Although he struck the man with his sword, he could not prevent him from cutting the reins, and had his right arm nearly severed by a sword stroke. The maddened animal reared up, surged through the mob and carried his half-dead rider up the hill to safety.

Churchill himself had a no less horrifying experience when, swinging his Mauser pistol, he shot two dervishes at point blank range, turned around – and saw another one, a fierce looking figure wearing the colourful robes of an Emir, riding straight at him, swinging his keen-edged sword menacingly, barely missing his throat. But Churchill shot him in a split second and saw him, hanging dead in the stirrups of his black mare, being dragged away.

By this time the bulk of Kitchener's army was on the march towards Omdurman. But yet another surprise was in store for them. As they were about to set off, his most westerly brigade under Colonel Hector MacDonald was attacked by 15,000 of the Khalifa's bodyguard, hitherto concealed in the sandhills, threatening the whole army. With incredible coolness MacDonald rallied his men and with their disciplined fire beat off this and a second even larger force, giving time for the other brigades and the artillery to redeploy to his assistance.

The battle was now truly won and the day ended in the capture of Omdurman, the Khalifa himself escaping on a single mule, just as Kitchener entered the town. The Khalifa's once proud army, which had fought so bravely, dissolved into a rabble of broken-spirited refugees seeking sanctuary in the endless desert. Some time later the Khalifa, once the sole ruler of his own man-made empire, was hunted down and killed by one of his former captives, who had headed an expedition to find him. So ended thirteen years of anarchy and tyranny.

The price was a heavy one. About 10,000 dervishes died in battle and almost twice that number were maimed, many of them to die later in great agony. Kitchener's losses were surprisingly low – 450 casualties of whom the Lancers alone lost 21 killed and 46 wounded, losing a third of their horses in the great charge. But this battle gained them fame as a fighting regiment, a fame which it retains to this day. General Gordon's death was avenged and honour restored to British arms in the Sudan.

CHAPTER TWO

DARING OVER THE DESERT

By 1914 the Turkish Empire, which once had ruled the Middle East from the Adriatic to the Indian Ocean and from Mount Ararat to Tunis, was in decline. Egypt had become the focus of interest since the opening of the Suez Canal in 1869 and Great Britain regarded it as a vital strategic asset to guard its lifeline to the far eastern colonies. When Germany went to war with Britain, one of its first targets was the Suez Canal, which it regarded as Britain's jugular vein. The Germans were already prodding their allies, the Turks, to attack the Suez as early as August 1914, with Bavarian Colonel Kress von Kressenstein and Baron Frankenburg-Proschlitz assisting Djemal Pasha's Fourth Army in an effort to hit Britain where it would hurt most.

But it took the Turks until February 1915 to finalise a plan for Suez. Their attack strategy was ambitious – perhaps too ambitious, in view of the lack of motivation of the Turkish army. Following a gale which had swept through the desert the night before, Captain von

Hagen of the German army crossed over the Suez Canal at 0325 on 3 February, having slid masses of pontoons and rafts into the dark water. His crossing point was Deversoir, which nearly sixty years later, in 1973, the Israelis used as their point to cross the Suez during the Yom Kippur War. The vigilant Indian sentries of the British Army were on the alert, however, and commenced rapid fire, sinking all but three rafts, which reached the opposite bank at Tussum Post, where they were soon swept up by the defenders.

At dawn a general assault was launched on Serapeum, but was defeated by a sharp counter-attack, again by Indian units, supported by naval guns of the French warships stationed on the Bitter Lake. A month after setting out on its expedition, the Turkish Army was back in Beersheba, having failed miserably in its attempt.

While the immediate threat to the canal had been removed, the British were concerned, and Egypt was placed under British martial law and declared a protectorate. In view of this threat to their vital lifeline, they even found troops to man a massive logistical base in Egypt to prepare a plan finally to remove the Turko-German threat to British interests in the Middle East.

In the summer of 1916, following a long period of British inactivity, von Kressenstein convinced his Turkish allies to have another try at the canal, this time without a crossing. The plan now was to occupy the east bank, which would enable them to blockade the canal to Allied traffic. The British were ready, however, and after a series of battles in northern Sinai, the main one being at Romani, von Kressenstein admitted defeat and withdrew his forces to the border of Palestine, opening the gateway for the British to enter – and eventually conquer – Palestine.

While the Palestine Campaign gained most of its fame from the magnificent feats of British and ANZAC horsed cavalry, the role of the newly formed Royal Flying Corps acquired growing importance. Air support was used mainly for reconnaissance at first, as the aircraft had only a limited range. For flying over the desert east of the Canal, a motley collection of aeroplanes had been assembled in Egypt. At the newly established airstrip near Qantara, Captain Massey of the 29th Punjabis had flown out from the Flying School at Sitapur, India with three Maurice Farman pusher aeroplanes. This would form the base for No. 30 Squadron RFC. The French contribution was a number of seaplanes which flew reconnaissance missions from converted freighters located on the Great Bitter Lake.

On the German side aerial activity began with the formation of Flight Detachment 300, later renamed 'Jildrim', which started off with a detachment of German Rumpler C1 and some Pfalz aeroplanes, these being what could be spared at the time.

In 1916 the British, realising that a major campaign was imminent, increased their airpower in Egypt, with the formation of two RFC squadrons under Lieutenant Colonel Geoffrey Salmond with Nos. 14 and 17 Squadrons at his disposal, but with only inferior aircraft – all the good planes were in France, there being none to spare for what was at that time considered a side show. In their new operational theatre the pilots encountered climatic conditions entirely unfamiliar to most of them. Just a few had been in India, and some had flown in the Italo-Turkish campaign a few years earlier when bombing Turkish installations from the air. But for most, the climate and topography were entirely different from what they had known in Europe. High temperatures, sand, fine dust, dry air and brackish water in the radiators, as well as rocky terrain for emergency landings, made flying extra hazardous, not to mention what would face them if they came down in the inhospitable desert wastes, where hostile Arab tribes out for loot would show no mercy for downed pilots. The planes had to be adapted to the new conditions, too, a big challenge for the inexperienced maintenance crews. Many pilots lost their lives even before the battle had begun, from one or several of the above causes. Air encounters were few at first since pilots from both sides were reluctant to open fire from their totally unsuitable aircraft. The British planes, although better constructed, could not mount Lewis guns for protection or attack, the observer's position being unsatisfactory for opening fire, to say the least, his view being almost entirely obstructed by the wings and engine, giving him the unattractive option of hitting either his own pilot or the tailplane!

On 29 June 1917, General Sir Edmund Allenby arrived in Egypt to take overall command of all British forces; soon after No. 5 Wing RFC was formed, incorporating the two squadrons already there with another one from Australia. This was No. 1 Squadron AFC which had trained on Caudrons and Box Kites at Cook Point in the Australian outback. On arrival at Heliopolis they were converted to fly BE-2Cs and taught to use the newly invented wireless and aerial photography to fly reconnaissance and artillery spotting support missions. The Australian pilots were more at home in the hot climate than their European comrades, and were soon in action over the Sinai desert. Major T. F. Rutledge, an Australian who had flown with the RFC in France and had some combat experience, was put in command of the Australian contingent, although the dominant personality there was a former light cavalry officer, Captain Richard Williams, who had taken command of a flight in the squadron when it had formed at Cook Point. Among his first pilots was Lieutenant Frank Hubert McNamara, newly graduated from the Royal Military College, Duntroon, Australia. The Aussies brought with them a kind of hilarious good humour which was sorely needed at a time when everyone else's morale was sagging badly as the horrendous news from the Somme began to seep through. For those in the Middle East, things were not so bad. True, they had to face the hot weather, the flies, the sand, but at least they were flying in clear skies, not the murk and fog which covered France. On the other hand, however, in France and Britain at least the pilots had some recreation and relaxation after the hardships of battle while, here in the desert, the best they had to hope for was a can of warm beer in the desert sands, if rations managed to get through the sandstorms, or were not looted by nomads.

There was not much action during the British Army's trek through the desert towards the Palestine border, most aerial operations being flown for reconnaissance purposes. When the Turkish garrison at El Arish, the northernmost desert oasis on the Mediterranean shore in Sinai, was captured, the German flight detachment withdrew and a forward airstrip for the RFC was soon established, known as 'Kilo 143'. It was here that a great act of bravery took place, hitting the headlines and bringing the Middle East, so long ignored, to the notice of a previously indifferent public.

On 20 March 1917 four aircraft of No. 1 Squadron took off to bomb the Turkish railway line across Wadi Hassa. Two were Martinsyde single-seaters flown by Lieutenants McNamara and Ellis, and two were BE-2C two-seaters, piloted by Captain D. Rutherford and Lieutenant Drummond, but flown without observers on this mission to save weight. Each aircraft carried six 4.5in howitzer shells with delayed 40-second fuses, activated after release, there being no regular bombs available at the forward airstrip.

The flight out to target was uneventful; no enemy aircraft were encountered. Soon the planes were flying in clear skies over the railway which stretched over the desert, its twin black lines clearly visible in the sand. Scattering a cloud of dust, a steam engine puffed into sight, towing a line of fully laden freight trucks, a tempting target to the airmen. Ellis spotted the train first and swooped down to attack but, as soon as he had released his shells, he caught sight of a German scouting plane and set off in hot pursuit, the German making a bee-line for home. McNamara followed him down for his own attack on the train. The modified shells were attached to a makeshift bomb rack with a pin tied to the rack, so that when the shell was released and dropped away from the aircraft, the rack remained, the shell becoming live only when far enough away for the safety of the pilot. But something went wrong this time! After McNamara had released three of his 'bombs' without mishap, dropping them onto the train, a fourth fell short but hit the tracks ahead; he then released his last one, but a violent explosion rocked his plane as soon as he had pulled the lever. Slivers of shell ripped through the fuselage and tore into the pilot's right buttock, but although racked with pain, McNamara kept his wits about him, realising that his engine was still purring happily away. Sensibly deciding that his future lay in getting his plane safely home to base, he turned and, dropping two smoke markers, set course for base. But then, taking one last look down at the ground, he saw that one of the BEs was down and that the pilot, Rutherford, was kneeling down by the plane, not far from the railway tracks, firing his Very pistol to attract attention. In the distance McNamara could see the dust from the hooves of the Turkish cavalry horses, racing to capture their prey while the stranded Rutherford could only helplessly watch them coming. McNamara, although himself almost fainting from pain and loss of blood, decided to do what he could. He switched off his engine and glided down to land. The engine sputtered and then fell silent... only the wind could be heard and, in the distance, the faint sound of rifle fire. The stricken aircraft grunted and groaned as it fluttered down, buffeted by the wind. McNamara, only vaguely aware by now of what was happening, searched for a place to land near Rutherford's crashed plane. He did not know how badly his own plane was damaged, but braced himself for the bumpy landing which he was sure would come. At near ground level, the pilot jerked the engine into action, to give him some control as he landed and, to his surprise, the engine responded. Levelling out, he hit the desert with a thud. The engine, blowing out acrid fumes, died as he slithered to a stop – only a few metres from Rutherford, who was still crouching behind his plane, pistol in hand.

As he saw the Martinsyde land, Rutherford raced over, climbed on to the engine cowl because there was no room for him in the single seater and hung on to the rigging of the centre section for support.

McNamara, his right leg now nearly paralysed, gritting his teeth against the searing pain, lost no time: he turned his aircraft into the wind and opened the throttle for take off. The ground was soggy and uneven, and he found it almost impossible to operate the rudder bar to keep the plane in a straight line. The heavily laden Martinsyde laboured over the rocky desert ground, McNamara virtually pulling it into the air. It had just gained flying speed when McNamara momentarily lost direction and hit a shallow ditch on a low ridge which he had not seen. The plane dipped its nose as the undercarriage collapsed and the stricken machine came to an abrupt halt. Rutherford, who had been holding on to the struts, was thrown off, while McNamara, now numb with pain, somehow managed to extricate himself from the wreckage. The two pilots immediately realised that this Martinsyde had had its day and would never fly again. McNamara fired a bullet into the petrol tank and set it alight.

Now the sound of shooting came nearer as the Turkish cavalry approached in a cloud. Certain that they would be taken prisoner and perhaps killed, the two pilots scrambled towards Rutherford's BE-2C, which was now their only hope of survival. They saw that the machine gun was intact and Rutherford and McNamara made their way across to the aircraft with the idea of stalling the Turks with machine gun fire. But just then help came from an unexpected quarter.

They had just reached the BE when the remaining shell in the Martinsyde exploded, causing a spectacular fire display and blowing splinters all over the place. This halted the Turks temporarily and McNamara meanwhile inspected Rutherford's plane and found, to his amazement, that it could still fly! In his forced landing the pilot had ripped a tyre from one of the wheels, broken centre section wires, and cracked a longeron in the fuselage. Shouting to Rutherford to swing the propeller, McNamara painfully climbed into the cockpit and, throwing some Lewis gun cartridge drums overboard to clear the rudders, he settled down to fire the engine. Watching the Turks out of the corner of his eye, Rutherford swung the propeller as if his life depended on it – which it did. He made several attempts until the engine, miraculously, spluttered into life, then he swung himself into the observer's cockpit, while McNamara turned into the wind for his second take off attempt, almost forgetting his pain in the excitement.

The sogginess of the ground nearly proved their undoing again – three times the plane pulled back but, with a sudden burst of power and superb flying skill from McNamara, the aircraft lifted into the air, by which time the pursuing Turks had almost reached the plane as it staggered into the air. Base was still a long way away and McNamara feared that he would lose consciousness before they could reach safety. His strength was leaving him, his eyesight fading by the moment. Bending sideways into the slipstream to cool his fevered head, he manhandled the aircraft with almost superhuman effort until Rutherford found the desert airstrip. McNamara made a perfect landing. Then, as he shut down the engine, he fainted over his controls!

After he was lifted gently out of his cockpit, the squadron leader examined the aircraft and was amazed to find one of the longerons completely fractured and much additional structural damage. McNamara had really flown on a wing and a prayer! Major Richard Williams, commander of No. 1 Squadron AFC, wrote a report praising his young pilot's courage. McNamara remained in hospital for several months, was promoted captain and, while convalescing in Australia, learned that he had been awarded the coveted Victoria Cross for gallantry, the only one gained by an Australian airman in the First World War. During the Second World War, McNamara, now an air vice marshal, served in Europe, commanding RAAF Headquarters in London, and terminated his long and distinguished career as AOC British Forces Aden and Director of Education at British Headquarters Germany. Major Williams, who was to become Air Marshal Sir Richard Williams, became known as the 'Father of the Royal Australian Air Force', which did so well during the Second World War, while Lieutenant Peter Drummond, who had also flown on that eventful mission, became an air marshal, serving in Cairo during the North African campaign.

One last, but no less interesting anecdote, may serve to illustrate what air fighting was like during those early days in Palestine when chivalry among warriors was still in style. Oberleutnant Georg Felmy, a younger brother of the commanding officer of Jildrim, had just forced down a British plane of No. 14 Squadron, when he saw that the British pilot was on the ground. Concerned that he might become the victim of a brutal attack by nomads, Felmy swooped low over the squadron's base, and dropped a note telling the British there of their comrade's plight, and his whereabouts! When the Englishman was captured soon after by a German patrol, Felmy flew once more to No. 14 Squadron's airstrip, and dropped another note, asking for some kit to be dropped for the captured pilot – a rare and commendable act of chivalrous humanity.

CHAPTER THREE

COLONEL PATTON LEADS THE WAY

The Saint Mihiel Salient, which had been bulging into the Allied lines since early in the First World War, had seen no serious fighting since 1916. In fact, the German high command regarded it as a kind of rest area for worn-out troops. But in 1918 33-year-old George Patton Jr. changed all that, and incidentally became known as a great military leader.

Patton was no stranger to military glory: During General John J. Pershing's 1916 punitive expedition into Mexico to put down the notorious border bandit, Pancho Villa, Patton, who was then a young lieutenant and personal aide to the general, led a party which chased the bandits into an isolated farmhouse just outside the village of San Miguelto. Patton was on his way to the building, pistol drawn, when three horsemen appeared and began to fire at him. One of the riders galloped straight for Patton, who promptly shot him out of his saddle! Another tried to ride him down, but was picked off by another well directed shot, and fell. The third man jumped off his horse to get a better aim, but missed, and Patton killed him as well. As he turned the dead man over, he identified him as one of Pancho Villa's top lieutenants, one of the men they had actually set out to find! Patton tied the three bodies to his car and drove into General Pershing's headquarters, where he received great praise for his courage from the Old Man himself. The general took his protégé to France when the USA joined in during the later stages of the Great War, but young Patton soon got tired of lounging around as the general's personal aide and HQ commandant. He wanted some real action, and badgered his superior to let him go, finally receiving the coveted assignment of commander of the first American Light Tank Center at Langres, where he started training recruits in tank combat.

Patton had been an enthusiastic Francophile since, accompanied by his wife, he had first visited France in 1911 on a private tour which took him over wide areas of the country; at that time he had also pursued a course of cavalry training at the French Cavalry School at Saumur, where he studied mobile warfare tactics from proponents of the great French military traditions. Now Patton was back in France, getting ready for his first battle. Promoted first to major, then swiftly to lieutenant colonel commanding the 304th Tank Brigade, the first American tank unit, he was raring to go. Aided by two able battalion commanders, Majors Sereno Brett and Ronulf Compton, he set out to bring his new unit to peak condition, driving them incessantly round the countryside of Bourg and Longeau until they had driven over every hill and copse and knew the area by heart.

Patton soon turned his unit into a crack formation, but he was no easy man to work under. He was an extreme disciplinarian, did not suffer fools gladly, and the word 'impossible' had no meaning for him. The gruelling pace of his training schedules had the men groaning, but they adored him, and would have followed him through hell, because he was always first to try everything.

Patton, wanting to know everything there was to know about tank fighting, had established close contact with the French tank school at Chaplieu, as well as with the British at Bovington in Dorset, where he actually drove the tanks and fired the guns. So by September 1918, he and his men were ready, and Patton set about preparing for the battle with his usual meticulous care. He had already reconnoitred the ground over which he was to lead his tanks, and knew every inch of it. But that was not enough for him. He wanted to see the enemy – and managed to persuade a friendly French commander to let him join a night patrol assigned to approach the German trenches. Having discarded his

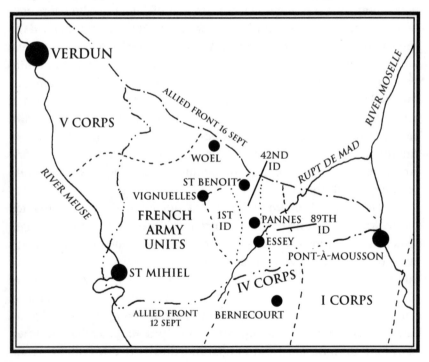

insignia and donned a French uniform for the occasion, Patton crawled along with the French soldiers into No Man's Land up to the German barbed wire, where they lay in a shellhole listening to the Germans chatting inside their trenches. Patton found the terrain suitable for his tanks to advance over, but noted that, should it rain, the ground could turn into impassable mud.

The St Mihiel offensive would be the first major battle for the Americans in France. Pershing, anxious to protect his forces, most of them untried in combat, deployed his three US corps with several French divisions backing them. Patton had in his brigade some 174 tanks, divided into two battalions, his mission being to support the attack of 1st US Infantry Division, commanded by General Joseph Dickman, who would attack on the left flank of the offensive.

An artillery barrage on a grand scale started an hour after midnight on 12 September 1918 and at 0500 the troops began to move forward under cover of a creeping bombardment. At once the lack of infantry-tank training became evident, when Major Brett's 326th Tank Battalion moved on to its first objective while the infantry was still bogged down, unable to follow. The same thing happened with Major Compton's 327th Tank Battalion. Patton, who had been watching the situation through his binoculars, at once left his observation post in order to help things along, and was soon drawn irresistibly into the vortex of battle. Going forward on foot, he saw that his tanks were delayed by what Compton had described as bad ground. It had been raining hard, the ground was soggy and shell holes were filled with water. Still on foot, Patton made his way through the mud, and through heavy German shelling, to a small ridge, which he climbed for a better view. Here, to his surprise, he found Brigadier General Douglas MacArthur, commander of the Rainbow Division, totally ignoring the German barrage which was dangerously near, even on some occasions, passing right over their heads. Neither man thought of budging! From his vantage point on the hill, Patton saw some Germans heading back towards the village of Essey; running down to where Major Compton stood, he ordered him to send five tanks into the village. A French sentry standing on the bridge leading to the village warned Patton, who accompanied the tanks, to stop, as the entire area was covered by enemy fire, but Patton ignored his caution and, leading the tanks on foot, waving his cane, he directed the tank commanders over the bridge and into the ruins of the village. Some of the Germans tried to make a stand, using a ruined house for cover, but a few carefully directed rounds persuaded them to surrender, and Patton sent them back to the main force. MacArthur now joined them with some of his runners, and Patton requested his permission to advance towards the next objective – Pannes, a few kilometres to the north-west. The brigadier agreed and Patton led the tanks on, still walking ahead of them, ignoring the sporadic sniper and machine gun fire which came down on them, most of it quite inaccurate.

Most of the tanks were now down to a few drops of fuel, and about to halt in their tracks. One, however, was still relatively full and Patton climbed on its turret, encouraging the nervous tank commander to go on. His aide, Lieutenant Joe Angelo, and a runner crouched on the back plate. Soon the tank was singled out by strong enemy machine gun fire; bullets pinged off the steel plates. Patton and his aides scrambled quickly off the tank and continued on foot. But by now the tank was totally isolated. Patton chased it and ordered the commander to turn round and return.

When night fell, Patton decided to go to the rear and get some fuel for his stalled tanks. He had realised that fuel would be a crucial problem in this battle, and had arranged with Captain Joseph Vincer, commandant of the tank training school at Langres, to establish a gasoline dump with sufficient reserves somewhere near the front line. Here he now walked in the darkness and, arranging for the fuel barrels to be loaded on sledges, had them towed by two tanks towards the night leaguer. By dawn the Renault tanks were ready for action once more.

Casualties during the first day of action had been relatively low, compared to what had been achieved: five men had been killed, mostly from sniper and shrapnel, another fifteen wounded and two tanks had taken direct hits from artillery fire and lost, together with three more stalled by mechanical failure.

Two days later Patton's tank men were in action again. Moving out of Vigneulles towards the village of Woel, 1st Division advanced with 51 tanks from Brett's battalion supporting them. As they advanced on the village, runners reported that the Germans were evacuating and that some French infantry were holding Woel. Meanwhile, on the Woel–St Benoit road, Major Compton's tanks were advancing in order to meet up with Brett's vanguard outside the village perimeter. Fifteen light Renault tanks of Major Compton's battalion, armed with small 37mm light guns, were advancing along the Benoit road, followed by some French Schneider medium tanks, armed with 75mm howitzers. Lieutenant Edwin A. McClure, commanding the lead tank, was just south of St Benoit when a runner came forward and banged on the steel door, telling him to get to Woel, where the 1st US Infantry Division was believed to be waiting for them. There was no contact with the division, as telephone cables had been disrupted by shellfire all along the road. The lead tanks had advanced to a point some two kilometres from the village when the supply column arrived with fuel, and McClure took the opportunity to top all his tanks up. Suddenly, German aeroplanes swooped down, strafed the fuel trucks and wounded several men.

McClure did manage to reach Woel, which he found to be clear of enemy troops, but, just as he was settling his men into position, he saw an enemy infantry battalion in full battle order coming straight at his position on the edge of the village. He sent a runner back to Battalion HQ, where Compton ordered McClure with another group of tanks forward; deploying into combat formation, they attacked – driving the Germans eastward as far as Jonville, destroying over a dozen machine guns and capturing four German 77mm guns abandoned by their crews. As they attempted to tow these battle gains back, however, McClure and the other officer were wounded by shrapnel, but they kept working on the guns and removed their breech blocks. Then, climbing onto their tanks, they withdrew under heavy artillery fire. Lieutenant McClure was awarded a DSC for this valiant action, but his luck did not last. A few weeks later, during another dash against the enemy, he was wounded again but carried on until, badly burned, he was evacuated, to live only one more day. He was one of the first tank aces, a fine tank commander with a lot of guts – a good example of Patton's influence on his junior officers.

Patton himself received a sharp reprimand from Brigadier General Samuel D. Rockenbach, the commander of the US Tank Corps in France and Patton's immediate superior. He did not mince his words as he told Patton exactly what he thought of Patton's conduct in leaving his command post at the height of battle and joining his forces in the firing line. Patton's attempts at explanation did not go down well and the senior officer was still in the process of castigating his junior when a messenger arrived and handed him a note. This was from Pershing himself; he had received an approving report from MacArthur about Patton's courageous conduct in battle, and he passed this on to Rockenbach together with his own enthusiastic support, confirming that Patton really had no choice but to lead from the front if he wished to control a mobile tank battle.

Patton's tank brigade was soon in action again. This time it was during the Meuse-Argonne offensive, when his tanks joined up with the French 14th and 17th Groupes des Chars. Patton once again did his best to familiarise himself with the terrain over which his tanks would be operating. In order to overcome the shortage of fuel, he ordered that each of his tanks should carry two fuel cans tied to its back plates. He also established another fuel dump behind the start line, and organised supply columns which would be on call to move forward to refuelling points.

On 26 September, following a three-hour preliminary artillery barrage, Patton's tanks moved up to their start line. Before dawn his 140 tanks advanced into enemy territory under a blanket of heavy mist and drizzling rain. Almost at once, Major Compton's battalion, working with the 28th US Infantry Division, stumbled upon a German minefield where the warning signs were still in place. The tanks managed to avoid the trap but, while they were groaning around the field, the mist had risen and the German fire became accurate and more intense. The infantry then came to a halt and some of the men panicked. Patton, appearing like a phantom from out of the mist, was furious with Compton for halting his advance and, never one to hide his feelings, told him so in as many words. Then, calling on the infantry commander, he suggested that they advance towards the village of Cheppy, situated inside a wood. It was only then that he realised what was halting the advance: downhill from where he stood were some deep trenches which the tanks could not pass. They had to be filled in and their earthen walls reduced. There was no earthworking material available but that did not stop Patton who, picking up a shovel, started digging, 'inviting' some of the men to join him. Although they were working under fire with bullets whizzing overhead, they soon had the walls down and Patton signalled Compton's tanks through the gap. Five of them managed to get through and Patton was about to follow them when, as he was climbing over the parapet, he saw a unit of German soldiers coming along the trench towards him and his small group. Waving his walking stick and by sheer force of his awe-inspiring personality, he soon had them under his control, disarmed, and being led back to HQ as prisoners. Then, still waving his stick, he ordered his men after him into battle.

Six men followed Patton into the thick of battle, among them his loyal aide, Lieutenant Angelo. One by one the men fell, hit by German machine gun fire, until only Angelo and one runner remained alive. Suddenly Angelo saw a bullet strike his colonel in the thigh, and Patton fell. Dragging him into an empty shellhole, Angelo started to bandage the wound, which was bleeding profusely. But Patton was still conscious, and ordered Angelo to stop some tanks which were passing and show them the nest of German machine guns which were sweeping the entire area. A sergeant jumped into Patton's shell-hole and was stunned to see his colonel writhing in pain, but Patton calmed him down, and ordered him to search for Major Brett and tell him to take command. It was near suicide for any one to attempt to get to Patton now, as the Germans were covering every inch of the ground with bullets, but a medical officer risked his life to come forward and patch up Patton's wounds. He was losing a lot of blood by now and some stretcher bearers came up, through the intense fire, and dragged him out, carrying him to safety through three kilometres of hell. Lieutenant Angelo, who had never left his side, remained with him until they reached the first aid station.

But Patton was furious. He ordered them to carry him to the divisional command post, where he remained to follow the conduct of battle until the end. Only then would he allow the medics to evacuate him to a hospital. When he awoke from a period of unconsciousness the next day, he found that two of his officers were lying in beds near him. They showed him newspapers in which he was described as 'America's Tank Hero'. It was not the last time that Patton would hit the headlines.

Patton was already a living legend. His men adored him for his courage and devotion, and would have followed him anywhere but, when he recovered from his wounds, it was 11 November 1918 and the Great War had ended. It was his 33rd birthday.

Twenty-five years later, in another war, General George S. Patton Jr. was to lead the greatest army the world had ever seen into a final victory, using the experience he had gained in his early battles in France. But that is another story...

CHAPTER FOUR

ZEEBRUGGE: THE ST GEORGE'S DAY RAID

In the spring of 1918 the Germans launched their offensives on the Somme and in Flanders and Allied casualties rocketed once more, draining British manpower. There was urgent need for a boost to the morale of the waterlogged British forces in France, but none was to hand. And then came Roger Keyes...

Keyes was a naval officer who had already earned some military glory during the abortive Dardanelles Campaign. He now provided the idea for the greatest combined naval and commando raid of the First World War. At 45 the youngest rear admiral in the Royal Navy, Keyes already had 32 years of naval service behind him and was now in charge of operational plans at the Admiralty. He now came up with a plan for a direct attack on Zeebrugge and Ostend, both of which had been a thorn in the side of their Lordships at the Admiralty for quite a while, providing as they did safe harbour for the German submarines which were a continual threat to Allied shipping in the English Channel. For years attempts by the Dover Patrol had failed to reduce this threat, and something drastic had to be done to keep the Germans at bay.

After many heated – and noisy – exchanges, Keyes got his way. He was promoted to vice-admiral and placed in charge of the Dover Patrol, where he set about bringing his plan to fruition. The harbour of Zeebrugge lay at the mouth of a canal running in a near-straight line towards Bruges, an inland port which housed the Kriegsmarine submarines and destroyers based in Belgium. The canal, tidal at the sea end, was navigable at high tide, the canal entrance being protected by a massive lock and two small stone piers. Bomb proof shelters provided added protection. In addition, the Germans had built a massive defensive line all along the 20-mile stretch of coastline between Zeebrugge and Ostend, with no less than 56 large calibre coastal guns, anti-aircraft batteries and heavy artillery, totalling 225 guns, bristling from well camouflaged concrete bunker emplacements in the cliffs. At Zeebrugge alone some 40 guns were emplaced to guard the outer port entrance. The entire system was linked by a modern signals network, allowing fast communications when necessary.

But the shore batteries were not the main obstacle to a British naval attack; far more threatening was the Zeebrugge mole, the largest of its kind in the world. This stone, steel and granite pier had been constructed originally to shelter the harbour entrance from shifting silt, but when the Germans had captured it in 1914 they had turned it into a virtual fortress. Curving north and east in a sickle shape, the mole was wide enough to carry a paved highway, a railway track and a footway. The entire construction was linked to the mainland by a steel viaduct set on iron piles. The height of the mole and its top parapet varied above sea level according to the tide, but even at high water it loomed some ten metres high. The German defences included several fortified

32

machine gun positions bristling with barbed wire fences, a garrison barracks and, at the end of the 100-metre extension, a large calibre gun position which guarded the port entrance with a 360 degree arc of fire.

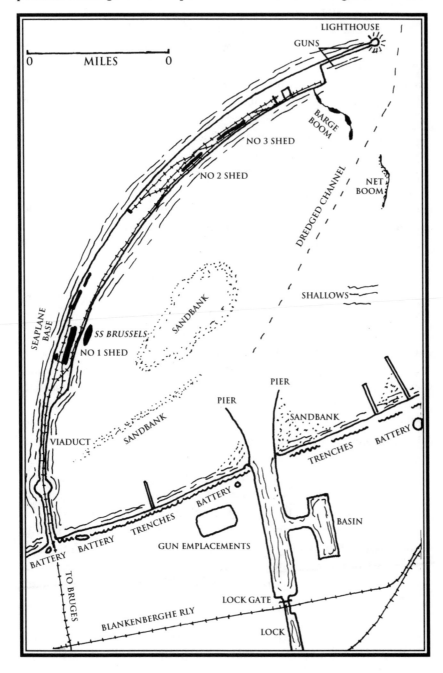

The garrison was manned by over 1,000 well-trained marines, with reserves based in the town. At night, at least two destroyers were known to be moored along the inner mole, ready to support any action necessary with their naval armoury.

Admiral Keyes' plan involved running some blockships into the harbour entrance, passing through the defences, penetrating the anti-submarine boom and reaching the heavy lock gates – thus, as he succinctly described it, 'putting the cork in the bottle'. It was planned to use obsolete vessels filled with concrete, to be sunk at carefully chosen spots so as to seal the entrance. In order to allow the blockships to penetrate the heavy defences, a commando attack would deal with the German fortification on the mole and destroy it, or at least divert attention from the ships during the critical phase of the operation. The steel viaduct linking the mole to the shore would have to be blown, and it was planned to do this by ramming a submarine filled with explosives under its girders. The most essential ingredient of the plan was surprise – so that the attacking party and the blockships could reach their objectives before being put out of action.

Keyes chose both his ships and his men carefully. Three ancient cruisers dating back to the end of the last century were selected as the blockships, each ballasted with 1,500 tons of concrete and fitted with scuttling charges to sink them when they reached their targets. Skeleton crews, all volunteers, would sail the ships into position, protected by specially fitted bullet-proof plating. For the main attack the admiral selected HMS *Vindictive*, a cruiser built in 1897 but – with her high freeboard and shallow draught – strong and fast enough for the job. In order to get the boarding parties onto the mole which would tower above, however, several modifications had to be made, including the addition of a new upper deck rigged to its port side, fitted with boarding ramps over which the assault troops would reach the mole's summit. Three howitzers were installed, each with two large flamethrowers, an ingenious invention of the remarkable Wing Commander F. A. Brock, RAF, son of the founder of the English fireworks company. Brock was also tasked with providing an efficient smokescreen, on which much of the success of the raid would depend. To manufacture his 'fog', Brock needed – and got – vast quantities of a chemical used to produce a sugar substitute. As a result, many British tea drinkers would bemoan the sudden disappearance of their national sweetener!

One more factor would be crucial for Keyes – the weather. Bad weather could make navigation through the treacherous offshore shoals extremely hazardous. Cross-currents could send the ships off course, preventing them from finding the narrow entrance. Worst of all, a sudden change in the wind could blow Brock's 'fog' seaward, exposing the fleet instead of hiding it from the German gunners.

For the commando force which was to storm the mole, Keyes selected 200 naval volunteers and 700 men from the Royal Marines, all of whom had undergone some gruelling training in close combat and demolition work, on a specially constructed full-scale model.

The start of the great adventure came on 11 April, 1918, when the 140-vessel fleet sailed out in perfect weather conditions, assembling off the Goodwin Sands in the early morning haze. Keyes, flying his battle flag on HMS *Warwick*, signalled the fleet to set off on the well-prepared route and they had reached the final buoy when suddenly, without warning, the wind changed, making the smokescreen totally useless. Keyes had to make the agonising decision to bring his entire armada back to port! Luckily, the Germans remained unaware of what was happening.

The young admiral now had the difficult task of persuading his sceptical superiors to give him another chance but in the end he succeeded and on 22 April, with the tides right, the operation set sail once again. It was the eve of St George's Day, the patron saint of England; Admiral Keyes hoisted the signal 'St George for England', to be answered by the captain of the *Vindictive*, Captain Alfred Francis Carpenter with the signal to give the 'dragon's tail a good twist'!

The force sailed in three columns towards their objective – only a few hours would decide for these men whether their mission would end in success or failure and, for many, in their death. At 2200 the final marker buoy was reached. In the distance gunfire could be heard as two British monitors shelled the coastal defences, which they had been doing nightly for some time until it became a matter of routine for the Germans. A projected air raid by four-engined Handley Page bombers of the RAF had to be cancelled at the last minute due to the heavily overcast sky over Zeebrugge and, although the raiders regretted the loss of air cover, the heavy cloud was welcome news. By now it was almost dark, the full moon having been obscured by cloud and rising mist. A slight drizzle was falling.

HMS *Vindictive* silently approached the mole which loomed up in the haze, while some of the fast motor boats raced forward, laying thick smoke. The German gunners, alerted by the throbbing of their engines, still held their fire, unable to identify anything in the murk. But suddenly a gust of wind blew the mist and fog offshore and the gunners atop the mole saw the *Vindictive* coming right at them like a giant ghost ship from earlier times. Searchlights and starshells illuminated the sky and soon a storm of shells and machine gun fire began to pound into the cruiser at point blank range.

The first salvo was disastrous for the boarding parties. Although most of the men were under cover, their officers – standing upright to find their objectives before the landing – were hit. Colonel Elliot and Major Cordner of the Royal Marines, Captain Halahan and Commander Harrington Edwards of the naval party were either killed or wounded. Men who rushed out from cover to help were mown down by machine gun fire from the top of the mole. Most of the boarding ramps were blown off, but over the two that remained the first troops stormed ashore, most of them being cut down before they reached the mole.

The captain of the *Vindictive* was facing another problem – it was virtually impossible to moor her. She had bumped against the mole at precisely 0001 on St George's Day, only one minute late, but she was rolling badly from side to side in the wash, bucking and rearing in the turmoil the water created in the narrowing space. The ship was also rocking from the impact of the shells coming at her from all directions and Carpenter virtually rammed the heavy ship to the mole. Then Lieutenant Harold Campbell, in the Mersey ferryboat *Daffodil* which had been brought along for this very purpose, rammed its bow against the *Vindictive*'s hull, pinning it onto the stone wall.

But by now the decks of the *Vindictive* were strewn with bodies; from everywhere the moans of the wounded could be heard, while medics risked their lives to pull them to safety despite the withering fire from above. The upper deck had been pierced like a sieve and, with all the senior officers of the assault parties dead or wounded, it fell to one of the junior officers to take the lead. Lieutenant Commander Bryan Adams was that man. He was first on top of the mole, leading a team of Bluejackets across the shuddering, heaving plank which rose and fell several feet every time the ship rolled. Once at the top, they still had to contend with the withering fire which swept right across their heads.

A few hundred metres to the west, Lieutenant Claude Hawkins balanced himself on one of the scaling ladders, trying to get up on to the stone wall from the ferryboat *Iris*, which bucked and rocked in the strong current. Held upright by his men from below, the young officer finally managed to grab the top of the parapet and pulled himself up to secure the ladder for the rest of his party. But he was immediately attacked by a German assault party and was last seen defending himself with his service revolver. Lieutenant Commander George Bradford followed him, carrying a grappling anchor; as he hooked it into position a stream of machine gun bullets lifted him off the parapet and he dropped down between the ship and the wall. Petty Officer Hallihan jumped after him in an effort to save him, but neither man was ever seen again.

The Germans were still pouring a tremendous amount of shellfire onto the protruding upper deck of the *Vindictive*, but Lieutenant Charles Rigby, Royal Marines, made his way through the suffocating smell of cordite, the smoke and the explosions, the blood-soaked bodies writhing around him screaming for help. He grabbed a Lewis gun mounted on the rail which was still functioning and opened fire, silencing a German machine gun.

Wing Commander Brock had decided to wait no longer. Hoping to get some important new range-finding equipment known to be in one of the German sheds from aerial photos he had seen, he rushed up the gangway and raised himself to the top of the mole, where he joined Lieutenant Commander Adams and whoever remained of his men behind one of the stone walls. It was hard to see how to proceed, for the Germans were pouring fire all along the mole, hitting anything that moved. There had already been many casualties. But Adams knew that in order to save the blockships now approaching the harbour entrance, the mole gun batteries had to be stormed. Every moment counted and he had 250 yards to cover to the target. Judging by the fire, Adams realised that only a few of his men would remain on their feet by the time they reached it – but they had no choice: Adams and his men were the only ones there.

Brock saw, 40 yards away from where they crouched, the concrete observation post that contained the German equipment he coveted. Signalling to Adams that he was going forward, he waited just long enough to lob a hand grenade, and was seen storming into the bunker, pistol in hand. Suddenly the entire area was covered by dense fire from one of the moored German destroyers, making any further move impossible. Adams looked at his watch restlessly: time was running out if he was to silence the mole guns before it was too late.

From the deck of the *Vindictive*, one of the gunnery officers, Lieutenant Young, saw Adams' plight and turned his own guns to engage the German destroyer, whose upper deck was protruding over the parapet and, with his support, Commander Adams led his remaining men forward. It was a gallant assault. As they stormed through the gauntlet of fire, explosions, starshells and flares lit up the sky, silhouetting the lighthouse which loomed at the end of the mole. Adams and his men had just reached the fortified zone on the narrow pier when the German gunners began to blaze away at them, while a small party of German sailors stormed right in front of Adams' men, only to be gunned down by equally fierce fire from the other side. Light artillery from the German destroyers was firing point blank at the Marines now, and Adams' group had dwindled to a few gallant survivors. But they were only a stone's throw away from their objective and, by some miracle, three new arrivals emerged from the smoke – Petty Officer Antell and two Lewis gunners, all wounded to some extent, but still able to fight. Then another figure swayed out of the mist: it was Lieutenant Commander Harrison, who had just recovered consciousness after fracturing his jaw while hurling himself over the gangway earlier. Now he came forward and threw himself by the side of the exhausted Adams. In a matter of seconds both officers and their men stormed on, covered by the Lewis guns which blazed away at the Germans. Able Seaman McKenzie raced beside Harrison, firing his Lewis as he went, but was cut down by enemy fire. Harrison picked up the machine gun and raced on, finally reaching the brilliantly lit German outpost. But luck ran out at last for the courageous officer and he fell, badly wounded, the Lewis gun still firing as he went down. McKenzie, however, was not dead. Crawling forward, bullets pinging around him, he picked up the gun and swept the enemy position, cutting down Germans, who could be seen running out of their positions away from the bullets. The other marine managed to hoist Harrison's body over his shoulders and run back to cover, but he did not make it, and they were taken prisoner by the Germans. Commander Adams, though, was still alive! On his way back to the ship to obtain some badly needed reinforcements, he stumbled upon a party of marines led by Lieutenant Underhill, and went back to the attack.

The German gunners on the mole extension had now seen the blockships steaming out of the mist towards the harbour, and turned their full attention to shooting them down, while German reinforcements rushed onto the mole from the shore and half a battalion of greyclad German bicycle troops converged on to the shore end. The situation was becoming critical.

Lieutenant Richard Sandford crept into the harbour exactly according to the timetable, guiding his explosive-filled submarine in the direction of the viaduct he was to blow up. Not far away, his elder brother Francis watched through his binoculars from his picket boat, stationed in a position where they could pick up the crew after they abandoned ship. Richard Sandford's approach was unnoticed by the German guards on the bridge, and he drove his boat right under the steel girders. Suddenly, a flare went up, and searchlights probed the sky for the intruder, but the submarine was already under the viaduct. The steel bridge towered high over the boat as it slammed into the steel of the bridgework, making a clang which reverberated over the dark waters. The boat's conning tower rammed right under the solid steel above and it juddered to an abrupt halt. Five tons of the deadly Amatol explosive were now in place. For a moment the only sound was the clatter of boots as the Germans rushed to the rails, sure that the English submarine captain had rammed the viaduct by mistake and they were about to become famous by capturing an enemy submarine intact! Their triumphant shouts and laughter rang out, while Sandford and his men quickly clambered into their rubber boats and turned away from the explosion they knew would come. The Germans were blazing away at them by now; Sandford was wounded twice, and others were hit, but they continued their escape. They were just far enough away when their submarine went up in a great roar, taking the entire viaduct and all the Germans with it. A German battalion pedalling their bicycles across the bridge were thrown into the air, twisted bodies falling like leaves into the dark waters below. From the dinghy the English sailors watched as cyclists somersaulted into the sea, still gripping their handlebars. Unable to stop in time, those Germans bringing up the rear shot over the edge of the gap and plunged to their deaths in the tangled steel below. Not a man escaped. The mole was cut off from land. After a frantic search, Francis Sandford finally detected his brother's boat and pulled them to safety.

Admiral Keyes, who had watched the entire operation from the bridge of HMS *Warwick* and seen the blockships enter the outer harbour, decided to start recalling the survivors from the mole to prevent them from being massacred. But first he wanted to make sure that the blockships would be able to run the gauntlet of the German gun battery and reach their assigned places.

On HMS *Vindictive*, Captain Carpenter was taking stock of his ship. It was a terrifying sight. But then he encountered the imperturbable Lieutenant Hilton Young, the gunnery officer, his right arm bandaged but puffing a cigar, which he removed just long enough to give Carpenter a wide grin – a real morale booster in the shambles all around. Carpenter saw the blockships passing the lighthouse, and decided to sound the recall signal and get the troops back on board his ship but, as the *Vindictive*'s hooters and sirens had long since been shot away, he signalled the ferryboat still holding the cruiser to sound its own siren. Within minutes the welcome signal began, starting as a low moan and rose in scale to an earsplitting yowl which could be heard over all the din of battle. The warriors still standing were reluctant to leave their dead and wounded comrades behind and, at risk of their lives, carried most of them back to the ship. In one of the most gallant feats of arms ever known, of the 1,700 men who took part in the Zeebrugge raid, only 49 failed to return to Dover and of these several were lost at sea or taken prisoner, an amazing achievement bearing in mind that the Germans were fighting to the last moment and the retreat was made in the face of full firepower both on the mole and onto the ship itself as she sailed for home. Captain Carpenter and his *Vindictive* had won more glory in a single hour at Zeebrugge than most warships do in their entire lifespan. Barely afloat, shot to pieces, the *Vindictive* sailed into Dover, received by a cheering crowd.

But the main purpose of the operation was to block the canal, and that still remained to be done – an enormous test of skill and seamanship. Captain Ralph Sneyd on the bridge of HMS *Thetis* heard the recall sign as he passed inside the harbour, having driven his ship through the gauntlet of guns, watching the firefight on the mole as he went. The firing from the mole was inaccurate and the commander paid a silent tribute to the brave men who fought there to make it so. *Thetis* continued to advance, guided by Lieutenant Commander Young RNVR in his launch. Then, suddenly, disaster struck: the small craft was struck by three large shells which exploded the calcium flares and turned the boat into a blazing wreck. Young was dying, but he refused to be evacuated until he saw his entire crew picked up. Commander Sneyd now had to guide his ship alone to the lock gates and, by sheer navigational skill, managed to pass the narrow gap in the anti-submarine nets. But his propellers fouled the netting, slowing the ship down – in full sight of the German 21cm naval guns of the Goeben Batterie which were located on the sea shore. *Thetis* was hit repeatedly and was heeling over badly as she reached her blocking position. Ordering his crew into the remaining lifeboat, Commander Sneyd fired his scuttling charges and signalled the other two blockships to pass through the nets and place their ships in position.

HMS *Intrepid* was scuttled across the narrowest part of the approach channel, while HMS *Iphigenia* found her last resting place close behind.

The operation was almost at an end, but Admiral Roger Keyes made one last sweep of Zeebrugge to make sure that all his ships still afloat were safely on their way. He then ordered his captain to sail for Dover – and home! The Zeebrugge raid was over.

There is controversy over the success of the Zeebrugge raid. On the minus side, the Germans had managed to dredge a narrow channel round the sunken blockships within 24 hours of the raid. A further raid on Ostend also failed to block the canal, although several German submarines and warships were bottled up at Bruges for several days, vulnerable to a massive bombing attack which, for various reasons, was not flown. Admiral Keyes was furious that the Bruges basin had not been sealed up as a result of his men's sacrifice – 600 killed, 220 wounded, and a few captured. However, on the plus side, Zeebrugge was disastrous for the Germans in the strategic sense. The attack came as a complete surprise to Ludendorff's staff, right in the middle of their spring offensive in Flanders. The raid signalled the vulnerability of the Belgian sea flank and made the Germans reluctant to go for the Channel Ports, a move which probably saved the lifeline of the British Expeditionary Forces.

No fewer than eight Victoria Crosses were awarded to the officers and men who risked their lives at Zeebrugge. Others received high decorations, too, while civilian morale received a much-needed boost when the news of the daring feat became public. Admiral Keyes became a full admiral, being appointed director of combined operations in 1940 and planning some of the earliest commando raids. He died in his sleep in 1945, a man deserving of the highest praise.

CHAPTER FIVE

WITH BLANK SABRE AGAINST THE TANKS

The tradition of the Polish cavalry dates back a long time. In August 1920 the Polish general Josef Pilsudski and his horsemen routed the Red Army's Cossack cavalry in a surprise counter attack near Warsaw. This was one of the most decisive victories of the century, blocking the communist advance in its westward thrust, just as Charles Martel had checked the Moslem surge into Europe at Tours in 732 AD.

Great traditions, however, are useless when they do not incorporate new methods and ignore modernisation. Anachronism in warfare often ends in disaster. This is what happened to Poland when it faced the massive German armour in 1939. Almost 30% of the Polish Army consisted of mounted regiments which, although well trained and highly motivated, were ill-equipped to fight a modern mobile war. Although, after the Russo-Polish war of 1920 the cavalry had gradually adopted a dragoon mode, using the horses for mobility but attacking on foot and thus at least preventing the previous suicidal charges against withering machine gun fire, the sabre had been retained as a weapon to supplement the Mauser Carbine. Strangely enough the Polish cavalry officers had re-adopted the pennant-adorned lance in 1939, just when a modern German panzer force was massed on their borders.

In spite of its shortcomings, however, the Polish army of 1939 was a force to be reckoned with, especially as the German Wehrmacht had not yet reached the level it later achieved. The Polish cavalry brigades, equipped with 37mm anti-tank guns, were actually superior to the German Mk III 37mm tank guns, of which there were in any case few in the panzer divisions, the bulk of their firepower being made up of lighter machine gun tanks. The Polish high command used their cavalry in a defensive role, in spite of its being their only manoeuvrable force, and concentrated all 70,000 men along the 1,500km border where they could play neither a strategic nor a tactical role against the Germans attacking by land and air. The Polish cavalrymen did have one ace up their sleeve. Their engineers had designed the first workable anti-tank rifle: the Maroczek was a lightweight, limited recoil weapon firing a tungsten carbide core bullet, capable of penetrating any German tank at 250 metres range. These were to prove of great help to the Poles when confronted with the German panzers.

At 0445 on Friday, 1 September 1939, the German warship *Schleswig Holstein* fired its first gun salvoes on the Westerplatte, a tongue of land in the Vistula river, and so began Hitler's onslaught on Poland. The *Wehrmacht* mounted its dawn attack with some 54 divisions, among them six panzer, four light and four motor divisions, in all a force of some 3,000 tanks, although only a mere hundred of them were 37mm-gun-mounted vehicles with sufficient armour protection. What decided the day for the Germans, however, was the Luftwaffe, extremely well trained to provide superb firepower in support of the advancing panzer units.

The Polish Army numbered some 40 infantry divisions and eleven cavalry brigades, with about 1,000 lightly armoured 'tankettes', armed only with machine guns. There were also some outmoded armoured cars mounting short-barrel 37mm guns – quite ineffective weapons in mobile combat.

0426 on 1 September.... At the Elbing forward airstrip Oberleutnant Bruno Dilley, leader of the 3rd Staffel in Stuka Squadron 1, gave the thumbs up sign to his pilots; all of them, revving their engines to full, throttle, lumbered into the morning fog over the bumpy grass field. They had arrived just the day before from their home base at Isterburg, landing in total darkness and surrounded by thick fog. Dilley had been given a difficult mission: to neutralise by air attack the explosive charges on the vital Vistula bridge at Dirschau to prevent it from being demolished! He was instructed *not* to bomb the bridge itself, which would have been difficult anyway in the weather conditions prevailing, but to attack and take out the Polish firing post which agents had pinpointed close to the nearby railway station. For days on end Dilley and his pilots had trained for their mission by flying low on a model target near base. Dilley himself had travelled in plain clothes by train over the bridge to Koenigsberg to see for himself where the demolition cables lay. Now, just fifteen minutes before the *Schleswig Holstein* was due to open

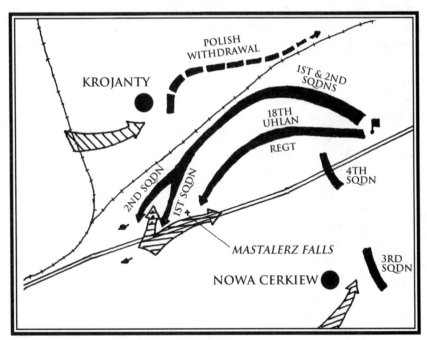

fire, Dilley's flight took off on their dangerous mission. With only 50 metres visibility, it took a lot of flying skill to retain formation, but the Stukas followed their leader. In only eight minutes of flying time they reached their target. Three Stukas, each carrying a single 250kg bomb, flew at treetop level, their pilots peering intently through the fog. Suddenly, the fog miraculously lifted and the river bend came into sight – right ahead of them! There was no sign of any enemy action as they roared towards the bridge. Rising sharply over the railway dam, Dilley and his two wingmen released their bombs and dragged their machines upwards to escape the blast. All three bombs were bulls-eyes and the first Stuka attack of the war was over. The bridge over the Vistula was safe, for the time being. Now it was up to the panzers to get there.

At 0445 Guderian's XIX Corps started out from its assembly area at Dobrinin in Pomerania. The long columns advanced over the border which was covered by heavy mist. To the east the sky showed its first streaks of colour as dawn broke. But no one had slept that night! Like a curled spring the regiments unwound, and sprang forward, the tension finally over – action at last! A sleepy Polish customs official emerged from the frontier hut in his shirtsleeves, staring in amazement at the advancing panzers.

The lead vehicle, driven by Rittmeister Freiherr von Esebeck, crashed through the barrier, the Pole jumped clear, falling into a ditch, and the invasion of Poland was on! The 3rd Panzer Division raced towards its first objective, the River Brahe which flowed into the Vistula to the south. Crossing the Brahe was vital so that the Germans could reach the Vistula to cut off the Polish defences along the border where they were strongest. General Guderian travelled with the first wave of the panzer regiment. He was standing in his command car when some artillery shells dropped right in front of it; the driver panicked, lost control and drove straight into a ditch. The general stopped a passing vehicle and, rushing back to his headquarters, took another command car which was standing by. As he crossed the path of the forward elements of his reconnaissance battalion, commanded by his younger son, Kurt, the two men waved to each other.

On the bank of the River Brahe, it was almost morning and Guderian was searching for the local commander when an officer approached, warning him that Polish snipers were busy on the far side and rifle fire was falling on the troops massed along the banks. For the moment, things were static. No one seemed to know where to go from there. The divisional commander, General Geyr von Schweppenburg, had been called to a conference at Army Group, exactly when he was most needed at the front. Just then a young officer, Leutnant Felix, came out of the river in his shirtsleeves and reported that he believed the river bank on the far side seemed weakly defended. Responding immediately, Guderian took charge and ordered a strong armoured column to cross the Brahe. Having succeeded in this, he pushed more and more troops and vehicles over and managed to create a strong bridgehead. Then, reorganising the troops, for most of whom this had been their first action, he began to prepare for the next objective.

By now, though, the Poles were recovering from their first shock and their resistance had stiffened considerably. The adjutant of the Polish 7th Mounted Light Infantry Regiment, Captain Szacherski, had been woken by a telephone call shortly before 0500 to be told by his commander, Major Kalwas, that the Germans had crossed the border and were on their way to his region. Even as he alerted his regiment, Kalwas could hear Stukas screaming overhead, dropping bombs which slammed into the assembly area, causing the Poles' first casualties. The horses screamed and reared in terror, the riderless racing wildly over the field.

Soon the first German vehicles appeared round a bend. Two hastily emplaced Polish anti-tank guns opened fire at point blank range and their effect against the thinly armoured German vehicles was lethal. But the Luftwaffe was soon in action, and some Stukas dived onto the Polish guns, which disappeared in a ball of fire and smoke. The panzers rolled onwards, avoiding two tanks which had been hit and were left burning at the roadside. Suddenly, from a side road, a Polish truck came at full speed, ignoring the German fire. Then the lead tank fired a burst of machine gun fire and the truck overturned, spilling wounded troops who dragged themselves painfully into the bush and scrub for cover.

While the Polish commander was trying to rally his troops, Guderian had received word of a forthcoming Polish cavalry attack on the German 2nd Motor Division. The divisional staff asked to withdraw to better defensive positions, only to be told quite forthrightly by their general that nothing of that sort would occur while he was around, and the advance was going to continue.

By noon the German vanguard had reached the outskirts of Krojanty in the Polish Corridor. Here the first serious clash occurred between German troops and Polish cavalry. The 18th Uhlan Regiment of Brigadier Stanislaw Starogard's Pomorska Cavalry was ordered to counter attack the German vanguard and stop its advance on Naklo and the railway line. The horsemen assembled in a nearby wood and, forming into battle order, the 1st Squadron, led by Captain Godlewski, emerged and galloped towards the German columns. Behind him Major Malecki raised his sabre defiantly to signal the assault – the first cavalry charge of the war! As they emerged, Leutnant Lossen saw them coming through his binoculars and, ordering his vehicles to halt, he directed merciless machine gun fire onto the men and the horses alike. A few fell, but the others raced on, moving over the open fields, waving their heavy sabres which shone in the sun. The 2nd Squadron joined them, forming a broad wave of horsemen across the fields. It was a magnificent display, but a hopeless one. For a moment Lossen and his gunners watched this knightly spectacle and, for a second, he hesitated, not wanting to destroy the horses and their brave riders. But then his sense of survival overruled his emotion and he and his men fired burst after burst. He had just pulled his two vehicles into a copse at the side of the road when the battalion commander arrived. He called over his portable radio for artillery fire and soon the shells came screaming over, crashing into the line of advancing cavalry which was now close to the road. At the same time some armoured cars appeared from the rear and opened fire too. The carnage was terrible. Horses crashed into the ground, while others bolted in terror. Men could be seen falling out of their saddles, while a bugle could be heard faintly, mingling with the screams.

The Polish regimental commander, Colonel Mastalerz, rushed forward with a reserve troop but he himself was shot from his horse and killed outright. The entire battle lasted only a few minutes but, to the horsemen in that inferno of fire, it seemed an eternity. Nearly half of the riders had been hit, many killed or seriously wounded. The fields of Krojanty were no longer fields, but an abattoir. The story of horses charging tanks swiftly spread but, in fact, the Polish command had not intended to create a legend. They had tried to rout the German infantry battalion of General Bader's 2nd Motorised Infantry, and would have succeeded but for the intervention of Leutnant Lossen and his armoured troop.

And that was not the end of the German-Polish tank versus horse battles. An even more savage one took place at Mokra, near Lodz not far from the German border between the 4th Panzer Division, led by General Georg Reinhardt, and the Wolynian Cavalry Brigade commanded by Colonel Julian Filipowicz. The main body of the Polish brigade was defending the woods surrounding three hamlets along the north/south railway line, with a gun-mounted armoured train in support. The terrain assigned to the cavalry was well suited for defence. In the north the River Liswarta offered security while the woods gave good cover across the entire length of the front. A hedgehog defence could thus be deployed, with troops dismounted in forward posts, a large reserve, and mobile scouts used as forward reconnaissance.

On the German side, 4th Panzer had two tank regiments, mostly of light machine gun tanks operating with Stuka support. 35th Panzer Regiment, commanded by Lieutenant Colonel Heinrich Eberbach, was in the lead. To the south, 1st Panzer Division, with General Rudolf Schmidt in command, was driving eastwards to take the railway junction.

At 0800 the vanguard of Colonel Eberbach's regiment rolled forward, encountering only isolated resistance which they quickly outflanked but, as the lead panzer column, led by motorcycles, edged toward the village of Rebielice, it was met by accurate fire from the Polish 12th Lancers shooting from well concealed positions on Hill 268 which afforded a good range of fire. The German troop leader halted and set up heavy machine gun fire on a small hamlet from where he thought the fire was coming, but he soon realised his mistake after losing one light tank and two motorcycles. The road filled with a mob of civilians attempting to flee from the surrounding villages and the Poles, fearing that this would endanger their room to manoeuvre, sent out a horse patrol to calm the panic, but they were forced to withdraw due to heavy German fire.

Some 25 German light tanks now advanced onto the hamlets, taking advantage of cover from isolated houses, but still coming under heavy fire from the Polish 2nd Horse Artillery. Colonel Eberbach came forward and took charge of the assault. With their 20mm automatic guns blazing, the panzers rushed on, burning the hamlets to the ground as they went. The Polish commander, though, decided to hold and, with the German tanks only 150 metres away, the 21st Lancers manhandled three of their anti-tank guns into position, knocking out six German tanks one after another. Colonel Filipowicz saw his chance! Seeing the Germans waver, he ordered his reserve under Captain Hollak to outflank the German column around a village called Wilowiecki, using an approach route which would have cover from the woods.

To the north, the German commander was trying to mount a three-pronged attack on the 19th Lancers' position, just south of the

Liswarta River but, encountering heavy fire from anti-tank and machine guns, the attack soon faltered. At 1000 General Reinhardt, realising that this time he was facing serious opposition, came forward to confer with Eberbach, and decided to resume the attack to the north of the 19th Lancers, through the forest. Here the German attack clashed head on with Hollak's squadron which was galloping towards Wilowiecki and the Poles were forced to withdraw into some buildings against strong German fire. Some of the horses stampeded and fled into the forest as a number of Stukas screamed down at zero height to strafe the cavalry. As they had no anti-aircraft guns available, the Poles could do little to defend themselves against the aeroplanes.

The fighting had now been going on for several hours – and no end was in sight. The Poles kept holding on and the Germans, now under pressure to keep up with their timetable, were trying to get through the cavalry positions, with no success, despite the incessant Stuka attacks and German artillery barrages which slammed into the wood and hamlets indiscriminately. Several guns and machine gun positions had been destroyed or overrun, but Captain Deszert and his group on Hill 268 had held out for over an hour, pinned down by German fire. Then he lifted his head, saw some German tanks rolling towards Opatow, and opened fire on them with his remaining gun.

But the Poles were fighting a losing battle against overwhelming odds. Reinhardt, no longer willing to waste valuable time, sought to out-flank the Polish blocking position. In a final attack he launched a com-bined air and armoured assault to break the deadlock. Around 1300 the Germans launched their final assault on Mokra, using over a hundred tanks in two waves, which overran the Polish anti-tank barrier and burst into Mokra, destroying the 2nd Horse Artillery position from the rear. The mêlée lasted for another hour, both sides suffering serious casualties in hand-to-hand fighting. As a last, desperate gesture of defiance Filipowicz even ordered the armoured train into action, but its move was spotted by the German air patrols, which swooped down and bombed it. In the late afternoon, Captain Hollak who had been trapped inside Wilowiecki fight-ing off German assaults all afternoon, managed to break out and rejoin the brigade – only to join them in their forced retreat.

Polish losses on that day were heavy: nearly 200 officers and men had been killed, 300 wounded; half their complement of horses had been killed, mostly by Stuka attack. But the Germans had suffered too. They had lost many men, some 75 tanks and armoured cars had been knocked out in combat, and more were damaged but repaired.

During the night the gallant survivors of the Polish cavalry withdrew in orderly fashion, still led by their commander, Colonel Filipowicz, ending a memorable battle, which had held up the German advance for almost a full day.

CHAPTER SIX

MASSACRE OVER THE MAASTRICHT BRIDGES

The Second World War had been going on for nine months; but not much was happening and many people, lulled into a sense of false security, were calling it 'The Phoney War'. All that was to change, however, on 10 May 1940 when the Wehrmacht finally struck in the West. At first light German bombers took off from their bases along the Rhine and, using the element of surprise, attacked French and British air bases. The Luftwaffe's air wings operated almost like clockwork as they swooped over the Allied airfields and supply depots near Nancy, Metz and Toul. There was one mishap, however – and it was a serious one, which would have even more serious consequences as the war went on.

At 1500 on the warm, cloudy afternoon of that Friday, 45 German Heinkel 111 bombers of Kampfgeschwader 51 took off from their base at Landsberg, near Augsburg, to bomb the large French air base at Dijon-Longvic. Leading the 8th Staffel was Leutnant Seidel. At first all went well but, as the formation entered into thick cloud, Seidel went off course...

The little south German town of Freiburg in Breisgau, not far from the Swiss border, was having a normal day. Suddenly, out of the clouds emerged three twin-engined bombers. They were still too high for their national identity to be verified by the air observers on Lorettoberg overlooking Freiburg. The watch commander, however, picked up his telephone and reported the flight to his superior at HQ, who tried to calm him by saying that the planes must be German. The three bombers could now be seen coming down in a shallow dive, and they were indeed German – they were Heinkel bombers! Out of the cumulonimbus clouds they came, going straight for Freiburg. Still holding the phone, the watch commander gasped as he saw explosions erupting in the centre of the town! Several bombs were falling near the Gallwatz barracks, others near the railway station and, worst of all, some fell on a children's playground in Kolmar Street. Within minutes 57 civilians were dead, among them 22 children. Seidel's three Heinkels which had strayed from their course were the first shot in a total war of indiscriminate bombing of civilian targets which culminated in the bombing of Germany into ruins five years later.

The German government was shocked when it learned of the error. But the Nazi Propaganda Ministry took advantage of the tragedy by blaming the French for an inhuman act of war, and then using it as an excuse four days later when the Luftwaffe devastated Rotterdam. But whispers of the true story were already circulating, as not only had the Freiburg police found bomb fragments which were easily traceable to the Luftwaffe's armoury at Lechberg, near Munich, but the watchmen of Lorettoberg had also spread the news. Strangely enough, however, no German sources have ever admitted to the Freiburg affair, and most postwar publications simply ignore it. It is true that even more dramatic events were taking place – and not very far away.

From dawn to dusk of 10 May, hell broke loose all over northern France. On the ground, the Luftwaffe crews could watch the magnificent sight of entire panzer divisions packing the roads leading to the River Meuse, a tempting target indeed for enemy bombers... if there had been any. But there were none about that day – the skies belonged entirely to the Germans.

For the French and British airmen, still lulled and unaware, the morning dawned just like many others. Not one of them could foresee the savage battles which were about to begin. Then suddenly at General d'Astier de la Vigerié's Northern Zone Headquarters at Chauny, telephones began to ring... Reports were coming in from all over the area. The Germans seemed to be everywhere at once. The French general was pacing up and down, unable to determine where the Germans' main thrust was coming from, when in walked Air Marshal Sir Arthur Barratt, commander of the British contingent in France, buttoning his tunic. One look at the map was enough to tell him what was at stake and Barratt was itching to counterattack. To unleash the combined French and British forces without more information would be dangerous, however, so GHQ remained silent, while the two commanders continued to chafe and fume for several hours and reports piled up indicating the havoc being caused to their precious airfields in northern France.

Meanwhile General Erich Hoeppner's XVI Panzer Corps was pouring over the Meuse at Maastricht, having captured the two bridges intact. As his two panzer divisions pushed on towards Tongeren, supported by a strong contingent of Stuka dive bombers, it seemed that nothing could stop their onslaught.

At 1100 GHQ finally gave the word to attack; Barratt raced to his telephone – connected to the Advanced Air Striking Force (AASF) headquarters in Champagne – and ordered No. 114 Squadron to stand by. The squadron, one of six RAF units equipped with Blenheims, was ready for take-off within the hour. At Condé Vraux airfield, on the River Aisne, a slight drizzle was falling and the air was fresh. Suddenly nine strange aircraft flew over the trees, coming straight at the bombers lined up on the ground as if on parade. The Dorniers, for that is what they were, thundered in at near zero feet. Leutnant Reimers, leading the 4/KG 2 formation, was an experienced airman but now he could hardly believe his luck! The English Blenheims were sitting ducks! Soon showers of 50kg fragmentation bombs were exploding on them, covering the machines with dense black, oily smoke. Reimers swung his bomber into a tight turn and returned within seconds, raking the remaining bombers with deadly accurate machine gun fire. By now nearly all the British bombers were in flames, some from the explosion of their own bomb loads. While all this was going on, only one lone Vickers gun sputtered in response, and Reimers led his formation, still very much intact, over the ridge and disappeared from sight.

But that was not the end of the story. In the last plane Sergeant Werner Borner, the radio operator, had filmed the entire scene – so the same evening General Bruno Loerzer was able to demonstrate to a euphoric Adolf Hitler the results of that smashing success. Down below, as the aircrews emerged from their dugouts, shaking the dust off their jackets, No. 114 Squadron was no more. In just 45 seconds a significant part of the Advanced Air Striking Force in France ceased to exist as a fighting force.

Meanwhile, the Belgians had been attacking the Maastricht bridges, trying to stem the seemingly endless flow of German panzers over them. But it was like trying to stop the ocean. Nine Fairey Battle bombers from 3 Air Regiment operating out of Aeltre airfield arrived, only to be struck by a shower of dense anti-aircraft fire. The mission was a complete disaster – six Battles were shot down before they could even drop their bombs, among the casualties was the dashing pilot Captain André Glorie; the other three planes crashed, badly damaged. They had managed to drop their bombs but had failed to do any damage to the bridges. The Germans just kept coming.

The French High Command was now very worried and d'Astier was ordered to stop the German panzers regardless of the cost. The aircrews, who had been champing at the bit for far too long, were soon in the air – most of them flying to certain death from the withering fire of the enemy air defences. The effectiveness of the German rifle and machine gun fire was one of the great surprises of the war for the Allied forces, who were completely unprepared for such ferocity. But as well as the small arms, the low level attackers faced highly accurate flak, which shot down scores of attackers even before they were ready to bomb their target.

The following day, 11 May, the massacre went on. The Germans' northerly thrust over Maastricht gained momentum, now endangering the entire northern flank of the French and British forces in Belgium and northern France. Hoeppner's panzers were racing towards Brussels; in the east, Sedan was about to fall to the panzers of General Heinz Guderian which had crossed the Meuse in a brilliant coup de main. The scarcity of Allied aircraft was becoming even more serious as, in addition to those lost the day before, others now lay mangled on the ground, shot down by flak, ground fire or fighters which filled the skies over the battlefield.

On 12 May, the Allies focused on the Maastricht area and in particular the bridges which they decided must be destroyed at all costs. But for 48 hours the Luftwaffe was still very much in control of the air all over Belgium and northern France. The Allied pilots took off again and again but were shot down in hordes. Something had to be done, and quickly...

The targets chosen were the two vital bridges over the Albert Canal, west of Maastricht, where the main thrust of the German advance was piling up behind Hoeppner's panzer corps, and very much dependent on its supply lines in the rear. The destruction of the Veldwezelt bridge on the Hasselt road and the southern bridge on the Tongres road would cut Hoeppner's lines of communication. He had no immediate alternative for feeding fuel and munitions to his panzers who were involved in the first major tank battle of the war, against French forces near Hannut.

At nightfall on 11 May, the French Air Force flew a final attack on the bridges, followed by RAF home-based Blenheims, all attacking from medium height. Four Blenheims were immediately attacked by German fighters and shot out of the sky. Several French bombers were damaged, and none of the bombs did any damage to the bridges.

At daylight on 12 May, Barratt made another attempt to send his remaining Blenheims to Maastricht. It was the turn of 139 Squadron, which despatched nine Blenheims to attack the enemy supply columns on the Tongres road... At 0700 that morning Hauptmann Joachim Schlichtig, commanding I/JG1, took off from Gymnich near Cologne to fly defending patrols over the Albert Canal bridges. As he flew over his assigned area, the flight leader could see several black dots below him, which he soon realised were twin-engined Blenheims, nine in number, flying serenely along, unaware that they had been observed. The Bf 109 leader immediately ordered an attack, swung into a dive and, followed by his wingman, closed range onto the British formation, whom he clearly identified from the RAF roundels on wings and fuselage. Leutnant Adolph, the second flight leader followed suit and soon the bombers appeared in their sights, as big as houses, still flying in perfect formation. The two German pilots raced towards their prey, guns cocked and eyes peering into the sights. At 80 metres – an unmissable range – they fired their guns and almost immediately flickers of flame appeared along the Blenheims' wings. Taking sharp evasive action so as not to collide with their victims, the Messerschmitts broke and dived down, but not before seeing one Blenheim burning, one of its wings folding like a bird's as it hurtled earthwards in flames. The other bomber reared up like a stricken horse and, for a brief moment, seemed to standing on its tail. Then it fell, spinning, to earth. One parachute was seen to emerge, but that was all. Within five minutes six Blenheims were blazing on the ground. The three survivors escaped, only to be pounced upon by another flight of Messerschmitts near Liège, when two more were shot down. Of the nine that had taken off just two hours before, only one Blenheim limped home to its base at Plivot.

At the green and pastoral airfield of No. 12 Squadron AASF, near the village of Amifontaine, tension was high. The 'Shiny Twelfth', as they had been nicknamed, had already gained some experience in the Blitzkrieg, but their own squadron had been spared the fate of No. 114, as their Battles were well camouflaged and dispersed in the surrounding trees. At dawn on Whit Sunday, 12 May, the crews of No. 12 were roused and told that an important mission was coming their way. As they assembled for their briefing they were in good spirits, as Squadron Leader Lowe told them what their mission was to be. Instructed by Air Marshal Barratt to destroy the Maastricht bridges once and for all, he called for volunteers only, to fly the mission – because it was almost certain suicide. Six crews were needed, but the entire squadron volunteered to a man. It was a difficult choice but, finally, the decision was made to select those on that day's operational roster. Those who were left out were deeply disappointed, some even trying to swap places with the 'lucky' ones, but to no avail.

The briefing was just coming to a close when the squadron leader was handed a note informing him of the disaster which had befallen the Blenheims near Maastricht. He immediately warned his men to look out for fighters. As the two flights were taking off, eight Hurricanes of No. 1 Squadron, led by their CO, 'Bull' Halahan, were already on their way to Maastricht to fly cover for the Battles, which could certainly not defend themselves in a dogfight.

Leading No. 12 Squadron was A Flight, commanded by Flying Officer Norman Thomas, ordered to attack the Vroenhoven Bridge, the southern one on the Tongres road. Flying in formation with him were Pilot Officer Davy and Pilot Officer Brereton. But the latter had mechanical trouble on take-off and was forced to turn back. Following was B Flight, commanded by Flying Officer Donald Garland, Flying Officer McIntosh and Sergeant Pilot Marland. It was a bright, fresh May morning but the pilots were under no illusions – they knew that they might not live out the day, but they were all too busy to be afraid. The aircraft they flew were in no way suitable for their hazardous task – indeed by 1940 the Fairey Battle had been in service for half a decade, and was already obsolescent, unable to confront German fighters or, for that matter, serious flak or ground fire and, as a day bomber, it would be a sitting duck. Garland and Thomas therefore depended on 'Bull' Halahan to carry out his task, that is, let them get to their targets. Then it would be up to them to use their not inconsiderable flying skills and, with a lot of luck, they would do their job *and* survive.

Thomas was aiming to cross the Meuse south of Tongres, then swing east to reach the Vroenhoven Bridge, his target, but was surprised to encounter heavy flak from below as he was flying east – Intelligence had not warned him of the intense enemy presence in that area. Another detour at that stage, however, would be pointless so the pilot decided to fly straight for the concrete bridge, which stood out clearly on the horizon. The flak thickened dangerously as he flew in and out of low clouds, which hid him for a few brief moments, but then the sky became a cotton wool inferno, with bursts of flak following them everywhere. None of Halahan's Hurricanes could be seen.

In fact, they were already involved in a fierce fight with a swarm of Messerschmitts of JG 21 which had swooped down on them in seconds. The Hurricane pilots were on the alert, though, and with their throttles at maximum, black smoke already pouring from their exhausts. Leutnant Gustav Roedel in his Bf 109 followed a Hurricane flown by Pilot Officer 'Hilly' Brown, who in turn was in pursuit of another Bf 109. Hilly opened fire, saw his prey breaking away sharply, going down in a steep glide, when he felt his plane shake from Roedel's guns. Not losing his nerve, the Englishman broke into a steep dive and, followed by his German pursuer, went down for the deck, swinging into cloud cover on his way. When he emerged, however, his foe was still after him. The two chased each other over some wooded hills, skimming over valleys and hillocks, but in the end the German gave up.

Overhead the battle was just reaching its climax. Halahan and his pilots were fighting for their lives, but at the end six Hurricanes and three Messerschmitts were burning on the ground. Interestingly, one of the German pilots involved in this battle was Hauptmann Adolf Galland, later to become the Luftwaffe's most senior fighter commander, who – bored with his office assignment – took a little holiday to fly this engagement ... and to shoot down his first enemy plane.

Under cover of the dog-fight going on, Flying Officer Thomas was already roaring onto his bridge. One German fighter swooped down on him, but left him for someone else to take care of, and veered off, going after Pilot Officer Davy, who hid himself behind a welcome cloud. Thomas pointed his Battle at the bridge, attempting to ignore the thick flak that was still coming up at him. Pointing the nose of his plane at the centre of his target, he eased the control column down, watching the altimeter in front of him start to unwind dangerously. As if hypnotised, he stared at the oncoming bridge as he released his bombs. Behind him the observer, lying prone on his belly, was monitoring the falling bombs, while the gunner struggled to hold his position. The bombs exploded while Thomas was still dangerously low, struggling to escape the dense flak now bursting all around him. But the bridge still stood, undamaged – all the effort had been for nothing. Pilot Officer Davy, having shaken off his pursuer, saw Thomas' bombs explode at the far end of the bridge. He turned in and dropped his own, but saw them explode in the water. On his way out, chased by flak, he was again attacked by a German fighter which swooped at him as if out of nowhere. His rear gunner, Sergeant Patterson, fired back and damaged the German plane, but not before Davy's own aircraft was hit by cannon shells which ruptured the fuel tank. Davy ordered his crew to bail out at once and held his course with his blazing plane until he saw them all drop away. Then suddenly the fire went out, and he struggled back to base alone, nursing his crippled plane down to a crash-landing _ from which he walked away unhurt!

It was not the only crash-landing that morning... Back near Maastricht, Thomas felt his aircraft staggering around in the sky like a punch-drunk boxer from the impact of flak. The wings were about to snap from the strain – so the pilot pushed the nose down and, virtually throwing his aircraft into the ground, flattened out at the very last minute as he saw the ground coming up. Touching down relatively smoothly, to everyone's surprise, he ground to a halt not far from the bridge he had been trying so hard to destroy. A convoy of German gunners had been firing wildly at his plane as it came down. They were still firing when the plane stopped. Thomas helped his crew to leave the plane. He was amazed to see Corporal Carey, his rear gunner, still in position to fire at the enemy, but Thomas ordered him to come away before the aircraft caught fire. Some of the German gunners raced to capture them, their first prisoners of the war. One of them, an elderly gunner, told Thomas that he thought the British pilots were totally mad – but grand! And mad they must have been, because almost none of the Battles returned from that suicide attack.

Five minutes after Thomas had crash-landed at the Vroenhoven Bridge, Flying Officer Garland approached his own bridge, the Veldwezelt. This one was a metal construction, a few kilometres to the north. Garland favoured a low level attack, so flew in at 50 feet, plunging directly into a dense cloud of flak and light arms fire. Flying Officer McIntosh's aircraft was hit and burst into flames, but the pilot managed to jettison his bombs before they exploded beneath him. He swooped into a perfect crash landing on the left bank of the Albert Canal and he and his crew emerged, shaken but whole. Sergeant Marland's Battle was the next to be hit. It staggered, heavy black smoke poured out, it climbed steeply then suddenly, flicking over, it flew straight into the ground. Here there were no survivors. McIntosh and his crew, who had survived by some miracle an equally certain death, watched in horror as the Battle plunged into the earth. They had barely recovered from the shock when they saw Garland's plane come into view over the top of the trees which lined the river. The Battle was still flying, twisting and turning, shedding fragments of metal as the flak tore into it, leaving a thin trail of smoke as it went. McIntosh and his crew watched spellbound, totally unaware of the German soldiers who had come to capture them and who stood equally amazed by the spectacle above them.

And what a spectacle it was! Although badly hit and barely in control of his aircraft, the pilot went straight for the end of the bridge.

Garland knew that his bombs, fuzed to only eleven seconds delay, would give him no chance to survive, but he knew that he could at least cause some damage to the bridge, so he kept as low as he could – and crashed, the western edge of the bridge exploding in a huge ball of fire. No one could be expected to survive but some German sappers managed to pull out one of the crew; he was mortally wounded, but they left him for dead. He was later secretly buried by some local Belgian patriots. This was Leading Aircraftman Reynolds, who lived long enough to reveal Garland's courageous act, and this filtered through the Underground back to Britain, leading to the award of the first two Victoria Crosses to aircrew in the Second World War – one to Flying Officer Donald Garland and one to Sergeant Thomas Grey, his observer. This was a boost to the sagging morale of the forces and especially to the AASF after the painful losses. Curiously, Reynolds received no mention at all, although he was as much part of the heroic act as the other two. Sadly, all three of Donald Garland's brothers, also serving in the RAF, were killed during the war.

By the end of the second day of the battle for France, the RAF contingent there was already shattered, having borne the brunt of the action to stem the German advance. It had lost some 200 of its aircraft, mostly Blenheims, Battles and Hurricanes, the latter having been devastated in dogfights with the Luftwaffe. The home based squadrons had to take over the fight, which caused concern in headquarters that too many aircraft would be frittered away in a battle which was already lost, thereby endangering Great Britain's home defence. This, of course, was precisely what the Luftwaffe were aiming for. Fortunately there were sufficient cool heads in Britain to make the right decision, so that the crucial Battle of Britain could be won a few months later. Meanwhile the French took partial revenge by winning one battle over the Meuse, when the famous Cigognes squadron destroyed an entire Luftwaffe Stuka squadron returning from a bombing run over Sedan a day after the Maastricht disaster.

The bridges over the Albert Canal were not damaged sufficiently to stop the flow of German supplies, but the repeated attacks, costly though they were to the Allies, did cause much concern to the German commanders with regard to their supply line at Maastricht. Matters got so bad that the 4th Panzer Division, which had run out of fuel and ammunition, had to be supplied by air-drops near Lens-Saint Rémy. But by then attention had already shifted to a new crisis, further south on that same river Meuse – the great breakthrough at Sedan.

CHAPTER SEVEN

CROSSING THE MEUSE: BLITZKRIEG IN ACTION

In May, 1940, when the Germans arrived at the River Meuse, they thought that all the bridges had been demolished by the Allied forces. But an alert intelligence officer, scanning the countryside from a Fieseler Storch reconnaissance plane, was amazed to find one bridge still intact, and jubilantly radioed his HQ with the good news: the bridge at Yvoir was passable!

Colonel Paul Werner commanding Panzer Regiment 31 was ordered to race to the river and take that bridge; at 1630 on 12 May 1940 – Whit Sunday – the vanguard, led by Leutnant Heinz Zobel approached, with an armoured car forward. But, as Werner watched from his command car, the enemy suddenly came to life.

Colonel Jean Tachet des Combes, commanding the defending French 129 Infantry Regiment, was trapped on the west bank, where he had gone to establish contact with some cavalry troops. As soon as he saw Werner's troops approaching he started to run back over the bridge, but was killed by a burst of machine gun fire from Zobel's car. The Belgian engineers sent to the bridge to set demolition charges saw the colonel fall on the girders, but were too stunned to act. Lieutenant Jean Wispelaere, the Belgian officer in charge, now showed great courage. Realising that everything was up to him, he rushed to the demolition desk and was about to pull the trigger when he saw a French cavalry unit racing towards the bridge, with Zobel's armoured car right behind, its 20mm cannon blazing. Making a split-second decision, the Belgian officer made to fire the explosive charges – but nothing happened! The electrical cables had been ripped.

The French soldiers had just passed him on the bridge when Zobel's armoured car arrived on it. A French anti-tank gun situated on the west bank now opened fire and stopped the vehicle in its tracks. Zobel bailed out and raced for cover, with a Belgian sapper shooting at him as he ran, but he miraculously survived. Wispelaere rushed forward, reached the explosive chamber, and lit the last fuse manually. As he raced back, ducking the fire from a second German car coming up to the bridge, he was hit by a 20mm cannon shot, but, at that moment, the bridge exploded like a thunderclap, taking with it both German cars as it fell into the river. The last bridge over the Meuse had been blown.

But that Whit Sunday was a lucky one for the Germans! Rommel's motorcyclists, patrolling along the river bank, found an old weir near Houx, which their commander, Leutnant Herbert Krause, immediately realised would give them at least a chance to cross the river. On checking the weir he thought that, although quite narrow, it might afford enough support to cross over to a small island in the river. He immediately set out with a party, only to encounter heavy fire from the far side of the river, where vantage positions overlooked his every move. As his men were only lightly armed, the heavy units still being far away, Leutnant Krause looked at the dominating heights from which the enemy fire was coming, and saw that it would be foolhardy to make the attempt in daylight. He was right – the Wastia heights turned out to be a major obstacle, too much for a small force to handle.

Not having the benefit of hindsight, however, Krause set out after dark, leading his men step by step over the narrow stone locks. They were unobserved, the French having decided that they had given up and, as dawn lit up the sky, the patrol had reached the heights and begun to fire on some very surprised Frenchmen. Krause now set up his only heavy weapons, his machine guns, and radioed that he was in control of the heights.

This news reached the divisional commander, Erwin Rommel, as he arrived at the east bank of the river, and he wryly reflected that it was the only good news he had had all day. Things were going very slowly everywhere else, only a single company having crossed during the night. The French were firing away from their artillery positions, and punctured rubber boats were strewn all around, the German sappers having hidden or run for cover. The advance seemed to have ground to a complete standstill.

Rommel now ordered that artillery fire be directed at the French positions to reduce some of the shelling, and that some of the houses on the river bank be set alight to supply a smoke screen for the sappers trying to get their boats into the water. By this time, too, Krause's small force was in urgent need of reinforcements so Rommel, not wanting to give up this vital spot on the high ground, decided to act fast. Running to the river bank, he boarded one of the rubber boats himself, shouting to the commander of the 2nd Battalion to get his men into the boats. Rommel took his adjutant, Captain Schraepler, with him, but the latter was wounded as he tried to board, and Leutnant Most joined the general instead. The two officers paddled across the bullet-torn water, reaching the far bank safely where the commander of the rifle company who was holding the small bridgehead welcomed him. Soon the entire battalion reached the river bank and took up positions below the hills.

Using a portable radio, Rommel directed his tanks on the eastern bank to fire point blank into the French bunkers on the hillside but, just as he did so, his adjutant informed him that some French tanks had been sighted by Krause's men on top of the heights. Rommel's small force on the west bank, still without tanks or even anti-tank weapons, was in serious jeopardy.

But Rommel was just the man for a challenge. Ordering machine gun fire against the advancing tanks, he also called for flare pistols to be shot at them, which the inexperienced French commanders mistook for anti-tank rounds with tracer – and decided to withdraw. Meanwhile the sapper officer had built a cable ferry and set it in motion to ferry some tanks over from the other side of the river. The first of these were the 75mm gun tanks with firepower to combat even the heavier French tanks if they were to come forward again. Some anti-tank guns were also brought over.

During the night the German sappers built a heavier bridge over which all of Rommel's panzer division would be able to cross – just in time, since urgent messages were arriving from HQ warning of a strong French counter attack. Two enemy armoured divisions were now on their way to the front, and would probably arrive at dawn. The transfer of German tanks across the river went on, but not without trouble. The French were still in vantage positions on the Wastia heights and sent a hail of explosive shells on to the targets below. One tank, commanded by Hauptmann Steffen, was hit by a French 25mm anti-tank round and the officer was killed. Another toppled into the river and all the crew drowned. Leutnant Heinz Zobel, the courageous officer who had escaped almost certain death at the Yvoir bridge the day before, miraculously escaped once more when his armoured car was blown into the water, only to drown later when guiding a Panzer IV onto a pontoon raft which collapsed under the excessive weight.

During the night Most sent a forward observer to join Krause on the heights. From this vantage point the Luftwaffe officer directed the Stuka pilots which came over at first light, pulverising the French bunkers on the same hill. It was at this point that the French counter attack came in. A combined tank and motor infantry attack rolled onto the German bridgehead but, with the aid of strong Stuka support, guided by Krause's men on the high ground, the supporting infantry was kept at bay and the cautious French commander broke off the action and withdrew. During the following night Rommel gained control of most of the high ground and was able to regroup for the advance into the French rear.

Dramatic events were also taking place in the south, where General Guderian's XIX Panzer Corps was trying to cross the Meuse at Sedan. This small garrison town, well known for its textile mills, was also famous as a battleground: in 1870 it had been the scene of France's most painful defeat at the hands of the Germans. Defending it in May 1940 were second class troops, mostly elderly reservists with no training in modern warfare. Some 450 modern anti-tank guns were still stored in army depots, but these men, with almost no heavy weapons available to them, had no chance against the highly trained, experienced German army fighting with the blitzkrieg tactics which were new and strange to the Frenchmen. The French deployment was even worse than their manpower because the most sensitive sector, the seam between two of their armies, was situated right to the west of the Meuse river bend and north of Sedan, probably one of the worst mistakes made by the French high command in the entire war – and they made a few! With their totally inadequate communications, such a deployment invited disaster, and the invitation was accepted.

Guderian reached the bank of the River Meuse and saw that it looked easy to cross, being only 25 metres wide at the Sedan bend, but French pillboxes cleverly placed in the overlooking cliffs made activity on the banks difficult, not to say impossible. Guderian set some of his tanks and 88mm flak to fire across the river and silenced one after another of the French positions with fire which penetrated right into the bunker slits.

Guderian's chief of staff, Colonel Walter Nehring, took charge of the Luftwaffe support, which had been well organised beforehand, with pre-arranged code names to mislead any enemy listeners. Soon the Stukas of VIII Fliegerkorps screamed into the fray. They were equipped with special screaming devices which they employed as they swooped to attack, dropping even louder screaming bombs on the enemy below, who had never before experienced such noise, and were completely shattered by it. A British liaison officer who was present, Major English, witnessed the terror and confusion: officers were trying to get their men into some kind of order, but the men, cowering in any corner they could find, just refused to listen. The actual damage was surprisingly light, but the effect on the men's morale was devastating, and the French commander was soon considering withdrawal.

But Guderian was not yet ready to move his tanks over the Meuse. The French defences were still functioning and heavy artillery fire was shelling the east bank continuously. What the Germans needed was a bridge. Three crossing sites were selected for their terrain suitability. The 1st Panzer Division was chosen for point attack, having been reinforced for the crossing with the crack Grossdeutschland Regiment, whose first action this would be. Major Walther Wenk, the division's operations officer, now gave his final briefing to the commanders, handing out an attack order based on a war game held earlier at Koblenz which had been eerily prophetic of the situation on the front right now!

The logistic staff had performed miracles and managed to get some collapsible rubber boats through the congested roads to the river bank, so 2nd Rifle Regiment of the panzer division was able to attempt a crossing. Commanding the Regiment was Guderian's good friend, Lieutenant Colonel Hermann Balck, who had worked under him during the creation of the Panzerwaffe years before. While Balck's boats moved into the water, Stukas pounded the French artillery positions, temporarily distracting their attention.

Not far away, the Grossdeutschland Regiment under Count von Schwerin also crossed the river in rubber boats, near Glaire, and formed a bridgehead. Once across, the grenadiers dodged through vegetable gardens, ramshackle tool sheds and barns which hid well-camouflaged enemy bunkers, most of which were knocked out with demolition charges.

By 1930 the lead battalion under Lieutenant Colonel Foellmer had reached and occupied the dominating Marlee Heights near Cheveuges. Colonel Balck was with them, although his river crossing had not been entirely without mishap. As he was organising the boats, a heavy artillery shell exploded right on a group of sappers and killed 29 men. Leaving the wounded in the hands of medical orderlies who rushed forward, Balck ordered his men into the boats and began the crossing. Rowing ahead was Staff Sergeant Heinz Rubarth, a member of the armoured engineer battalion. With eleven of his men he stormed into a fortified French position on the west bank and hurled demolition charges into the slits, destroying two of the gun emplacements. Balck and his men were finally able to cross in safety.

Some of the French, though, were still defending their positions. Just as Rubarth was rushing another bunker, he was confronted by several giant Frenchmen, who stormed up, rifles blazing, hurling hand grenades. One corporal fell, two other soldiers were wounded and fell to the ground, screaming in pain. Although nearly out of ammunition by this time, Rubarth stormed them, using only his rifle butt. Amazingly, the Frenchmen hesitated and then withdrew.

By nightfall the crossing of the Meuse had been achieved, but Colonel Balck decided to enlarge the bridgehead during the night in order to get some armour over. He had information of an enemy counter attack expected the following morning, and wanted heavy weapons and tanks, knowing they would be vital to block a strong enemy armour attack.

In Rommel's sector, to the north of Balck, a bridge had been established by dawn of Tuesday 14 May. In an attempt to head off the expected French counter attack, he ordered an advance towards Onhaye, where his riflemen had already occupied some high ground. As General Max von Hartlieb's 5th Panzer Division was massing to cross over the same bridge, Rommel 'adopted' some of von Hartlieb's panzers which were better armed, crossed with them and raced on, just behind Colonel Otto von Bismarck's rifle regiment. Just then the French attacked. Two

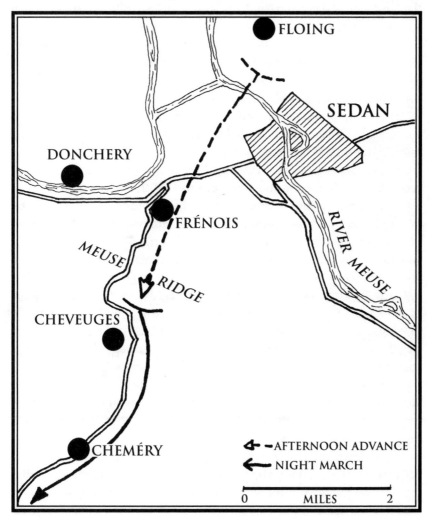

companies of infantry supported by eight gun-mounting armoured cars attacked von Bismarck's men, who were still devoid of tanks. Rommel, hearing von Bismarck's urgent call for help, ordered his tank driver to speed up and, going to the front of a battalion of tanks from Panzer Regiment 31, rushed to confront the French attack. His tank was just bumping through a hollow when it received a direct hit from two anti-tank rounds which shattered the glass of the periscope while the general was actually peering through it. He received a superficial cut from glass splinters, but was quickly in action again. But the driver, opening the throttle too wide in his panic, drove the tank into a ditch; it slid down a slope and nearly overturned. Rommel quickly bailed out and climbed back up to the road, hailed a passing car, leapt in, and drove on, just as some French soldiers had moved an anti-tank gun into position against his tank. Further on, Rommel saw a stationary tank by the roadside, a crew member wounded and receiving attention from medics. Rommel clambered up to the turret and ordered the driver to start up and soon he had reached his command group. After this, for Rommel, fairly uneventful journey he was in his element and ordered both of his forward commanders to mount a concentrated attack which pushed the enemy back and opened the way towards the important target of Morville.

That same morning, Tuesday 14 May, the battle near Sedan was reaching its climax. During the previous day the French had been in total disarray, having suffered more from shock than actual losses. The panic caused by the screaming Stukas had remained and several senior officers had lost their nerve. Rumours of German tanks approaching spread rapidly although, in fact, no German tanks had actually crossed; what had caused the rumours were actually French tanks driving towards the front. By morning it was too late to save the situation. Most of the French 55th Infantry Division had retreated, and only the brave defenders of the 213th Regiment were still holding the position to which they had been assigned, and which they only reached by dint of forcing their way through their fleeing compatriots. General Lafontaine, commander of the 55th, had managed to concentrate sufficient forces for a strong counter attack and, if one had been mounted early enough, it could have dislodged the Germans from their still precarious bridgehead. But it was too little, too late.

At dawn the first tanks of the panzer regiment crossed the River Meuse and were refuelling by the roadside. Just then Captain Pierre Billotte, the son of the commander of French forces on the north-east front, was leading his company of powerful B tanks along the same road.

Rounding a corner, he caught sight of the German column dead ahead – a tank commander's dream! Billotte wasted no time in attacking; they were only 50 metres away. Firing his 47mm gun at the first tank, a Pz IV, he knocked it out before the crew could even clamber into the turret, and two more German tanks were knocked out, including that of the German colonel, who was killed. But then his deputy took charge: manhandling an 88mm flak into position and firing at short range, he destroyed several of the heavily armoured French tanks. After a short battle, well over half the French tanks were knocked out, some of them by Stukas who had joined the fray. The French colonel was taken prisoner and the surviving tanks withdrew.

General Guderian now made a strategic decision, which would decide the outcome of the entire campaign. His armour having ripped through the main enemy defences, Guderian ordered two of his panzer divisions to drive westward, ignoring or evading all enemy counter attacks, and traverse the open ground of the Aisne and Somme rivers to the Channel, thus cutting off all the Allied forces still trapped in Belgium. His brilliant conduct of the campaign and the dismal French response – their armoured divisions never coming into battle – decided the issue and led directly to the fall of France.

CHAPTER EIGHT

THE LAST DETACHMENT: THE CADETS OF SAUMUR

The evacuation of Dunkirk lasted for less than a week, during which time some 350,000 Allied troops were ferried to safety in England. The German divisional commanders, who had been stopped by Hitler's own orders, were given the green light at last, but failed to break through the defence cordon formed by the French rearguard, who sacrificed themselves to save their allies. In any case the German panzer commanders badly needed a breathing space before going back into battle.

This time they were called for the second part of the French campaign whose goal was to push south and reduce the last Allied resistance which was building up fast. While the main units of the BEF were embarking under German fire from the Dunkirk beaches, other elements were landing at Cherbourg, among them armoured units from 1st British Armoured Division, but half of the tanks which were landed were obsolete, almost useless hulks. The French, too, were hastily putting together tank forces from the remnants of those that had taken such a battering in northern France.

While all this Allied activity went on, the German Army had not sat idly by. It had undergone a major regrouping process, in which five panzer corps had been created, ready for the next onslaught – this time on the River Somme, that old battleground from the First World War which became the new French line of resistance. General Guderian was given command of two panzer corps with four armoured divisions, General von Hoth's XV Panzer Corps still had Rommel's 7th Panzer and the 5th Panzer Divisions with it to operate along the coast towards the Channel ports, and two other corps were poised to strike inland with four more divisions. Against such an overwhelming armoured force, the French Army and its allies had little chance.

And indeed, after some fierce battles over the River Somme, including some local counter attacks, the German panzer spearheads were on the move once more – heading for the final kill. Paris was taken by two mighty armoured pincers, while Guderian's divisions outflanked the French defences near Rheims and raced south-east towards the Swiss border. The Cherbourg peninsula was taken by Rommel's 7th Panzer Division on 19 June; some of the British troops there, including some members of the armoured division, tried to embark for England, but many were taken into captivity.

Only on the River Loire were the Germans halted temporarily. Here the 9th Région Militaire was charged with the defence of the river line, with the cadets of the world-famous French cavalry school at Saumur being given a 40-kilometre stretch of the river to defend, due to the scarcity of reinforcements. The school's commander, Colonel François Michon, had under his command less than 1,300 men, including some 750 officer cadets and their instructors. In their support he could muster a bare handful of obsolete tanks from the school's arsenal and some hastily commandeered Hotchkiss tanks from elements of the 19th Dragoons who had retreated to that region. The school's defence sector spanned from Montsoreau to le Thoureil, and contained several bridges, the most important being at Gennes to the north-west, at Saumur itself and at Port Boulet. The most dangerous sector was at Saumur, where a major road from the north crossed the river leading south.

Shortly before the arrival of the German spearheads on the northern riverbank, it was decided to evacuate the famous Cadre Noir horses and their riding instructors. They left the city in a long convoy heading south; civilians stood by the roadside, sadly watching as these precious animals left them, seemingly for ever. After they had gone, the towns-people went to seek shelter from the impending battle in the lime caves near the river.

Colonel Michon's only specific orders were to defend the river line, using groups of cadets, each under the command of an instructor, each group in a different position. Michon set up headquarters in a villa near a château which overlooked the river line and the island over which the main road passed between the two parts of the town. The school's chief instructor, Major Lemoyne, was placed in charge of the command post, while a cadet was sent to the castle's tower to observe and report developments by field telephone.

The island at Saumur proper, where two bridges spanned the river, was defended by Lieutenant Gerard de Buffevent. He was sup-ported by a group of men from the school, who set up blocking positions on the south bank near the city square. Further west, at Gennes, Lieu-tenant Jacques Desplats with another group of officer cadets set up defences on an island. To lend some mobility to the defence, Colonel Michon organised a mobile force which included the few available tanks as well as some Panhard armoured cars. This force he placed under the command of Captain Foltz, a senior instructor, who selected the best trained men from his class to man the vehicles.

The first contact with the enemy, advance elements of the 1st Ger-man Cavalry Division, was made in Lieutenant de Buffevent's sector. At about midnight on 19 June, a German reconnaissance group advanced cautiously towards the railway station on the northern riverbank while an officer went on foot towards the nearby Napoleon bridge. De Buffevent saw the Germans coming, but decided to hold his fire to prevent the enemy from discovering his position. Only when the German column started forward towards the bridge was Cadet Houbie, commanding a 25mm cannon, ordered to open fire; within minutes seven German light tanks were destroyed, impeding the progress of the other tanks massed behind. There was confusion in the German column, whose commander had not expected such fierce opposition. He called frantically for artillery support, but the guns failed to arrive until dawn – hampered by the traf-fic jam building up on the road behind. De Buffevent and his cadets were encouraged and astonished by their early success, for this was their first combat. But at dawn the German artillery began to range in on the island. Suddenly a light armoured vehicle appeared on the river bank and from it emerged a German officer together with a French prisoner, waving a white flag. Shouting across the water, the German demanded the surrender of the city but de Buffevent's men failed to recognise the white flag and fired on him, whereupon he withdrew hastily.

By now the main force of the German division had arrived at the river line and deployed along the bank. Tanks and anti-tank guns were taking up firing positions, covered by the houses on the river bank. From his vantage point the cadet who was observing from the castle tower saw the fight on the island and pinpointed the enemy's gun positions, but Colonel Michon did not have enough guns to be effective against the massive fire power that the Germans were bringing up. The dreaded Stukas had arrived by this time and the first bombs fell near Michon's command post, forcing him to withdraw to another house inside the town. The cadet in the castle tower also came under gunfire and left hurriedly. He managed to drive his motorcycle combination to safety.

Lieutenant de Buffevent's force held fast on the island, preventing any Germans from advancing towards the Napoleon bridge. At dawn it was blown, but German fire intensified, causing the first casualties to the cadets. The German commander, seeing the demolished bridge, decided to outflank the town, and sent a task force along the river to the east while another turned west towards Gennes.

A few kilometres to the east was the railway viaduct, defended by a group of cadets commanded by Lieutenant La Lance. As the German advance guard, commanded by Captain Holste, reached the railway bridge, it was blown by Lieutenant La Lance's sappers. The Germans only managed to repair it a year later. Interestingly, in 1944, shortly before the Normandy invasion, the Royal Air Force destroyed that same bridge plus a nearby tunnel with earthquake bombs dropped by No. 617 Dambuster squadron.

Further to the east, at Port Boulet, another German force tried to cross the river, but it was kept at bay for several hours. Here, too, the bridge was blown, but the charges were badly placed and only part of the bridge demolished. German sappers went to work immediately while direct fire from tanks on the opposite bank covered their operations.

Some time later, another attempt was made to force a crossing and at dawn on 20 June, an infantry battalion crossed the water in rubber boats and created a small beachhead on the far side. However, under heavy fire the small French detachment there withdrew and set up defensive positions near Fontevrault, a large training area. Realising the threat, Colonel Michon sent his only reserves to the endangered region. Some Panhard armoured cars came under fire as they drove along the open river road, but they reached the Fontevrault detachment with three 75mm guns and started firing on the German bridgehead.

Lieutenant de Buffevent's dwindling force was still fighting fiercely on the island, but the air attacks increased as the Germans poised for an all-out attack. De Buffevent himself realised the hopelessness of their situation and ordered his remaining men to withdraw to the south bank and join the detachment defending the bank under the command of Lieutenant Perin. As the survivors started to withdraw the entire island seemed to be on fire. De Buffevent remained in his place, rendering covering fire. With him were some of his men who refused to leave him. With darkness falling, de Buffevent decided on one last audacious coup against the Germans now massing on the approaches to the northern bridge. He led a small force, armed with light weapons and hand grenades, to the northern side of the river. Approaching the Germans unnoticed, the French cadets stormed the German positions, throwing grenades into a group of German trucks from which troops were just dismounting. The carnage was terrific. However, a passing motorcycle turned round and gave the alarm, and fierce fire was immediately directed against the French. De Buffevent had just thrown a grenade into a German mortar position when he was mortally wounded by a burst of machine gun fire, and fell. Two more of his cadets fell nearby but the rest of the small group managed to retire over the river to safety, although some were badly wounded.

The German commander now decided to give up his attempt to cross over to the town of Saumur and increased his efforts to outflank it. On the afternoon of 20 June, a strong battle group stormed les Rosiers and approached the stronghold of Lieutenant Jacques Desplats who was defending the Gennes sector. It was this area that was to bear the brunt of the fighting over the next few hours. Desplats blew the bridge to the north and held on in his position on the island, keeping the southern bridge intact for the present. Meanwhile Colonel Michon had received word by telephone that Gennes was under attack and sent his armoured car squadron there under the command of Captain Foltz. The colonel was still confident that his men could hold off the Germans, at least for the time being, and he reported this to his superiors at Azay-le-Rideau. It was perhaps one of the few optimistic combat reports to come from that region for a long time.

But time was running out for the courageous French cadets. The Germans, frustrated by their inability to cross the River Loire, pressed the higher command at 1st Cavalry Division HQ to solve the problem without further delay. Strong artillery elements were now rushed forward and put into action, together with repeated dive bomber attacks. The French were feeling the pressure and, under cover of the deluge of fire, another crossing was attempted in three places simultaneously. Lieutenant Perin, in charge of the defence of the far bank, blew the southern bridge, thus cutting off the island from Saumur, but at Gennes the enemy forced a crossing and finally captured the island. Lieutenant Desplats fell throwing his last grenade at the advancing Germans and with him fell most of his cadets, only a handful managing to reach the southern bank on board the armoured cars, which had passed by shortly before the second bridge was blown.

Once they had taken the island, the Germans had no trouble in reaching the farther river bank, scarcely hampered by some of Michon's obsolete Hotchkiss tanks. Michon realised that the end was near, and played his last card – a counter attack aimed at dislodging the Germans from their hold on the south bank. Captain Delmotte from Michon's headquarters was placed in charge and given all the mobile forces which were still intact. Delmotte's motley force included some H-39 tanks, some of the remaining Panhards and two platoons of cadets from the infantry school at St Maixens. The French armour had little chance against the better-armed Germans but they drove off defiantly to the attack, the young cadets willing to die for the honour of their school. As they approached a German column advancing along the river road, the vanguard tank commanded by Lieutenant Pitiot came under anti-tank fire, killing the young officer outright in his turret. Another tank was set ablaze, the entire crew being killed. But the French infantry cadets stormed forward, led by Captain Delmotte, and overran the German machine guns guarding the road. Most of the cadets, however, fell during the 300-metre rush and the survivors sustained a sharp counter attack. Some rallied under their commander who was, miraculously, still on his feet.

But by now heavy mortar fire was coming down. There was no more hope for the French defenders and, having received orders to withdraw, Colonel Michon called off any further attempts to defend the Loire, with the resultant massacre of his young cadets that would ensue. An order was given to withdraw southwards towards the River Vienne and, even during the withdrawal, Captain Foltz's armour managed to destroy two more German tanks.

The cadets of Saumur had fought heroically for over two days without respite, and had held the Germans' elite cavalry division at the river's edge. Although losses had been severe, these young officer cadets had shown what a motivated force, even a lightly armed one, could do when called upon. The battle for Saumur may have been just a skirmish – no more than a footnote in the battle annals of the Second World War – but it remains to this day an example of human courage and devotion, and it saved the honour of the French cavalry. In honour of the brave cadets, the Napoleon Bridge at Saumur was renamed *Pont des Cadets*, a name which it proudly bears to this day.

CHAPTER NINE

COLD STEEL AND BLAZING CHARIOTS

On 18 November 1941 the British launched their largest – and most ferocious – offensive yet, codenamed 'Crusader', against General Erwin Rommel's Afrika Korps. Their objective was to liberate the garrison besieged at Tobruk, by first destroying the bulk of the German armour and then linking up with the British troops inside the fortress. The fighting went on for almost a week, with the tanks on both sides grappling in confused mêlées during the hours of daylight and then retiring to lick their wounds and regroup during the night.

On 24 November, following some savage fighting at Sidi Rezegh, the battle appeared to have reached a climax, although neither Rommel nor his counterparts at the British Eighth Army really knew what was going on after the confused tank battles of the day before. There had been terrible losses both of men and tanks; some regiments had dwindled to a handful of 'runners', others had ceased to exist as fighting units, and the battlefield was strewn with the wrecks of hundreds of burnt-out tanks and other vehicles.

Rommel acted first, to make the most of what he thought then was a heaven-sent opportunity to strike a final blow at the British before they could recover. General Ludwig Cruewell, commanding the Afrika Korps, had conducted the battle in a masterly fashion and, while having suffered severe casualties, he still maintained a strong grip on his dwindling forces. Rommel had not been in touch with the detailed operations so, on receipt of Cruewell's slightly rose-tinted after-battle report, he decided to mount yet another of his daring coups, which had been so successful throughout the war. Assembling the entire force of armour remaining to him, he ordered an all-out dash eastwards, maintaining a token force to guard the Tobruk perimeter, and then moving at high speed *through* the British rear, exploiting the shock effects of his mobility to cut off what remained of the British forces in the area of the previous battle. His instinct, bolstered by the monitoring reports handed to him by the German 'listeners' to the British radio traffic, convinced Rommel that the British commanders were in total disarray, receiving faulty, late and erratic information which only served to confuse, and that most of their tanks were either destroyed or dispersed. It was this situation that Rommel wanted to exploit before his enemies could rally.

Rommel's daring counter stroke nearly worked. It resulted in total chaos in the British rear, where the forces scattered and fled towards the Egyptian border but, even worse, it affected the morale of the British command so badly that General Cunningham, commander of the Eighth Army, actually thought of calling off 'Crusader' and withdrawing to the east. It was a strange paradox: Rommel's tactical situation was very bad; the number of tanks in his two panzer divisions had dwindled to a handful, with no reserves available. On the British side, the entire XIII Corps, with the 2nd New Zealand Division, 4th Indian Division and Brigadier Bill Watkins' 1st Army Tank Brigade, with nearly a hundred infantry tanks were making good progress. The British situation was therefore far better than the German, but the Desert Fox had once again gained the psychological upper hand!

However, this time Rommel did not have it all his own way. While he personally spearheaded the advance of his mobile columns, spreading confusion and panic through the Eighth Army rear, General Sir Claude Auchinleck, the Commander-in-Chief, arrived at Cunningham's forward command post. Cunningham had been shelled by German panzers while conferring with General Gott, commander of 7th Armoured Division. On his way back to his command post at Maddalena by plane, Cunningham had seen with his own eyes the British stampede and the German tanks lining up on the next ridge. No wonder then that when he met Auchinleck, Cunningham was a shaken man.

But General Auchinleck was made of sterner stuff. He realised that the situation called for decisive action and that under no circumstances should a withdrawal take place, leaving the strategic fortress of Tobruk to its fate. He was convinced that, with XIII Corps intact and Rommel's forces near the end of their strength, this was a golden opportunity to exploit the situation and make a push to link up with the Tobruk garrison.

The focal point in achieving this link-up was the Belhammed ridge, overlooking the plain leading up to the Tobruk perimeter. This would be the Eighth Army's next objective and accordingly orders were issued to both XIII and XXX Corps, the remnants of which were slowly reorganising after the battles which had dispersed them. While Rommel roamed around the British rear, his vehicles fast running out of fuel, the British recovery crews worked feverishly to repair as many damaged tanks as they could – and they performed wonders.

While XXX Corps was reorganising, the spotlight turned to the New Zealanders of General Bernard Freyberg's 2nd New Zealand Division. The battle for Belhammed was to be a major test of endurance and courage, but the New Zealand reservists were up to the job, showing once more the fervour and dedication demonstrated at Gallipoli.

On the morning of 25 November, the 4th New Zealand Brigade reached Zaafran, about 12 kilometres from El Duda, the place scheduled for the breakout of the Tobruk garrison, thus setting the stage for their link-up with the other British forces after their long siege. Only 12 kilometres – but they would see some of the most savage fighting of the 'Crusader' operation. The Eighth Army's directives for the link-up attack were specific: the New Zealanders were to capture the Sidi Rezegh–El Duda ridge and join up with the break-out assault from Tobruk, exploiting the fact that the main body of Rommel's Afrika Korps was still roaming about in the British rear and only a token force remained to guard the Tobruk perimeter.

Belhammed was a tall, sausage-shaped ridge overlooking the Sidi Rezegh airstrip, over which most of the tank battles of the previous days had raged. On this ridge the German Battle Group Boettcher, the Afrika Korps towed artillery and elements of Infantry Regiment 155 were emplaced in strong positions. To the south, the ridge was strongly held by the crack 9th Bersaglieri, the best infantry regiment the Italians were able to field. Thus, even in the absence of Rommel's armour, there were sufficient enemy troops to fight it out with Freyberg's New Zealanders and hold out until Rommel could come to the rescue.

General Freyberg decided to mount a night assault. His infantry would go in with bayonets, leaving the Matildas of 44th Royal Tank Regiment and the Valentines of 8th Royal Tank Regiment to follow in a supporting role. Lieutenant Colonel Howard Kippenberger's 20th Infantry Battalion, attached to Brigadier Lindsey Inglis' 4th Brigade, and Lieutenant Colonel John Peart's 18th Infantry Battalion – assigned to spearhead the assault – set off in the dark in battle formation, side by side, at precisely measured distances to follow the guiding strips laid out by sappers. The advance was slow, with company navigators leading by compass. Two kilometres out, the lead companies reached a depression, and radio contact between the company and battalion HQ advancing with the other troops was lost. The lead navigator lost his bearing, veered too far right, and reached a paved road, part of the German bypass route round the Tobruk perimeter. Within seconds, the New Zealanders had been detected by elements of Boettcher's troops, who first shot illuminating flares into the sky and then opened automatic fire. Colonel Kippenberger, with a small command group, not yet aware of the mistake, could see a battle going on below him, which he believed to be Brigadier Barraclough's 6th Infantry Brigade attacking Sidi Rezegh. Suddenly a maze of tracer bullets flew over his head, coming, apparently from Belhammed. As Kippenberger and his small group climbed the ridge, they encountered a group of Germans rushing to meet them head on. Having dealt with them, they continued in the direction of the firing which could now be heard from the top of the ridge. Once at the top, they joined up with their men again but soon the entire hilltop was covered by Boettcher's heavy artillery barrage. Colonel Kippenberger was wounded, hid in a foxhole and was reached by a daring radio operator who crawled in and handed him a microphone. The senior company commander was ordered to take over – and the attack continued.

By now it was almost daylight, although morning mist still reduced visibility. Major Leeds, leading C Squadron of the 44th Royal Tank Regiment, was hit and badly wounded, while two of his crew were killed outright. They had run into the range of strong German anti-tank defences on Belhammed ridge. Pinned down all morning in exposed positions, the New Zealanders could only watch in frustration as the infantry attack from Tobruk on El Duda took their objective. The German Battle Group Boettcher began to mount a counter attack on the 4th New Zealand Brigade when fighter bombers of the Desert Air Force came in low over the southern ridge and strafed the Germans to spectacular effect. But the respite was short-lived and soon all the New Zealand positions came under heavy fire from all directions at once. The situation was fast becoming critical.

Further to the west, at his headquarters at El Adem airfield, Lieutenant Colonel Siegfried Westphal, Rommel's chief of operations, was watching developments with ever-increasing concern. Unable to communicate with his commander, who was far away and out of radio contact, Westphal faced a serious situation. The breaking of the Tobruk siege would allow the British to cut off the withdrawal of Rommel's armour – which would mean the end of the Afrika Korps! Through the single radio link still operating to General Johann von Ravenstein's 21st Panzer Division in the Bardia region, Westphal sent him a summary of the situation, suggesting that von Ravenstein rally as much armour as he could to move westward and counter the British infantry attack on the Belhammed and Sidi Rezegh ridges, thus cutting off the New Zealanders from their rear and improving the critical situation around Tobruk. Von Ravenstein agreed in principle, but was reluctant to act at first without Rommel's consent, knowing that this would bring to naught the latter's aim of rounding up the British Eighth Army although, in view of the changing situation this was no longer feasible in any case. A quick decision was required, and only Westphal was there to take it.

On the British side, the new situation also called for some decisive action: not only was the planned link-up with the besieged Tobruk garrison within reach, but a strategic outcome in sight in which Rommel's armour could be destroyed and 'Crusader' brought to a decisive victory. But once again the Desert Fox refused to admit defeat. As soon as he linked up with his armour near Bardia and learned the reality of the situation, he unhesitatingly pushed all the remnants of his depleted armour force in a westward march toward the scene of battle on the ridges of Tobruk.

The time factor once again became crucial for the British: the link-up between the New Zealanders and the Tobruk garrison now had to be effected without delay before Rommel's panzers arrived. Consequently, General Freyberg ordered 4th New Zealand Brigade to attack with the support of 44th Royal Tank Regiment and force the link-up at El Duda 'at all costs'. Four miles of fire-swept ground still separated the two forces and Boettcher's gunners were determined to prevent any advance. Lieutenant Colonel Bill Yeo commanding the 44th, suggested mounting a combined tank–infantry attack at night, but the infantry commanders, who were suspicious of tank tactics, vehemently opposed the suggestion. The New Zealanders had never worked closely with tanks and their experiences to date had been mainly bad ones. Brigadier 'Booming Bill' Watkins was called in to support Yeo's idea, one which Watkins not only endorsed but had actually pioneered in the Royal Tanks.

Watkins had got the concept of night tank attacks from Major General Percy Hobart, who had used this unconventional method during exercises in the Egyptian desert before the Second World War when he trained the Mobile Division in long desert marches. Watkins, then commander of 1st Royal Tank Regiment under Hobart, took up the idea with great enthusiasm. At that time the brigade's Matilda infantry tanks were still superior to the German panzers, and their heavy armour was the only thing able to stand up to the lethal, accurate German anti-tank guns, which wrought havoc among all other British tanks of that period. Two months before Operation 'Battleaxe', 1st Army Tank Brigade had temporarily replaced 7th Armoured Brigade, undergoing reorganisation in the Canal Zone. The 1st Army Tank Brigade took part in the defence of Egypt, blocking Rommel's advance eastwards. Watkins had then reached the inevitable conclusion that his brigade was inferior in speed, which precluded his heavy armoured tanks from fighting effectively in daytime, but he was convinced that they could successfully take on the German panzers during late afternoon, using an armoured car screen, which would trace the German panzers into their night leaguer and pinpoint their positions. Once the Germans thought themselves secure, thought Watkins, accustomed as they were to the British practice of breaking off the engagement after dark, his Matildas would have a perfect opportunity to attack the German tanks inside their leaguer and inflict serious losses on them.

Having worked out his new strategy, Watkins now set about training his tank squadrons in long, exhausting night marches until officers and men were not only fully familiar with the night, but experts in celestial navigation techniques. Acting on intelligence information, he built a dummy leaguer and on this he drilled his tank crews until they each knew their mission by heart. Each night a different squadron would carry out a 24-kilometre night march and then attack a dummy camp. Each squadron had an expert navigator and each a specialist in night fighting techniques, which were perfected as time went by. By the end of his training scheme, Brigadier Watkins had brought his 1st Army Tank Brigade to a fighting pitch in darkness, and now only had to wait until providence would test his plans in a real battle. Unfortunately, Watkins' seniors were hostile to these new ideas, and lacked the imagination to visualise their potential.

So on that afternoon in November 1941, Colonel Yeo and Brigadier Watkins, the two night attack proponents, confronted General Freyberg's staff, who were reluctant to try anything new. But Freyberg himself, although an infantry officer – and a noted one, having won a distinguished Victoria Cross in the First World War – was a man of vision and listened even to junior officers, if they had something interesting to say. What these two tank commanders had to say made sense, and was finally adopted, much against the will of the infantry officers who resisted to the end.

The method devised was that a spearhead of one squadron should lead the way and a second squadron would follow ten minutes later, escorting an infantry battalion. The attack was to be silent, without artillery support, and Watkins' night fighting techniques would be applied for communication and direction finding in the dark.

The attack jumped off at zero hour, with a well directed stream of tracer bullets guiding the way from the tanks' Besa machine guns. From the start, the German defenders were utterly surprised by the night attack with tanks, and responded with ill-directed counter fire, which caused no casualties. The New Zealanders marched behind the tanks, suffering only a single man wounded, in contrast to the horrors of their infantry assault the night before. Tank commanders did not close down, and went through the entire attack with their heads out of their hatches, with the infantry commanders marching alongside in close contact or, in some cases, even riding behind on the rear engine deck. The tanks sent out withering machine gun fire, scattering the enemy soldiers before them, while British prisoners-of-war, captured in last night's battle, crawled out of foxholes, their German captors having left them behind in their hurry.

By midnight the 44th had joined up with Colonel O'Carrol's 4th Royal Tank Regiment on El Duda ridge. The link-up was completed, at least for the time being. Colonel Yeo's night attack had been an unqualified success, carried out precisely as planned and with great skill, according to 'Booming Bill' Watkins' concept. His efforts had paid off and with this success the stage was set for the next attack which was to come a few weeks later at Bardia.

The Axis garrisons of Bardia and Halfaya sat astride the main supply route along the coastal road from Egypt. They had both held out stubbornly throughout the 'Crusader' campaign, and now the time arrived to tackle them once and for all. Of the two, Bardia was the tougher nut to crack, with some 20,000 troops in a strong, fortress-like perimeter. The perimeter defence consisted of several mined, barbed-wire fences, pitted with well-concealed anti-tank and machine gun positions and a strong artillery concentration in the rear.

The village of Bardia itself was perched on high ground overlooking the Mediterranean Sea, but the defended area stretched some ten kilometres inland, and contained many strongpoints manned by forces of platoon strength. A metalled road, the Iponticelli, bisected the position, running north-west towards Tobruk and south to Capuzzo.

The Allied attack was to be mounted jointly by four battalions of the 2nd South African Division, supported by the 44th Royal Tank Regiment and 8th Royal Tank Regiment of Brigadier Watkins' 1st Army

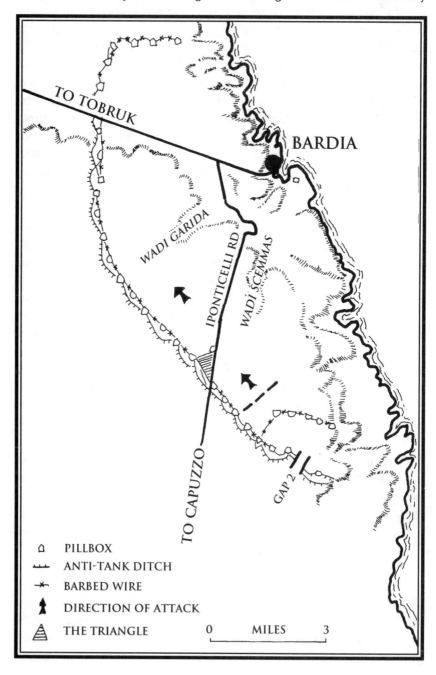

PILLBOX

ANTI-TANK DITCH

BARBED WIRE

DIRECTION OF ATTACK

THE TRIANGLE

0   MILES   3

Tank Brigade. The attack was to be in two stages, the first to be a break-in, the seizure of a consolidated start-line, from which the second stage, a night assault, would penetrate and capture the fortress itself. The first stage was planned to start at dawn on 31 December 1941, and involved South African sappers blowing the wire, which would allow 8th Royal Tank Regiment supporting two infantry battalions, to get through. The second stage would see 44th Royal Tank Regiment advancing with two squadrons up front, without infantry, behind a creeping artillery barrage, while engineers advanced before the tanks to clear mines. The vanguard, having dealt with the enemy positions, would be followed by a second wave of tanks shepherding two South African infantry battalions for mopping up operations.

At 0430, shortly before dawn on 31 December, 8th Royal Tank Regiment set off very quietly, without artillery support, while the engineers cut the first wire fence, fired Bangalore torpedoes and, working feverishly, started to fill the forward anti-tank ditch, over which the leading squadron of Valentine tanks passed. One of the men moving through the gap was Lieutenant Stuart Hamilton, leading his troop, while his gunner fired short bursts from the coaxial Besa to keep the enemy from shooting. They were making good progress when the driver spotted the muzzle flash of an anti-tank gun. A second later, the left side of the turret was hit by a heavy crash, which temporarily concussed the turret crew. When the tank gunner regained consciousness, he found himself staring at the red hot nose of a 50mm anti-tank round stuck in the turret armour – just above his head! The driver, reacting automatically, swung the tank in the direction of the gun and, putting his foot down on the accelerator, raced right into the gun position, scattering its crew, which fled as the heavy tank smashed the anti-tank gun into the ground. Moving on, Hamilton's tank reached the top of the escarpment overlooking Bardia's harbour which was bathed in the pearly Mediterranean morning light. But they did not have much time to enjoy the scenery; swinging left to continue towards their next objective, the tank hit a German anti-tank mine, which exploded, smashing the tracks and suspension. The Valentine lurched to a halt – in a place most likely to win the title of the place you would least like to be: totally exposed in the middle of a minefield.

The South Africans had advanced with the tanks and captured the high ground, as planned. But the enemy now put in a strong counter attack, causing severe casualties and forcing the infantry to leave the ground they had captured. The disorganised infantry was now incapable of mounting the second stage of the attack and, after a hasty discussion, the commanders decided that it would have to be postponed for at least 24 hours. Colonel Bill Yeo was against postponement, convinced that if the night attack were delayed, the defenders would have time to reorganise and would be much stronger against the assault forces, thus causing more casualties. He and Brigadier Watkins persuaded Major General de Villiers, commanding the 2nd South African Division, to go ahead on 1 January 1942 at 2200. Shortly before the attack Colonel Yeo contacted the two South African battalion commanders, Lieutenant Colonel Palmer, commanding 1st South African Police Infantry, and Lieutenant Colonel Page, of the 1st Kaffir Rifles. Both were keen to cooperate with Yeo's tanks but, as time was short, little was achieved by this meeting, apart from a discussion on communication aspects of the coming battle.

Zero hour approached. The night was bright, with a half moon making the tanks all too visible as they lumbered slowly into their start-line position, two squadrons in night battle formation, with the infantry forming up behind. At precisely 2200 the Allies began their barrage while the Matildas moved majestically forward over the sand and disappeared over the first ridge into the enemy compound.

For Sergeant John Holley of the Kaffirs, it was his first time under hostile fire. As he led his section of infantry he could hear the thunder of the artillery; the flashes, illuminating the night sky, silhouetted the hill in front. Before him was the reassuring sight of the big tanks ploughing ahead, spitting fire from their guns, and he followed one of them through the barbed wire. His men scrambled behind, rifles pointing forward, bayonets glinting in the moonlight, their mouths dry from that fear of the unknown that every soldier knows. Suddenly the silvery landscape turned into a scene from hell as shells began to fall all over the area, making a terrifying noise. Shrapnel flew all around – the first men fell, some moaning, some without a sound. Holley froze for one split second, but then his training took over and he began to run forward, passing a tank which had careened over and was lying on its side in a tangle of barbed wire. One of the crew was scrambling down, but was caught by a short burst of fire and fell off the tank. Holley saw three men crouching behind a light machine gun, only metres away. He realised that they were Germans and, firing from the hip, he advanced like a robot on the enemy position. The Germans saw him coming and wrestled with their gun to turn it in Holley's direction, but they were still trying when Holley, with two of his men close behind, charged into them. Two of the Germans died instantly; another stumbled to his feet and, eyes wide with terror, disappeared into the darkness.

While this drama was taking place, the tanks were going forward, finally reaching the paved road, but there the lead tank exploded, hit by an anti-tank round. They had come up against a strong enemy tank obstacle, and in consequence the tanks had to change direction, a difficult task in a night attack. This caused further delay as signals were exchanged between the tanks and the infantry commanders but finally the tanks were on their way again. At 0230 the units of the leading echelon reached their objectives, but came under heavy mortar fire as they stood on an exposed ridge which overlooked Bardia harbour. However, within an hour dense smoke could be seen rising from the direction of the village and harbour installations, a clear sign that the enemy was about to give in and had started to incinerate the supply dumps.

As dawn broke a message came through that the German commander, General Arthur Schmitt, was ready to surrender and with him some 9,000 German and Italian troops went into captivity. Since Bardia had been one of Rommel's main supply bases, huge quantities of stores, guns and ammunition fell to the victors, an irreplaceable loss for Rommel and one from which, despite his subsequent tactical victories in 1942, he never fully recovered.

Despite this victory, Brigadier Watkins' concept of night fighting, so brilliantly executed by Colonel Bill Yeo and his 44th Royal Tank Regiment reservists, gained little attention from their masters. Moreover, surprisingly little has been written in the military annals of the Desert War giving credit to these two men who had done so much for the Allied forces, and could have done even more if their ideas had been put into further use. Sadly, both Watkins and Yeo were forced to leave the scene of battle shortly after Bardia, and neither of them saw active service with tank forces again.

CHAPTER TEN

ATTACK OF THE COCKLESHELL HEROES

One of the major challenges facing the Germans in the Second World War was the provision of vital raw materials to their military industries. One of these materials was natural rubber, only to be found in the Far East. Although German scientists had come up with a wonderful substitute called 'Buna S', even this had to be blended with a certain amount of the real thing in order to manufacture tyres of acceptable quality. After Japan had occupied the Far East, therefore, its vast rubber plantations called to the rubber-hungry Germans, and they opened a lifeline of merchant ships to transport large quantities of the material, evading the ever-growing menace from Allied warships and aircraft whose task it was it was to blockade the vessels and stop them from reaching Europe.

By the summer of 1942 the problem of these 'blockade runners' was causing the British naval strategists much concern. The Germans were getting their valuable cargoes through the western approaches of the Atlantic and into the harbour of Bordeaux which, with its excellent port facilities and lying as it did well-protected by its long river approaches, proved to be a perfect collecting base. It was estimated that it would take nearly two divisions to mount even a limited attack on the port, an assault landing being far beyond what was available to the British at that period. Moreover, since the town itself was right next to the harbour, any high altitude bombing attack would cause tremendous casualties to the French civilian population, a consequence which could have disastrous effects on inter-Allied relations. However, *something* would have to be done, since intelligence reports received at this time made it clear how much the German war industry was depending on this important lifeline.

Major H. G. Hasler, better known as 'Blondie', due to the impressive Guards moustache which he proudly sported, already had a distinguished career behind him by the summer of 1942. He had been in charge of landing operations during the abortive Allied invasion of Norway in 1940, and using his boats had put ashore troops from the French Foreign Legion, Polish forces landing on Norwegian shores and, later, took off young Norwegians joining the Underground in their homeland. Hasler had already gained an OBE as well as the French Croix de Guerre for his deeds, a remarkable accomplishment for a young officer so early in the war. Before the war Hasler had been a small boat enthusiast, believing, with Mr. Rat, that 'there is *nothing* – absolutely nothing – half so much worth doing as simply messing about in boats.'* He had gained considerable experience, and in 1940 had written a professional paper emphasising the importance of small boats in the conveyance of powerful explosives into enemy ports to destroy shipping moored at berth. Their Lordships at the Admiralty

---

* *The Wind in the Willows* by Kenneth Grahame, Oxford University Press.

had regarded the idea as too dangerous to execute but, when Combined Operations Headquarters was formed, Hasler's paper was put forward once again for assessment and, when the problem of the Bordeaux blockade runners became acute, Hasler was called into the Chief, Admiral Lord Louis Mountbatten, who was impressed both by the young man's enthusiasm and by his expertise.

Within 24 hours of his meeting with Mountbatten at Whitehall, Hasler had put forward a detailed plan for an attack by small boats into the Gironde River. Mountbatten approved the plan and set about form-

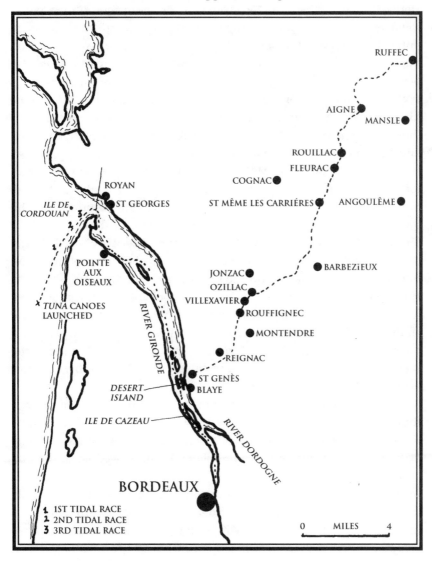

ing the Royal Marines Boom Patrol, putting Major Hasler in charge. Now began a long and gruelling training schedule, with a team of volunteers specially selected from the Royal Marines Small Arms School at Gosport, who would carry out this extremely dangerous, some might say suicidal, mission under his leadership. There were numerous problems involved in getting a small force of assault canoes as far upriver as they would have to go, to attack a target known to be defended by massive amounts of German troops, bristling with gun positions. Not the least of their troubles would be Kapitan zur See Erdinger's 8th Zerstoerer Flotilla based in the Gironde River with its many gun-armed patrol launches. To get through this superb defensive cordon, which was supported by a dense net of observation and radar stations, would need all the luck and expertise there was. But Hasler trusted his men and his own experience, and his more cautious superiors were infected by his enormous confidence. He got his way, together with the tools to do the job, a remarkable feat in view of the history of previous operations of that kind – operations which had died before they ever came to fruition, killed by the caution of the red-tape bureaucrats.

By December 1942 Major Hasler was ready. His force of volunteers had been trained to the hilt, all of them highly motivated, although they knew that their chances of survival were practically nil, the best they could hope for being imprisonment for the remainder of the war. They did not know of Hitler's latest directive, issued shortly after the raid on Dieppe, in which he ordered that all captured commandos should be handed over to the Gestapo and shot without mercy. Hitler's orders were a serious breach of the conventions of war, but were followed without question by his forces. Thus, despite the painstaking efforts made by Hasler's team to sew on their 'Combined Operations' badges, insignia and 'Royal Marines' shoulder patches against the event of their capture, this would be of very little help to them in view of Hitler's order.

Hasler had organised his small force into two sections, each with three two-man boats. Instead of using the Special Boat Squadron Folbot, Hasler had looked for – and found – something more robust: a specially developed Cockle, which could be collapsed and placed on to the hull of a submarine. The Mk II Cockles which were to be used in the raid were a new departure in small boat operation. The loaded canoes could carry 215kg of weight, two men, and stores in five compartments – two in front of the forward man, one in front of the rear crewman, and two behind him, side by side. These compartments carried weapons, limpet mines, magnetic holders, rations, camouflage netting, navigating gear, and spares. The limpet mine was a specially designed explosive device which could be attached to a ship's hull; it consisted of a canister of high explosives fitted with six horseshoe magnets. To prime the mine a glass bulb had to be broken, releasing acid into a washer holding the striking pin, which fired the detonator. For maximum effectiveness, the mine should be placed below the ship's waterline, and this was achieved with the aid of a magnetic holder and steel rod which lowered the mine into position. This was a precision operation needing both composure and courage – those flimsy boats would be travelling from the Atlantic up the Gironde river to Bordeaux – over a hundred kilometres!

The operation, codenamed 'Frankton', began on 1 December when Hasler and his team embarked into the submarine HMS *Tuna*, stowing their flimsy craft into the forward torpedo room, where the men settled down in their cramped surroundings. It was only when the submarine had pulled away and slipped out of harbour that Hasler held his first briefing and told the men their target – Bordeaux. There was a collective gasp of surprise. In fact, throughout the training period, the major had disseminated the rumour that they would be aiming at the *Tirpitz* in a Norwegian fjord.

It took the *Tuna* five days to reach the point of disembarkation – the Bay of Biscay off the French coast – and what a journey it was for the 'Frankton' team. The first three days the boat was on surface in a stormy sea, which pitched and rolled the rounded hull from side to side. Most of the men were seasick, suffering not only from the foul air inside their cramped quarters, but from bouts of claustrophobia. The men would have faced anything just to get out of this tin can. On the third day, the *Tuna*'s captain, Lieutenant Commander Roger Raikes, DSO, decided to submerge, having reached enemy waters, and the boat dived into the calmness of the deep, much to the relief of Hasler's team.

On 6 December the *Tuna* reached its destination and at periscope height the captain surveyed the sea and the coastline, which was in sight. But the sea was high, a terrific gale blowing which made the boat roll heavily. Unable to launch the canoes in such conditions, Raikes submerged to wait another day, in the hope that the weather would improve.

At 1930 on Monday 7 December 1942, the submarine broke through the surface with a crash and settled on an even keel in perfectly calm seas and under cloudless skies. The forward torpedo hatch was opened and the heavily laden canoes lifted onto the upper deck. Major Hasler had realised from the outset that it would be impossible to launch the Cockles over the side in the normal way, and he had talked the naval engineers into building a sort of improvised crane on the submarine's deck gun to hoist the canoes and their crews over the side, thus preventing them from hitting the waves which would crunch them against the submarine's hull. The contraption worked – as would now be proved under operational conditions off the French coast.

First to go over were Major Hasler and Marine William Sparks, his team mate. As they hung over the water on the hoist, Sparks could see in the distance farmhouses on the French shoreline, their lights blinking reassuringly in the dark, as was the phare from the lighthouse at Pointe de Grave, signalling the entrance to the Gironde estuary. The canoe met the water with a slight splash, its heavy load causing it to settle low in the water. Then misfortune struck – the boat of Bill Elley and Eric Fisher knocked against the submarine's hatch clamp, tearing a long gash in the rubber fabric. Hasler had no alternative but to leave the two men on deck, in tears as they waved the rest of the canoes out of sight. Major Hasler and his remaining canoes rallied, and began paddling towards the coast, a full fifteen kilometres away.

There were now five canoes in his small force: Corporal Albert Laver and Marine Bill Mills in *Crayfish*, Corporal G. Sheard and Marine David Moffat in *Conger*, Lieutenant J. Mackinnon and Marine James Conway in *Cuttlefish*, Sergeant Samuel Wallace and Marine Robert Ewart in *Coalfish*. Hasler and Sparks were in their own canoe, *Catfish*. While he paddled, Marine Sparks was speculating on his chances of returning. Major Hasler had briefed them on their escape route, making it clear that any return by canoe over the near 100-kilometre trip along the river would be impossible, and that their survival would depend on their making an overland escape with the help of the French Resistance, if, indeed, contact could be made before they were captured. In other words, their chances were flimsy. But Sparks was reassured by the sight of Hasler in front of him. He and the rest of his team would follow him through hell, if necessary.

Paddling inshore, there were no enemy ships in sight, but suddenly a mighty roar could be heard ahead. Major Hasler signalled his canoes to raft up around him and told his men that the sound was the oncoming tidal race, with several currents of water meeting at this point. The crews secured their cockpit covers and braced themselves for the onslaught of the water. They did not have long to wait! Within minutes they were fighting to control their flimsy boats, which tossed about like corks on the huge waves which seethed around them. When the canoes finally assembled around their leader, one was missing – *Coalfish*, carrying Wallace and Ewart. The major attempted to find them, paddling back into the surging waters and blowing his signalling whistle, but there was no trace of them. Again there was that leaden feeling – they had lost two friends – friends who represented a large portion of the attacking force. Their chances of success were dwindling fast. Soon yet another disaster was to follow...

As they neared the Gironde estuary, the unmistakable roar of another tidal race was heard. This one was even worse than the first. Within just seconds the craft were pitching and bucking as the water boiled around them. The men paddled for their lives to prevent the canoes from capsizing in the huge waves but when, once clear of the danger, the major halted to await the others, only two came out of the shadows. This time it was *Conger*, with Sheard and Moffat, which failed to appear. Once again the major headed back into the dangerous currents and found the men clinging to their capsized boat. It was impossible to turn the boat upright, for it was too heavily laden, and in spite of everyone's efforts, it had to be abandoned, and it sank. Sheard and Moffat hung on to Hasler's canoe, which would tow the men as near as possible to the beach. By now the water was calm, but it was freezing, and their chances of survival depended on the time they would have to spend in the water.

Although the additional weight of the two men clinging on slowed the canoes, they managed to pass the revolving beams of the Pointe de Grave lighthouse without being noticed. Once inside the Gironde, Hasler swung as near as he dared to the river bank and the two men let go and started to swim ashore, encouraged before they left by a tot of rum. The men in the canoes watched their exhausted comrades disappear from sight – never to be seen again.

Now only three of the original six canoes were left to carry out Operation Frankton, and they had only been afloat for less than two hours since leaving the submarine. But they paddled on, crouching low to reduce their silhouettes as they slid through the water. Naval Intelligence had warned Hasler of German patrol boats which might be encountered in the estuary and sure enough one soon emerged out of the darkness, sweeping the water with its searchlight. Hasler and his men were unaware that the German radar station on the river mouth had picked up the *Tuna* as it surfaced and the German naval patrols were on high alert. The first German launch was followed by two more. Although it was too late for them to turn round, Hasler and his men kept their wits about them and, crouching low over their cockpit covers, they let the currents drag them upriver, managing to dodge the German boats which slid past them.

The three canoes had barely escaped the German launches when, as they paddled past a jetty, they saw a German sentry standing right on the waterline, only metres from where they would be passing. Hasler's group held their breath and, in spite of the freezing cold of that December night, drops of sweat ran down their blackened faces. But for the moment luck was on their side and they managed to slip past the jetty unnoticed.

Behind them, Wallace and Ewart in *Coalfish* were still alive. They had lost their way in the tidal race and nearly capsized in the second tidal race. With their strength ebbing, they dragged themselves onto the beach not far from the lighthouse while their boat rolled over and sank like a stone. Unfortunately, the exact spot where they landed was a Luftwaffe flak position; an alert sentry saw the two marines, and several German soldiers pounded along the beach and captured them.

Captain Max Gebauer, the German officer commanding the Marine Inshore Squadron, was immediately informed of the capture. He had already been informed of the spotting of a British submarine off the Gironde estuary a few hours before, and he now put two and two together, and ordered an immediate search for more possible intruders. A German patrol boat retrieved Wallace's canoe and dragged it ashore and a specialist crew found the limpet mines, together with some maps, but they were not marked, so the real aims of the operation went undiscovered. German intelligence believed that the canoe was on a British intelligence operation and not a full scale commando attack. Neither Wallace nor Ewart gave any information about their mission, but let the Germans believe that they were the only crew working in the area.

Meanwhile, totally unaware of what had befallen their comrades only a few kilometres to the north, Hasler's force was paddling on. It was now well past midnight and Hasler knew he would have to start searching for a place to spend the hours of daylight before continuing the next night. But the tide was beginning to turn, making the work more difficult, while the men were very tired and bitterly cold. Their hiding place was near Bordeaux-Merignac. On their first night, they had paddled 36 kilometres and they were all badly in need of rest. Having camouflaged their boats in some bushes, the men, soaked and chilled to the bone, crawled into their sleeping bags and fell asleep like logs.

Dawn broke and Hasler awoke. He passed a bottle of rum around to warm up the numbed limbs of the men who were still in their damp clothes, but it was of little help in that bitter cold. Just as they were settling down in their hiding place, some French fishermen came into view, shouting to each other as they went towards their boats moored along the river bank. The commandos lay under their nets, watching in agony as the Frenchmen came within metres of them. At the last minute, just before they actually stumbled upon them, Hasler, who spoke fluent French, came out of hiding and spoke to the amazed Frenchmen, who promised to keep their secret. They kept their promise, in spite of the danger to themselves if the commandos had been captured later.

The rest of the day passed without further incident and at nightfall, having surveyed the river carefully, Major Hasler ordered the canoes launched again for the night. Heading out into the river they began paddling south towards their target. The current was with them this time, helping to quicken their pace, and towards dawn they found a hiding place just north of Port de Calogne. It was now 9 December and two days remained in which to reach Bordeaux – still a considerable distance upriver. The day passed quietly, apart from an intrusion by a Frenchman who was walking his dog and stumbled on their hiding place. He too promised to keep his mouth shut but Major Hasler, not placing too much confidence in his word, decided to launch earlier than planned, and they took off again. They had not gone far when the throb of engines brought them to a halt. A German naval patrol boat was chugging along – straight for them! At the last minute the major led his boats into some tall reeds at the water's edge and the Germans passed them by downriver. But for the rest of the night the river was filled with Germans frantically searching the Gironde for more commandos, under orders from Captain Gebauer. Towards morning the commandos found a hiding place on a small uninhabited island close to the vineyards of St Julien where they slept peacefully for the entire day.

The dawn of the following day found them a considerable way upriver, approaching Ile de Cazeau, a large island in the fork of the Garonne and Dordogne rivers. They were about to land on the bank when the major, who had gone first, rushed back, signalling the canoes back into the water. It turned out that the site they had chosen was none other than a Luftwaffe anti-aircraft site. Paddling fast, they hid in some tall reeds as far away as they could get from the German positions, but not so far that they could not hear the Germans talking! In the morning some curious cows approached, and a German gunner began to look in their direction, no doubt wondering what the cows found so interesting. Sweat poured down the faces of the British commandos but, after a time, the German lost interest and disappeared into the woods.

After dark the group started on the last lap of their long odyssey, turning right into the Garonne river and heading for the harbour of Bordeaux. A steady drizzle began and at Bassens, only a stone's throw from the port, they rested for the last time. As the day grew brighter they took stock of their position. Their hiding place was just off the main highway, where heavy traffic could be heard rolling along. On the opposite bank of the river were two German merchantmen, the *Alabama* and the *Portland*, moored alongside a jetty.

During the day the men primed their limpet mines, setting the fuzes at eight hours' delay which, hopefully, would give them time to escape before the explosions went off. Then, at dusk, came the moment for which they had been planning and working. They made their final arrangements for the attack and set off, each one to his assigned target. Major Hasler and Marine Sparks paddled for Bordeaux harbour, which was bathed in light. Apparently the Germans felt so secure here from the RAF that no blackout was observed at all! Paddling up the middle of the river the commandos approached their objective undetected. There was so much activity going on along the piers, with the loading and offloading of ships in full swing, that no one took any notice of them! Soon they were right inside the harbour basin where several ships were moored in a row, a tempting sight for the attackers! *Catfish* approached its first target, the 7,800-ton cargo ship *Tannenfels*. This vessel had only just arrived from a tour of duty as a blockade runner from Japan, having picked up on its way the survivors of the commerce raider *Stier*, which had sunk after an encounter with an American warship. Sparks sent the canoe drifting towards the ship where Hasler, gripping the hull firmly, fixed three limpet mines into position below the waterline. Then they went upriver to a Sperrbrecher minesweeper, fixing two mines on her. Finally, they approached the 8,600-ton *Dresden*, moored alongside a tanker, but passage between the two ships was difficult, due to a swirling current. Suddenly they were bathed in light from above! A

German sailor was leaning over the railing, shining his powerful torch right on them. The two men froze, their breathing almost stopping as they clung to the side of the hull, while the German walked along the deck searching the surface of the water with his torch but, amazingly, after a while he walked away and the welcome darkness closed in on the raiders once more.

The German sailor had hardly gone, however, when another – and even more deadly – threat confronted them. The two ships, which were tied together, began to move without warning, coming together with the shifting tide and almost crushing the flimsy craft between them! The canoe began to crack and was about to capsize when, just as suddenly as they had come together, the two ships drifted apart. Quickly fixing their last mines to the hull, the *Catfish* crew broke away. Just then they heard splashing in the dark. It was *Crayfish*, carrying Laver and Mills, who reported having placed their mines on the *Alabama* and the *Portland*. It was time to go. Shaking hands for the last time, the men paddled off into the darkness, each to his own fate.

At that time, not very many miles away, Wallace and Ewart were led to a waiting truck. They drove off out of the town, and then stopped. The two men were hustled out and, in the light of the truck's headlights, Leutnant Theodor Pahm, adjutant of the Naval base, gave the order, and the two men were shot.

A few hours later, the first explosions ripped through the *Alabama* followed by others as the mines exploded. The *Dresden* sank, the *Tannenfels* was badly damaged and the other ships listed badly. By then Hasler and Sparks were already out of the place, having scuttled their canoe downriver and began an escape which would eventually, after a month of constant danger, bring both men home – the only survivors.

The other men were all captured. None of them betrayed their comrades and, on Hitler's specific orders, Lieutenant Mackinnon and James Conway were executed in the courtyard of Paris Gestapo Headquarters a few days later, after a harrowing interrogation. Petty Officer Laver and Bill Mills were also shot. Wallace and Ewart were already dead and Sheard and Moffat had been lost from the start. Moffat's body was washed up on the French coast as far away as Brest, and nothing was ever heard of Sheard.

The only survivors, Hasler and Sparks, were decorated for their deeds – Hasler with the DSO, Sparks the DSM, but none of the others, sadly, received posthumous awards. It took 40 years for public recognition of the brave men of Operation Frankton, with the unveiling of a modest memorial at Poole in 1982. But this attack put paid to the German blockade runners, since it made the Germans realise that Bordeaux was no longer a safe haven for them.

CHAPTER ELEVEN

THE CHANNEL DASH

One of the most audacious feats of the Second World War should never have happened at all, but it did, and right on Great Britain's doorstep – the English Channel. For 300 years, ever since the Spanish Armada had sailed with banners flying to invade Great Britain one fateful Friday in July 1588, only to be beaten off with terrible losses, no one had dared to challenge Britain's sovereignty over the Channel – that is, no one had until 12 February 1942...

In March 1941, following a joint sortie into the North Atlantic during which they sank some 22 merchant ships, the German battle-cruisers *Scharnhorst* and *Gneisenau* slipped quietly into the shelter of Brest Harbour in Brittany to refit and rest after several hectic months at sea evading the Home Fleet. Although the Germans realised that their haven was within operational range of RAF bombers, experience had shown that well defended shipping targets were difficult to hit from the air. In any case, the German battle fleet was in urgent need of repairs, and there were few alternative naval facilities available for the repair of 30,000-ton vessels.

An air of anxiety, almost of panic, pervaded the corridors of the British Admiralty at this time. Losses at sea were rising and Britain's vital lifeline – the Atlantic – was in danger of being cut by the German submarines and surface raiders. It seemed that this would be an ideal opportunity to destroy, or at least paralyse for as long as possible, the two German capital ships in their harbour. After heated discussions, Winston Churchill overruled Bomber Command's reservations, and ordered a massive attack on Brest.

Updated reports were coming in via the French Underground, in particular from a former naval officer, codenamed 'Hilarion', who was now working as a dockyard fitter in Brest Harbour – the right man in the right place; he was later to attain high rank in the postwar French navy. Armed with this intelligence, Bomber Command ordered the bombing attacks to start almost immediately and thereafter photo-reconnaissance Spitfires flew constant missions to follow the repair work and enable British naval experts to estimate when the ships would be ready to sail again.

Although most of the attacks were unsuccessful and losses increased, owing to a terrifyingly accurate air defence, made up of hundreds of anti-aircraft guns, flak ships and the formidable firepower of the ships themselves, the British planes continued to fly against the odds of both firepower and awful weather. Seeing that the night attacks were a miserable failure, the RAF switched to daylight sorties. Thousands of bomber sorties were flown but, although a tremendous number of bombs were dropped, only five actually hit the ships!

One bomb dropped near the *Gneisenau*, failed to explode, but caused the great ship to be moved out of dry dock to evade the danger. Thus she was moored alongside a long stone mole when Flying Officer Kenneth Campbell arrived at dawn on 6 April 1941 in his 22 Squadron Beaufort torpedo bomber, having crossed the Ile Longue, surprisingly, undetected. The weather was atrocious, with a thick early morning haze almost blotting out visibility. Campbell flew in at near sea level to penetrate the harbour. Circling nearby was Flying Officer Jimmy Hyde, an Australian pilot flying the other Beaufort. Out of the corner of his eye, he could see Campbell's Beaufort flashing beneath him, going all out for the mole. Campbell was flying right between the two narrow arms of land encircling the outer harbour when suddenly all the shore batteries and flak ships opened up with deadly, withering fire. Campbell climbed up sharply to a cloud, then steered a roundabout course for his target, although every gun in the harbour was now on the alert. Down to less than 100 metres, with a flak ship ahead of him, he raced straight into the barrels of their guns – which pumped shells into the Beaufort as it roared overhead at the height of their masthead.

All at once, the awe inspiring shadow of the giant battleship came into view, like a beached whale, spitting fire from every gun. Down now to less than ten metres, the water spraying from the wash of his churning propellers, Campbell released his torpedo and pulled up sharply, thundering at full speed over the stern of the *Gneisenau*, whose gunners were now firing point blank into the plane. Hyde, cruising nearby, saw Campbell's plane, engulfed in flames, crash into the harbour. No one emerged. When the Germans later lifted the wreck out of the water, they found the navigator, Sergeant Scott, in the pilot's seat. No one was left alive to tell what had happened in those last terrible seconds; the gallant crew took their secret to the grave. Campbell was awarded a well deserved Victoria Cross for his supreme courage. Not yet

21 he had already flown over twenty missions. But Campbell's torpedo had run true and struck the great ship, and the damage to the *Gneisenau* was substantial, taking nearly eight months to repair. This time the attack had not been in vain.

In July the two battlecruisers were joined by the heavy cruiser *Prinz Eugen*, which had been cruising the Atlantic in company with the capital ship *Bismarck*, but, by a stroke of luck, had escaped that ship's fate. Later, however, she was hit by a British bomb and the *Scharnhorst*, which in the meantime had left Brest, was attacked and damaged at la Pallice on 24 July in a heavy – and successful this time – RAF Halifax raid, forcing her back to Brest where repairs were scheduled to take until the end of the year. Thus, in the summer of 1941, all three ships were immobilised. Hilarion sent a constant stream of clandestine reports, containing vital information on the progress of the ships in harbour, and his reports, combined with those from ULTRA and ENIGMA signal monitoring, gave British Intelligence a very good idea of what was happening in Brest Harbour.

Following the Germans' Operation Barbarossa on 22 June that year, which had begun the massive invasion of Russia, Hitler became obsessively worried about his northern flank; he feared that the British might repeat their attempt to invade Norway, thus securing the lifeline to Murmansk. For this reason, the Germans wanted to make an all-out effort to get their capital ships into operation on the northern routes in the Norwegian fjords, where they thought the ships would also be shielded from air attack. In January 1942, therefore, Hitler gave final orders for the movement of the Brest squadron. He had two choices for the voyage, neither of them very attractive: the northern route, heading out into the Atlantic to round the British Isles through the Iceland-Faroes gap, which would involve a probable clash with the Home Fleet, or a dash straight up the English Channel, an extremely dangerous venture which could bring the entire resources of Britain's war effort into play – if they were alerted in time. But Hitler was a gambler, and he relied on his instinct and his knowledge of human nature more than on logic. He believed that the British, with their cumbersome command and control system, would be unable to move into action instantly when faced with an unexpected situation, if strict security measures on the side of the Germans prevented early detection. It was an impudent decision – but it paid off.

Operation 'Cerberus', as the Channel Dash was codenamed (Cerberus was the three-headed dog which, according to Greek mythology, guarded the gates of hell), was a simple, but brilliantly conceived, military feat, admirably led by Vice Admiral Otto Ciliax, who commanded the Atlantic squadron. Not a popular man, a stickler for protocol and suffering from a painful ulcer, which made him even more short-tempered, he was, however, a superb organiser, and a veteran sailor. Given the awesome task of running the gauntlet of British defences, he weighed the alternatives and decided that his best chance of succeeding was to break out under cover of darkness, covering the most dangerous stretch through the Straits of Dover in full daylight, with maximum cover from his own defences, as well as a powerful umbrella from the Luftwaffe, which would deploy all along the planned route.

On 12 January 1942, at a special meeting in his headquarters in the Wolfschanze in East Prussia, Hitler sanctioned Ciliax's plan in the presence of Colonel Adolf Galland, the fighter leader responsible for the air cover. Captain Friedrich Ruge was given the difficult, and crucial, task of securing a passage through the dense minefields in the Straits, and told that, as the entire operation depended on keeping the British unaware of the break-out for as long as possible, secrecy was essential. However, the British High Command had been aware of the danger of a break-out from the first moment the German ships had arrived in Brest. There was no shortage of information. On 5 February, ENIGMA revealed that Admiral Ciliax had hoisted his flag on the *Scharnhorst* and that land-based flak crews had boarded the vessels to beef up the air

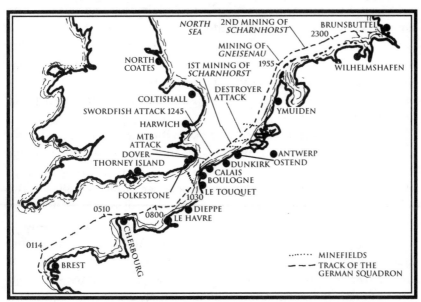

defence. On 8 February, a break in the wintry weather allowed photo-reconnaissance Spitfires to establish that all three capital ships were still in harbour, the *Scharnhorst* even being in dock.

An operational appreciation estimated that the Germans would sail from Brest in daylight so as to traverse the Dover Straits under cover of darkness. The RAF was convinced that, with their radar, there would be sufficient warning time to meet the challenge, even if Ciliax were to use adverse weather conditions to cloak his move. Given that British intelligence had not only managed to obtain precise information on the German plans to sweep the channel, but had actually established what route they would take, it was strange that the British High Command so completely misconstrued the German plans. Thus the British plan to counter the Germans' Channel Dash was faulty from the start.

Operation Cerberus started on the evening of 11 February 1942. Colonel Galland had placed a fighter controller on each capital ship, equipped with a short-wave radio for contact with the pilots and inter-ship coordination. The senior controller, Colonel Walter Ibel, a First World War veteran pilot, was aboard the *Scharnhorst*, while the wing commander himself set up shop at le Touquet, from where he would direct his fighters.

Off Brest, in a watching position, was the British submarine *Sealion*, submerged with its periscope on vigil. Lieutenant Commander Colvin had been watching the approaches for hours, but nothing had been seen. He remained on station until darkness fell and was about to surface in order to recharge his batteries, when the roar of bombers was heard in the distance. The submarine was already half out of the water when a Dornier bomber roared overhead, its navigation lights aglow. As it passed, searchlights flicked on and probed near the submarine – too near. Colvin sent the submarine tumbling into an emergency dive until the aircraft left.

As the ships prepared to move out of Brest, the roar of boiler room fans could be clearly heard in the surrounding area and the harbour came to life after many months of inactivity. Hilarion was desperately trying to contact London, but was unable to penetrate the tight security cordon of German military police which blocked all exits from the town. He could hear orders being shouted, and could see signals blinking as the fleet began to steam off into the Channel. At that moment air raid sirens began to wail and all movement ceased. Soon the bombers droned overhead while a barrage of flak shot lethal showers of shells into the night sky. For two hours bombs fell on the docks, but none of

Omdurman

Left: Lieutenant Winston Churchill, 4th Hussars, taken in 1895. Winston Churchill took part as a young subaltern in the cavalry charge of the 21st Lancers at Omdurman.

Below: British Infantry in action in the zareba at Omdurman.

Daring over the Desert

Left: The dramatic scene in Sinai, during the gallant rescue of Captain Rutherford, as McNamara's BE2, takes off at the last moment, just avoiding being caught by galloping Turkish cavalry.

Left: Captain Frank Hubert McNamara VC, AFC.

Patton

Above: French FT Renault tank in service with Patton's tank brigade taken on 4 October 1918, after salvage, having been damaged in battle.

Zeebrugge

Below: The British fleet going in to attack Zeebrugge Harbour on St George's Eve 1918.

Maastricht Bridges

Above: Fairey Battle bombers flown by No. 12 Squadron which carried the main responsibility for the suicide attacks on the Maastricht bridges.

Below: No. 12 Squadron officers. Flying Officer Garland stands in the middle back row; to his left is Flying Officer Thomas, who crash-landed but survived as a prisoner-of-war.

Crossing the Meuse

Above: A German panzer unit is fording the river bend, while in the forefront a mobile light flak unit gives cover against attacking enemy aircraft.

Cadets of Saumur

Above right: Cadets of the French Armour and Cavalry School at Saumur with their proud banner.

Cockleshell Heroes

Right: Major H. G. 'Blondie' Hasler, the leader of the Cockleshell Heroes.

Cold Steel and Blazing Chariots

Above: A squadron of Matilda 'I' tanks advancing in battle line. These tanks were used in the attacks on the El Duda Ridge and Bardia in 1941.

Below: Valentine tanks of the 8 RTR at Bardia, 1941.

Channel Dash

Above: Lieutenant Commander Eugene Esmonde, VC, a little man but a giant of courage who led the attack on the German Fleet dashing through the English Channel. His Swordfish crews flying their flimsy 'Stringbags' followed him into hell.

Some of the officers of the Royal Navy who took part in the attacks on the German fleet in those fateful 24 hours on 12 February 1942. **Top right:** Lieutenant Edgar Lee of No 825 Squadron. **Right:** Commander Anthony Law commander of MTB 48. **Bottom right:** Admiral Sir Bertram Ramsey. **Below:** Lieutenant Commander E. N. Pumphrey, M.T.B. flotilla leader.

Amiens Prison

Left: Flight Lieutenant Alan Broadley, Group Captain Pickard's faithful navigator who flew with him through thick and thin on many hazardous combat missions, here assists Pickard with his flight gear. Both men were to die at Amiens.

Left: A dramatic photo taken by one of the Mosquito crews, right over Amiens prison during the attack. The next 'Mossie' can be seen rising after dropping its bombs.

Schweinfurt Raid

Below: A B-17 Flying Fortress of the High Formation over the target: Bombs away!

Monte Cassino

Right: Monte Cassino – Mountain of Death. The monastery can be seen uphill, still intact before the heavy bombing attacks, but the 'castle' half way down the slope is under heavy artillery bombardment.

Right: New Zealand infantry fighting in the battered ruins of the town. The fighting was close, savage and desperate. No one asked for quarter and no one gave any.

Night Jump

Left: An American paratrooper after having landed in the Cotentin Peninsula, France, 6 June 1944.

Below: Two American paratroopers of the US 82nd Airborne Division with a captured young German Waffen SS soldier, Normandy 1944. Note the tension of the men, right in the midst of the battle.

Jewish Brigade Group

Top: A fighting patrol of the brigade comes under enemy fire at La Giorgetta, in no-man's-land. The nearby farm house was one of many occupied by German observation outposts, over which many hot engagements were fought by patrols.

Above: A night patrol returning to its base after an ambush, Italy 1945.

Right: The Jewish Brigade Group's shoulder patch personally authorized by Winston Churchill on 1 November 1944.

Calvary Hill

Left: Kurt 'Panzermeyer' Meyer, the veteran commander of the crack 12th SS Panzer Division which bore the brunt of the fighting in this hot combat sector. His young Hitlerjugend troops were the most vicious enemy that British soldiers in Normandy were to fight against. Meyer, shown here plainly as an exhausted commander, nevertheless was always up front in the thick of battle.

Below: A Kangaroo APC towing a damaged German Panzer IV through a Normandy village ruins during Operation 'Epsom'. These APCs were based on the turretless chassis of the Sherman tank and proved excellent protection for infantry under heavy fire. The well known halftrack could hardly provide adequate protection under the close-in fighting in the Normandy bocage.

Divine Wind

Above: A group of kamikaze pilots posing for a last picture, before taking off on their suicide mission against the American Pacific Fleet. Note the quiet resignation of those courageous men who are about to fly their last mission with no return ticket to get them home.

Right: A dramatic shot taken on board an American warship in the Pacific just seconds before a kamikaze fighter is about to strick.

Iwo Jima

Left: A group of the US Marines of the 28th Marine Regiment are raising the flag on Mount Suribachi in a sign of defiance after four days of desperate fighting for this heavily defended hill.

Left: US Marines of Colonel Harry Liversedge's 28th Marine Regiment pinned down on Iwo Jima beach soon after their landing. With Mount Suribachi towering over them, the men fought every inch through the deep black volcanic sand drenching it red with their blood in the heaviest fighting the marines encountered so far.

St Simon Monastery

Below left: Men of the 4th Palmach Battalion fighting their way into the monastery under a smoke screen, which only partly protected them from withering Arab counter fire. Note the locally produced Sten guns which, with hand grenades, made up the majority of the small arms available for Palmach fighters at the time – no match for rifles and machine guns which the Arab defenders had in abundance in Jerusalem in 1948.

Above: A group of Palmach fighters rejoice after the battle. Note the motley collection of uniforms, arms and weapons, some of them captured from the Arabs and put into use. Most of the Palmach youngsters fighting in and around Jerusalem were in their teens, but what they lacked in experience they made up in courage and motivation.

Wire Cutters

Right: Mustang P-51 pilots rejoicing after their return to base following a successful mission during Operation 'Kadesh', where they flew in at zero level to cut the Egyptian telephone lines in Sinai shortly before the Israeli push started out.

Company 'C'

Above: A young IDF tank platoon commander signalling during an engagement in Sinai during the first days of the 1973 Yom Kippur War. Some commanders controlled operations from their tanks, others preferred to use more spacious APCs like the M113 for command vehicles, but moved into their tank as soon as the battle was joined. In an M113 more radios could be installed to monitor the various nets.

Camp Nafakh

Below: The battle scene near Nafakh Camp soon after the Syrian attack was beaten off by Colonel Orr's reserve brigade. Note the terrible devastation on the battered track, which demonstrates the devastating ordeal that tank crews on both sides had to undergo. Many died in their steel coffins on this October day.

the ships was hit. Dozens of flashlight bombs exploded as bomber aimers photographed the harbour; ironically, analysts scrutinising the pictures a few hours later found nothing abnormal. But as soon as the drone of aircraft faded away, the signal came from the *Scharnhorst's* bridge to set sail – and the huge sleek shapes drifted silently through the watery haze, propellers churning the choppy sea as they began their dangerous voyage home. The time was 2145 – two hours had already been lost.

Commander Colvin's *Sealion* had now left its station, under the impression that there would be no German breakout that night. If it had remained, it would have been in a perfect position to torpedo at least one of the German ships! But that was not the only mishap which befell the British: the breakout was also missed by the special night patrols flown by Coastal Command Hudsons. Just as they reached their assigned patrol area off the bay of Brest, one of the planes signalled that his radar was defective and aborted, unable to see anything below. As luck would have it, at that very moment the German ships were actually passing below him. Another Hudson was sent out, but by then the ships were already out of range and his radar registered nothing. Because of this combination of coincidences, no warning was given during the night.

On the bridge of the *Scharnhorst*, Admiral Ciliax stood and sipped a cup of hot coffee as he peered through the starlit night sky. His ships were steaming at breakneck speed to make good the delay caused by the bomber attack; by midnight 30 minutes had already been regained. Maintaining strict radio silence, the German coastal radars followed every move, with Galland glued to his telephone receiver taking in progress reports. But not far away, in England, all was quiet...

In his headquarters at Dover Castle, Admiral Sir Bertram Ramsay had experienced strange forebodings that evening but, not hearing anything, he retired at midnight. For several days the Germans had been jamming all British radars along the south coast. This was the work of General Wolfgang Martini, the German Chief of Signals and a real wizard at electronics, and his 'tricks' achieved the desired effect by keeping the British in the dark for that night and most of the next morning as to what was going on beneath their noses.

The weather in the English Channel was abominable just before dawn: it was grey and misty, with low cloud; and moderate winds were beating up the icy sea, spraying the decks of the great battleships. Admiral Ciliax, still on the bridge of his ship, stood hunched beneath his greatcoat. His ulcer was active, signalled by a dull pain in his abdomen. But he had other, more urgent matters on his mind: he was facing the most crucial day of his career; if he failed, it would be the end for him, but if his gamble should succeed.... If the German admiral had known how firmly the British were fixed in their misconceptions of his plans, he would have felt much more relaxed!

The German fleet had sailed undisturbed into the narrows; in a few hours they would be off the Straits of Dover. The tidal stream was in their favour, adding some knots to the already respectable speed the engines were managing to obtain at full power setting. As daylight dawned the great armada, with a few more escorts tacked on, sailed in perfect formation while the German officers peered tensely through their binoculars to the west, wondering where on earth the British were!

Wing Commander Michael Jarvis, senior commander of the radar filter room at Fighter Command, had just received reports from Newhaven of movements in the Channel. Strangely enough, he took no notice at first – but he had an excuse: a training exercise was scheduled for that exact morning, and he thought the message related to it. However, Jarvis, a veteran fighter pilot, wanted to check, but he was unable to do so, since a signal officer told him that recent atmospheric interference had played havoc with their radar sets. This in fact was not atmospheric interference but Martini's 'box of tricks' and, as Jarvis vainly tried to read the radars, the ships passed Le Havre almost exactly on time, having made good the night's delay, and protected by the Luftwaffe 'umbrella' ordered aloft by Colonel Galland. At 0830 the German escort commander broke radio silence, but even this vital information was not received by the British because of their still-jammed radios. So, since nothing had been reported, British naval readiness was called off and everyone went for morning tea, ignorant of the German battle group sailing only a few kilometres to the east!

By 1000 Wing Commander Jarvis, whose instinct told him that something was going on in the Channel, despite his radars, sent out a reconnaissance sortie by No. 11 Group, 'just to make sure'. Ten minutes later the radar station at Beachy Head plotted two surface ships in the vicinity of Boulogne. The operator tried to phone Dover control, but was unable to get through. Even the 'scrambler' phone had been cut. So more valuable time was lost, while Jarvis awaited the return of his Spitfire patrol.

At 1030 Squadron Leader Bobby Oxspring, leading his wingman Sergeant Pilot Beaumont, came through cloud over the Channel 15 miles off Le Touquet and suddenly saw below him a large number of ships. But they did not have time to check, as they were pounced upon by a flight of Messerschmitts from JG I/26 flying in from St Omer-Arques. Oxspring broke contact and, followed by his wingman, hurried home. In the meantime the Beachy Head radar crew had finally managed to get their message through, and at 1040 the flap was on! Oxspring had landed and immediately phoned in his report: his wingman had positively identified a capital ship and, when faced with capital ship silhouettes, immediately put his finger on the outlines of the *Scharnhorst*.

Still, by the time the first alarm was sounded it was 1100. By that time Ciliax had been sailing undetected for the astonishing period of nearly fifteen hours, four of them in full daylight! Martini had indeed performed miracles.

The Germans' concern now was to cross the dense minefield, and Captain Ruge's minesweepers had barely cleared it when the great ships hove into sight. For twenty nerve-racking minutes the gap in the minefield was crossed at reduced speed, but as soon as they were through Ciliax ordered full speed ahead – the danger was over. There was still no sign of any British reaction, but the German admiral felt that he must be entering a trap; he was approaching the Dover narrows and only eighteen miles separated his squadron from British naval and air power. Making smoke to his port side to screen his fleet from the white cliffs of Dover which could be seen hazily in the distance, the admiral saw that the fog was thickening. Soon it almost covered the ships. At 1200 the Dover coastal guns opened fire but hit nothing, the shells raising great showers of grey water. Soon, however, the firing ceased as visibility was reduced to nil.

As soon as Oxspring's report was received by Admiral Ramsay at Dover, he acted with speed and resolution. The air liaison officer at Naval Headquarters, Wing Commander Bobby Constable-Roberts, immediately put his available forces on full alert. Ramsay ordered his Motor Torpedo Boat flotilla to race for the German battle fleet and attack as soon as contact was made. At RAF Manston in the Kentish countryside, Wing Commander Tom Gleave, a veteran fighter pilot who had recently returned to duty after months of suffering from frightful burns, alerted Lieutenant Commander Eugene Esmonde, commanding the depleted 825 Fleet Air Arm Swordfish Squadron, to immediate readiness. Gleave knew full well that their mission meant almost certain suicide, as the slow-moving biplanes would have well-nigh no chance of surviving the withering fire from the battle fleet, even if they were able to penetrate the protective outer defensive circle. But there was no choice – the attack had to be flown.

Esmonde was older than most RAF pilots, and had lot of experience; he was already famous for a daring attack on the *Bismarck* a few months earlier. Now, veteran that he was, he realised that this mission could well be his last. While he was briefing his young pilots, the drama in the Channel had finally begun in earnest.

Lieutenant Commander Edward Pumphrey, leader of the Motor Torpedo Boat flotilla, was racing towards several dimly seen shapes some 10,000 metres ahead, closing fast. On a parallel course, some German E Boats fired wildly to try and stop his advance through the German fleet's outer screen, but thanks to their greater speed the MTBs raced on. Suddenly, the great battle cruisers loomed out of the smoke screen. Pumphrey glanced anxiously upwards for some sign of fighter cover but, seeing none, grimly took his boat to maximum speed, stern well down, bows inclined upwards, the waves beating a tattoo on the boat's hull. His other boats stuck to him like glue and on they raced in battle formation, trying to elude the enemy shells which exploded ahead of them, throwing up huge showers of water and spray. Passing two E boats attempting to block the advance, Pumphrey crashed through the outer screen, going all out for the big ships, whose shapes increased alarmingly until they towered like skyscrapers above the little boats.

It was *Scharnhorst* which came into sight first. Pumphrey pointed his boat's nose at her, calculating the range for his torpedoes. As he was about to press the firing lever, one of the gunners shouted something, and the officer turned to two E boats right in front, shells pumping out of their guns. He ignored the danger and turned his full attention on to the battleship, hand jerking at the firing lever and, satisfyingly, saw two long torpedoes hurtling from the bows, streaking towards the enemy ship. Now he had time for the E boats, and turned away, only to receive withering gun fire from the *Scharnhorst*, which was by now firing full broadsides, smoke billowing from the heavy gun muzzles – a terrifying sight. Sadly, Pumphrey's torpedoes had missed but, as he turned into the haze, he saw his other boats attack, dodging and twisting through the German barrage. As one of the MTBs approached, it was chased by a German destroyer which, towering above the small boat, charged it at point blank range, guns firing, tearing the boat into shreds, but the young lieutenant ignored the mortal danger and doggedly pressed on with his attack. The captain of the German destroyer was impressed by his courage, even while he chased the attacker. Suddenly two Dover gun boats appeared out of the smog and raced between the MTB and the destroyer, their guns blazing. For a moment the destroyer captain's attention was diverted – just long enough for the MTB to launch its torpedoes.

On the *Scharnhorst*'s bridge, officers could see the trail of the torpedoes blasting right towards the ship, but they managed to evade them at the very last moment by only a few metres. Another gallant effort had failed. It was not to be the last. But, in fact, the Germans had already won the day. The slowness of the British reaction had proved decisive in the events of the day and what ensued was only a series of desperate attempts to try and undo the results of all the bungling. As the battered MTBs were staggering home, Commander Esmonde's Swordfish were skimming in to attack. Some of the boat crews waved to the slow-flying 'stringbags', wishing them godspeed in the impossible mission which they themselves had miraculously survived.

An hour before, Wing Commander Gleave had watched the squadron take off from Manston. Esmonde knew exactly what he and his men were facing and only a man of his calibre could instil so much courage and devotion into untried youngsters as he did that day. But even Gleave, an experienced officer, was moved as he walked with Esmonde to his plane. Esmonde was deep in thought, his face grey and haggard, as he waved with a forced, almost automatic grin. He looked very small in his dark blue uniform as he climbed into his flimsy cockpit.

The original plan had been to provide a large Spitfire escort to get Esmonde's Swordfish through the outer cordon, but the escort failed to report on time, so the Swordfish set off alone seawards. The weather was deteriorating fast, with clouds and fog nearly at sea level. East of Ramsgate, two flights of Bf 109s swooped down on the meagre force, which only at the last minute was joined by some Spitfires. However, the Messerschmitts did no real harm and they were soon forced to break off their attack. At 1230 the formation sighted the enemy battlefleet – and the enemy saw them. Aboard the *Prinz Eugen*, Leutnant Rothenberg, the fighter controller of JG I/26, saw them coming and grabbed his microphone. Flying straight into the smoke and fumes which surrounded the battle cruisers came Esmonde, together with Lieutenant Brian Rose – only a thousand metres separated them from the giants ahead of them. Lieutenant Edgar Lee, Rose's observer, looked back and saw that their gunner was slumped over his weapon, dead. With no time to reach the gun, he stood up and shouted to his pilot, who swerved at the last minute away from the attacking Focke Wulf, and they overshot the ships, climbing sharply to avoid collision. Below, they could see Esmonde's plane going straight for the German cruiser, still apparently under control, in spite of its flapping fabric. Above, Flight Lieutenant Michael Cromby in an escorting Spitfire had just shot down a German fighter when he nearly collided with another. Both of them could clearly see the awful spectacle unfolding below.

Edgar Lee was still standing, waving his arms, while on Esmonde's Swordfish the gunner was sitting astride the fuselage, trying to beat out the flames which licked the fabric. Tracer bullets passed through the fuselage, while the heavy naval shells threw huge fountains of water up into the sky. The planes were flying through a virtual wall of fire and water. Rose was hit in the back by an exploding shell which blew the back of his cockpit to pieces. Lee saw his pilot hunched over the controls but he was still moving, so Lee shouted at him to rouse him from his unconscious state; finally he responded and managed to pull the nose up.

In front, only a short distance away, was Esmonde's plane. Its lower port wing had nearly vanished, shot clean away by a shell. Esmonde, wounded in the back, still fought his controls and headed towards his target, while tracer bullets streamed into the stricken aircraft. His observer and gunner were already dead. He was seen to release his torpedo, but life drained from him as he desperately tried to pull up the nose, and the plane crashed into the sea, while his torpedo ran for the *Scharnhorst*.

On the bridge of the battlecruiser, Admiral Ciliax had watched silently but the captain ordered evasive action and the torpedo flashed by like a hungry shark. Now it was up to Rose to finish the job. Guided by Lee, still upright in his cockpit, they struggled on, the pilot barely conscious, petrol streaming from the bullet-punctured tank. Straight in front of them loomed the *Prinz Eugen*. Rose, at Lee's urging, launched his weapon and the plane passed over the German cruiser – so close that they could see the white faces of the German gunners as the plane scraped the deck. As they completed their task, the Swordfish burst into flames, its engine shot away, and flopped into the sea, where Lee, using his last ounce of strength, pulled his wounded pilot into a rubber dinghy. Luckily they were seen not only by the Germans but from the bridge of an MTB, where Lieutenant Saunders, its commander, had watched them ditch. Although they had to endure a low level attack from some German fighters which strafed the dinghy, they were finally picked up and brought home. Edgar Lee was one of five survivors of the sixteen of Esmonde's pilots who had flown that noon suicide mission – a magnificent failure, as not one of the torpedoes hit home.

An air battle was now in full swing overhead. Oberst Josef Priller's JG 26 was flying cover when it came upon a squadron of Spitfires, led by Australian ace, Squadron Leader 'Bluey' Truscott. As he wove his way through the storm of flak around him, he was confronted with Priller, coming straight at him. Both pilots saw each other at the same second. Truscott dived first and, going for the *Gneisenau*, he held his thumb firmly down, firing all his guns while flying through the spray from the battlecruiser's shells. Glued to his tail and also trying to escape the fire, Priller and his wingmen were blasting away too. Truscott saw them out of the corner of his eye and, wrenching his stick back hard, he rocketed upward, followed by the rest of his flight. For a moment Priller lost them; it was enough for Truscott and his mates: they reached sea level still intact, attacked without loss, and were off! On the deck of the warship several gunners lay dead, guns silenced, and some of the superstructure had been hit. This, the first damage to the ships that day, had been done by fighters! But there now occurred yet another of the serious mistakes made by the British – a crucial lull until the next attack, which came from Coastal Command Beauforts, but much too late to prevent the German ships, now relatively safe, from speeding for home waters. Fifteen of the Beauforts made contact, ten dropped their torpedoes but no hits were observed, and three Beauforts were shot out of the sky. Had they attacked in time, they might have caused great damage to the fleet, but now it was too late.

One hour later, however, the *Scharnhorst* struck a large mine, which exploded and damaged the great ship, bringing her to a virtual standstill. Having lost electrical power, her guns and engines were useless, and she sat like a huge sitting duck in the water, a dream target for enemy bombers which could now sink her at will. Admiral Ciliax was forced to transfer to a nearby destroyer and left with a heavy heart, forced to leave his flagship at the enemy's mercy. But no one came! Given this respite, the crew worked feverishly to repair the damage and they had the ship going again, under full power, in 40 minutes. As the familiar shape appeared over the horizon, the Germans aboard the battle fleet cheered, and even Ciliax appeared to relax for a moment – he was in sight of sanctuary at last. But one last attack had to be beaten off...

The final assault was made in the afternoon by the Harwich based destroyer flotilla, led by Captain Pizey in HMS *Campbell*. Having survived an attack by an RAF Hampden bomber which swooped on them, mistaking them for the enemy, Pizey set course to intercept the German fleet, which was now passing the Belgian coastline, keeping close to the Luftwaffe umbrella and shore-based gun batteries. With the speed of desperation Pizey and his destroyers attacked the *Gneisenau*, which first came into range. The Germans, who now believed themselves to be almost home, were totally surprised as the little British warships raced, guns blazing, towards the German giants. Scattering the E Boat screen they came within torpedo range. The *Prinz Eugen* and the *Gneisenau* thundered out their broadsides simultaneously. Incredibly, both missed, although towers of water burst high over the bridge where Captain Pizey stood steadfast, his eyes glued to his binoculars as he rapped out orders to launch torpedoes. Then a German destroyer raced out of the mist and fired its own torpedo, which missed the side of HMS *Campbell* by inches.

Nearby, HMS *Worcester* was coming into range, her captain, Commander Eric Coates, focusing intently on the *Prinz Eugen*, totally oblivious of the shells pounding his ship. The screams of the wounded combined with the hissing of steam from damaged boilers could be heard as Coates, himself wounded, fired his torpedoes. The *Worcester* was listing badly, with only two guns remaining intact. Still, the ship survived, although she could barely move by now. But the German battle fleet had had enough excitement for one day, and steamed on, leaving the stricken destroyer to its fate. Miraculously, she reached port still afloat.

The drama was nearly over... Dusk fell, giving cover to the German fleet as it passed the Frisian islands into the mouth of the River Elbe, where it received a hero's welcome. But fate was to strike Admiral Ciliax one final blow: just as he was sipping his coffee, justifiably proud of having achieved the impossible, a brilliant flash bathed the *Gneisenau* in a red glow. A terrific explosion followed and, floundering in the river, she limped to a stop. Another mine had struck and there she lay, drifting helplessly, only six miles from sanctuary.

Well after midnight the rest of the fleet steamed quietly into Heligoland Bight. The *Gneisenau* followed slowly behind, her crew having carried out hasty repairs. The last ship to enter was the *Scharnhorst*, which had just turned past the marker boats when she struck another mine right in the middle of the bight. She suffered even greater damage than before and her repair crews had to work under arc lamps to get her finally in to berth.

Although the Channel Dash was irrefutably a great victory for the German fleet – casualties suffered by them were negligible, and the three capital ships were home – still they were paralysed for a long time, vulnerable once again to RAF bombers which were not long in coming. Nevertheless what Admiral Ciliax had achieved would be remembered as one of the most daring feats in military history. The German admiral had succeeded in doing what the great Duke of Medina Sidonia had failed to do 300 years before.

CHAPTER TWELVE

THE DEATH OR GLORY JOB: AMIENS PRISON

It was the autumn of 1943 and a trainload of Wehrmacht soldiers sped through the cold French night. Some men were sleeping, others daydreamed about their forthcoming vacation and looked forward to a reunion with their families at home in Germany. A rude shock awaited them. Suddenly, metal grinding, the fast-moving train telescoped into a stationary eastbound goods train halted at Miremont station and within minutes the bodies of over a hundred SS troops lay amid the smoking debris.

This was the work of Jean Beaurin and his men, who belonged to one of France's most successful underground organisations. Only twenty years old, he was an expert rail buster, having already derailed several German troop trains. One of his feats was already legend among the Maquis. Travelling at high speed one night, a packed trooptrain headed for the Eastern Front was approaching a bend in the line at Frieulles on the le Tréport-Abbeville line when it suddenly derailed, spilling hundreds of German soldiers onto the railway embankment. When the dust had settled, 200 Germans were found dead and double that number severely injured. An entire combat brigade had been devastated, including five trainloads of tanks and other military equipment.

Jean Beaurin's luck had held out for a surprisingly long time, but the Gestapo was on his heels, searching for the man who had caused them so much damage. Beaurin's superior was Dominique Ponchardier, a courageous and resourceful leader who had been working his organisation since 1940. Among his activities, he had established the evasion route over which thousands of Allied airmen and escaping soldiers were helped to reach a neutral country before returning home. At present the Germans were attempting to eliminate this network, called SOSIES, which was causing them a great deal of trouble and, with the help of informers, several members of Ponchardier's network were captured and imprisoned within the heavily guarded prison of Amiens, awaiting their fate.

Young Beaurin was one of them. He had been bidden to a secret meeting at the Beaulot café behind Amiens station, but the Germans had set a trap and Beaurin was caught; Dominique Ponchardier, who was also supposed to be at the meeting, was warned only seconds before entering the café, and managed to escape. Ponchardier and Beaurin had agreed that, if one of their group was captured, the others would move heaven and earth to help him to escape. Now Beaurin himself was in prison and, following an abortive attempt to free prisoners from the Underground from the St Quentin prison, the Germans were known to have taken special precautions at Amiens to prevent such an attempt from being repeated. In January 1944, twelve members of their group had been shot inside those prison walls and Ponchardier knew that a similar fate awaited Jean Beaurin.

Dominique Ponchardier had close relations with British Intelligence in London and was on personal terms with some of the top men at Baker Street, which he had visited. Now the time had come to ask them for help. He sent a coded message to his friends in London requesting the help of the Royal Air Force in an attack on Amiens prison, to take place not later than mid-February, a date known by the French Underground to be the one on which their friends were to be executed. The request was passed through the British grapevine until it reached the desk of Air Marshal Sir Arthur Coningham, commanding 2nd Tactical Air Force. Coningham (known as 'Mary' – a corruption of the word Maori, hinting at his New Zealand upbringing), a man of quick decisions, lost no time in contacting Air Vice Marshal Basil Embry, commanding 2 Group, for an urgent consultation. Embry was one of the most remarkable combat leaders in the RAF, perhaps even the entire Allied air forces and, by a twist of fate, he owed his own life to the helping hands of the French resistance. In May 1940, as a group captain, he had been shot down near St Omer and helped by loyal Frenchmen, who risked their own lives to bring him to safety in Spain. Embry was in fact the first British airman to return home after escaping from German prison!

Four times awarded the coveted DSO for personal acts of bravery in action, he was the best possible leader by example that his aircrews could ask for but, quite apart from his great personal courage, he was also one of the RAF's top low-level operations experts. Never regarding his high rank as a hindrance to operational flying, he was one of the few who led, or at least flew along with, his aircrews on no less than nineteen dangerous low level precision attacks. His crews feared his wrath, which recognised neither age nor rank when things went wrong, but they also adored him and were willing to follow him anywhere.

Embry was under no illusions as to the task he had been given. He had led some tricky operations before; low flying was second nature to him and his crews, but this was something else – this was life *saving*, not destroying, and if the prisoners were killed in the attack, it would defeat the whole object, which was to get them as far away from the prison as possible, and in one piece. He realised that the attack had to be planned on the most precise information available, close to real time, and executed with the best crews at his command. These were the criteria that Embry had adopted as he started planning the operation, codenamed 'Jericho' – an apt one for the task!

Embry's group was flying the versatile de Havilland Mosquito, its sleek plywood construction making it one of the most remarkable combat aircraft of the war. With its maximum speed of over 300mph, it could evade most of the contemporary Luftwaffe fighters and reach long distance targets with a substantial margin for safe return. The Group's pilots had already flown some daring attacks on the German V1 launching sites, racing in at treetop level to score with pinpoint accuracy, but the bombing of a point target like the Amiens prison would test their skills even more. Embry, however, was a cautious planner, and evaluated carefully the chances of success. Following receipt of some updated aerial photos taken by reconnaissance Spitfires which flew specially for this mission, he examined the target in minute detail and came to the conclusion that the Maquis should be warned that there was a grave risk that many of the prisoners might be killed in the attack. The answer came within hours from Ponchardier: to all intents and purposes the prison inmates were already dead, and they would prefer to take their chances with the RAF bombs rather than die from German bullets inside the prison walls! This courageous statement, which was actually smuggled out of Amiens prison, decided Embry, and he set about planning Operation Jericho.

The prison at Amiens was situated outside the town on the road to Albert. This is a long, ruler-straight highway lined with poplar trees and telegraph poles, an easily defined approach route with no obstructions along its entire length up to the prison compound, which stood out clearly even from a distance, making it perfect for a low level flying approach. As one of the planners happily put it, 'You couldn't miss it even if you were totally blind'. But the approach route was the least of Embry's problems, as he soon realised. The main prison building was cruciform in shape, with a long vertical arm at right angles lying parallel to the Albert road. It was a three-storey building, twenty metres in height. The prison was surrounded by a wall which was six metres high and one metre thick. Embry concluded that there would be two main tasks – the breaching of the outer walls and the opening of the prison, to allow the inmates, or those of them who survived the attack, to escape. Having consulted his armament experts, without disclosing the name of the objective which he decided to keep secret until the very last moment, Embry decided to breach the outer wall in two places, thus creating an exit at both sides. Furthermore, as many of the German guards had to be eliminated to prevent their reacting after the initial shock, the building housing the German garrison was given special attention.

It was of prime importance to hit the target at a time when many of the prisoners would be assembled, together with their guards, and – going on information received from Ponchardier, consulted by clandestine radio – lunchtime was believed to be the best time. The hour selected was therefore 12 noon; the date chosen, any day after 10 February, but not later than the 18th, as the Germans were to execute the next batch of prisoners on the 19th!

On the afternoon of 8 February Air Vice Marshal Embry flew to RAF Hunsdon, the base of 140 Wing, which was commanded by Group Captain Charles Pickard. Coincidentally, Pickard was one of the men Ponchardier had met on his visit to London. His special operations squadron assisted the French Underground in its work. The group selected to fly the mission was a combined nations affair, with handpicked airmen from the resident New Zealand, Australian and British squadrons specially selected by Pickard. Charles Pickard himself was one of the most experienced bomber pilots of the day. Although he was only 28 years old, young for his rank, he had already been decorated with no less than three DSOs. He was quite famous, due to his having starred in a wartime publicity film, *Target For Tonight*, in which he played a Wellington pilot on a night bombing mission. But Pickard was certainly not just a film star. He had flown Major John Frost's party to parachute into France in their attack on the Bruneval radar in 1942* and later flew some extremely daring clandestine missions into occupied France in support of the Maquis from RAF Tempsford. He was well known to many of the French Underground leaders, among them at least one now imprisoned in the notorious Amiens prison. So, when confronted with the challenging job of bombing his former friends to freedom, no British officer could have been happier to fly the mission, even though it was a hazardous one.

Embry had decided to lead the mission himself. Convinced that the most experienced man should lead, Embry saw no reason why he, the senior combat leader, should not fly. But his bosses thought otherwise, a matter which would become crucial to the whole operation. Pickard himself had the highest regard for Basil Embry, and was quite happy to fly as Embry's deputy. But the top brass did not agree. This time Air Marshal Sir Trafford Leigh-Mallory put his foot down, hard! Leigh-Mallory, who commanded the Allied Expeditionary Air Force already preparing for 'Overlord' – the forthcoming invasion of Normandy – was very reluctant to let Embry fly, for two reasons: First, he feared the loss of such an experienced leader at this crucial stage of the war. Second, in the event of Embry's capture and questioning by the Germans, his already intimate knowledge of Overlord could prove a real disaster, and a much more serious one than a possible failure of Jericho. So when Embry returned to his headquarters after an inspection tour, he found a telegram on his desk stating that on no account was he to lead the Amiens mission. Embry was furious and raised the matter with his own boss, Air Marshal 'Mary' Coningham who sympathised – but denied all his pleas, and there the matter rested.

Embry now faced the most crucial decision of his long career. The operation had been planned according to a very strict timetable, and any deviation could mean the difference between success and failure. The requirements for leading a low level attack were quite different from those of normal bombing missions and, although Embry held Charles Pickard in high regard as a bomber pilot, he had flown most of his missions at night and had flown only six combat missions at low level. It was the general rule in 2 Group Mosquito operations that, by day, attacking formations went in at less than treetop level with full throttle and, once bombs were away, they got the hell out without

---

* For details, see *Daring to Win*, by the same author.

delay, *never* going round the target, whatever happened – there were no second chances in this dangerous game! Previous attacks on the German V1 rocket launch sites had demonstrated that the main threat was not from Luftwaffe fighters, which rarely got down to that level to attack a speeding Mosquito at full throttle, but from light flak or hitting an obstruction when the pilot's attention was temporarily diverted. The decision was a hard one, but Embry had to select a leader whom the crews would follow and, in the end, there was no other choice but Charles Pickard to lead Jericho.

Having made his decision, Embry gave Pickard his complete backing, and the two men went to see the specially prepared scale model which had been constructed by RAF Intelligence on a low level aerial photo. Pickard immediately set to work to familiarise himself with the target and the approach route, adequate knowledge of which would mean the success or failure of the operation.

Eighteen Mosquitoes were to take part in Operation Jericho, six each from 487 Squadron, Royal New Zealand Air Force, 464 RAAF Squadron and 21 Squadron RAF. Embry arranged for fighter cover from a mixed squadron of Typhoons from 174 and 245 Squadrons, flying from RAF Westhampnett, to rendezvous with the Mosquitoes and escort them all the way. The detailed plan, hammered out by Embry and Pickard together, envisaged 487 RNZAF Squadron leading the attack and breaching the outer wall. The second wave, led by 464 RAAF Squadron, in which Pickard would fly the last Mosquito, would be detailed to place their bombs against the walls of the prison buildings, while 21 Squadron RAF was to stand by, ready to flatten the compound if the two preceding attacks failed to breach the walls and no prisoners could be seen escaping outside. If it came to it, this would be the grimmest job of all.

The weather deteriorated steadily after 10 February but a message was sent to Dominique Ponchardier instructing him to have his men stand by at midday any day after the 15th, as it was impossible to predict exactly when the attack would take place, due to the weather conditions. For days heavy snow had been falling on northern France and East Anglia; the entire area was just one vast expanse of white, the sky a leaden grey, through which the rays of the sun could only occasionally be glimpsed. The usually crowded airspace over the bomber bases in East Anglia was strangely empty and quiet, all flying operations suspended as the weather clamped down. But at RAF Hunsdon, near Ware in Hertfordshire, the airfield was buzzing with activity.

Flying Officer Martin Sparks, a 23-year-old New Zealander, was lying on his bunk, looking out of the window at the morning sky. Low cloud and thick ground mist was drifting across the bleak airfield. Even Pickard would not be crazy enough to have them fly on a day like this, he thought. But a knock on the door dispelled this illusion. He was told to report to the briefing room forthwith.

Shortly before, Pickard and Embry had conferred. The weather was as bad as it could be. A photographic reconnaissance aircraft had barely managed to land in the mist; it brought updated information from France, where the weather was equally abominable. This was certainly no day for flying such a sensitive low level mission. But the two senior officers knew that they had no option – it was 18 February and next day the Germans would shoot the prisoners – the weather would be no problem to them! So if the attack was to go at all, it must go now!

As the eighteen selected aircrews shuffled, shivering, into the damp briefing hut, the weather looked even worse, if possible, and Sparks, a veteran of earlier low-level raids, calmed his friend, Pilot Officer Darrel with his opinion that the mission would certainly be scrubbed – only a fool would mount a raid under such conditions. But, as both the Group Captain and Air Vice Marshal Embry entered the hut and took their places on the raised platform, Sparks realised that, weather or not, they would be flying that day. Embry unveiled a strange-looking wooden box on the table, and displayed the model of Amiens prison. On the wall was a detailed map indicating the flight path and the target area. The Mosquito crews had been training for weeks on low flying, but no one, even the squadron commanders, had been aware until now what the target was. As the briefing went on, the crews, professionals all, became more and more serious. They worked for hours, each crew approaching the model and maps so that they could become familiar with the area. Pickard summed up the briefing with the words: 'It's a death or glory job, boys'. Every man present knew that he was probably facing his last day on earth. But they were young and, as they filed out of the smoky room into the snow-covered airfield, they began to recover their spirits.

The ground crews had already bomb-loaded the Mosquitoes, which looked like the ghosts of planes as they stood on the tarmac in the snow and fog. It was nearly 1100 and only two hours were left to rendezvous with Ponchardier's men on the ground at Amiens. With a last look at the weather, which did nothing to improve his mood, Embry gave the order to mount into the waiting aircraft. Hating the role of onlooker, longing to go with them, he took his leave of Pickard and went to the control tower to see them off.

The crews of the Mosquitoes were already strapped into their seats when they saw the group captain's staff car approach and stop. He climbed up into his cockpit. Flight Lieutenant Alan Broadley, his navigator, who had flown with him since early in the war, was already settled in his seat, having made pre-flight checks, as he had done on countless previous missions. Pickard attached himself to the 'Mossie', the parachute, safety harness (this, he noted grimly, would be of little use, as they would be flying much too low to bail out!), oxygen tubes. He fiddled with his radio cord and Broadley helped him to strap it on; he always did, it was a sort of good luck ritual which had brought them safely home so far.

All over the misty airfield, pilots were now starting engines until the air was filled with their thunderous roar. Then the first Mosquito taxied out towards the end of the flarepath which was lit up in spite of the so-called daylight, followed one after another by all the Mosquitoes. From the control tower Embry watched them go, straining his eyes to see them all rise into the air and disappear into the foggy sky. Operation Jericho was airborne.

Squadron Leader Dick Sugden of 464 Squadron was flying with boss Wing Commander Bob Iredale at the controls. No sooner had they lifted from the runway than they immediately entered a blinding snowstorm. It was the worst weather that any of them had ever encountered. To get into formation under such conditions seemed hopeless and, indeed, as they came through the overcast Iredale found to his dismay that four aircraft were missing from the wing of eighteen. It was a bad start but they were already nearing Littlehampton, where they would meet the Typhoon escort, led by Squadron Leader Mike Collins' Typhoons, but these fared little better on take-off, four of the twelve fighters becoming detached in the heavy overcast.

The total force of 30 aircraft was now down to 22, but Pickard, having seen the rest forming up nicely, set course for France. His problems, however, were far from over. As Bob Iredale was emerging from the cloud and snow, he could see a Mosquito weaving right in front of him, close enough for him to run into. Struggling with his controls in order to prevent certain collision, he shouted to the other pilot to break, cursing him loudly in the process. As the other obligingly complied, the Australian found to his dismay that he had just been telling off his group captain!

The weather improved quite a bit as the formation headed for Dieppe-le-Tréport on the French coastline; there were even a few moments of blinding sunshine. But this did not last and soon they were diving down to sea level, flying so low that the waves nearly touched their churning propellers. At 400 miles per hour, Flying Officer Sparks was trying to come out of his long dive seawards. The needles of his barometric altimeters, although totally unreliable, trembled around the hundred foot mark. He tried to ignore them, and scanned the wave tops, trying to fly level and avoid the propwash of the Mosquitoes in front of him. The fog lying close to the water made it difficult to see, and less than a dozen feet could make the difference between staying in the air – and a cold, watery death in the Channel. In front of him, somewhat to his left, he could see a Mosquito flying onward, leaving in its wake a spray of water from the sea-skimming propellers. He couldn't see the others, but he knew that they were flying in formation with him, all experts at that dangerous game.

The formation neared the French coast, and Flight Lieutenant Alan Broadley's precise navigation paid off as they roared over the cliffs near Dieppe, hugging the contours behind as they flew into the Somme Valley and the flat, snow-covered plains of Picardy. Squadron Leader Collins' Typhoons covered the Mosquitoes from every possible angle, while their pilots scanned the sky for the Luftwaffe fighters which they knew could not be far away.

The airfields at St Omer and its neighbourhood housed some of the top German aces in JG 26 Schlageter, and their boss, Colonel Josef Priller, was already well known to the RAF fighter pilots who had fought it out with his pilots in many dogfights. On that particular morning, however, the usually alert Priller was still asleep, confident that in such atrocious weather even the crazy English would not venture out of their snow-covered bases. He was looking forward to a quiet day to relax and enjoy the French wine in the officer's mess.

For Pickard's formation, now well inside France, disaster struck when a Mosquito flown by Flight Lieutenant Tich Hanafin from 487 Squadron was seen trailing smoke from its port engine, the propeller being feathered. Hanafin could not maintain speed on one engine, and was forced to abort. He was seen to turn away, a bad omen, as Hanafin was one of the most experienced New Zealand pilots. Wing Commander Ian 'Black' Smith led the Mosquitoes from 487 NZ Squadron, and saw Hanafin disappear. Smith, a veteran pilot, had been the first to shoot down a German aircraft with a Mosquito back in June 1942, when he caught a Do-217 and a Heinkel bomber within ten minutes of each other. Now, leading his remaining aircraft, he sped towards Amiens at tree-top height. Flying Officer Sparks flew right along with his leader, keeping formation as best he could. They were nearing the target. Passing the little town of Albert, its buildings looking like black dots in the white snow, Smith immediately recognised the ruler-straight road, lined by tall poplar trees, which stood out clearly in the snow.

At Amiens cathedral the clock showed 12 noon precisely. On the frozen ground next to it, hiding in some bushes, the leaves dripping icy water down their necks, Dominique Ponchardier and some of his men were waiting anxiously, looking eastwards in the direction of Route 29 to Albert. For several days now, the little group of Frenchmen had waited for the RAF to appear, but in vain. This was the last day before the execution and their hopes were fading. Then, suddenly, a faint engine noise was heard from the east, and soon some black dots appeared in the wintry sky, soon growing into the shape of aeroplanes, flying fast, almost at treetop level and coming straight at them! It was one minute past noon, and the chimes of the cathedral bell were just fading away when the aircraft roared in, dipping even lower. The hearts of the French resistance fighters beat with fierce joy and hope.

Flying Officer Sparks was flying so low that his wings almost touched the poplars as he swished by. Rain was beating at the perspex windshield, almost blotting out the view ahead and Sparks and his navigator had to peer hard at the view in front to avoid flying into one of the trees. As he tilted his Mosquito at a sharp angle, one wing lower than the other, to avoid hitting the trees, suddenly a Typhoon passed right across his front. Sparks nearly jumped out of his seat at the scare, but recovered and managed to straighten out. In front of him he could see the leader, Wing Commander Smith, dropping to a mere three metres as they approached the unmistakable shape of the prison building which loomed grimly before them. Sparks just had time to note that it looked exactly like the model he had studied – and then they were on top of the outer walls. As briefed, the New Zealanders now split into two sections. Smith's Mosquito went in straight and he hurled his bombs into the prison walls which were rearing up at him. Sparks was flying right beside him and, as one, both pilots pulled sharply over the walls, shot up and roared over the prison's rooftops. As they pulled away they saw that two pilots from the other section were going in for their bombing run to blow in the other side of the wall from the north. The two New Zealand pilots and the Australians standing by had been watching the attack of Smith's section, and saw with astonishment that the bombs hurtled through the eastern wall, careered across the courtyard, and crashed into the wall where they exploded in a pall of smoke and debris.

464 Squadron followed hard on the heels of the New Zealanders, too close in fact for safety. Although Pickard had taken care to use eleven-second delay bombs to prevent them exploding below the attacking aircraft, Wing Commander Bob Iredale, who was leading his first section in a straight run to the target, saw that to attack now would be sheer suicide. Breaking sharply to the left, he screamed over the city centre, passing over the Luftwaffe airfield at Glisy, from which light flak was coming up.

On the airfield, there was chaos as the Mosquitoes roared over. Pilots rushed to their parked aircraft and gunners let fly with everything they had but, the Mosquitoes disappeared as soon as they had come, leaving in their wake the Typhoons which screamed over, strafing the airfield and preventing the German fighters from taking off.

Iredale was back on track now, and lining up for his section's attack on the prison building. The debris thrown up by the first wave had scarcely settled when he dropped his own bombs. Down below, it was as if an earthquake had struck. Only moments before, the daily routine in progress; two men had started to ladle out the watery soup under the eyes of Oberfeldwebel Otto, the mean, elderly German guard, when suddenly the noise of powerful engines shattered the silence. The exploding bombs blew in the walls of the building, the upper floor collapsed and the whole building disintegrated into a mass of bricks, concrete and beams. Men were flung into the air, some buried under the rubble where they choked from the dust.

Belatedly the air raid warning sounded in Amiens, mingling with the drone of the aeroplane engines. Now bombs were falling from the Australian planes attacking the German guard house, and dramatic events were taking place within the prison walls. As cell doors were blown open, some of the prisoners rushed out, choking and coughing from the dust which swirled about, trying frantically to reach the open air. Jean Beaurin and three men from the same cell were thrown on the floor by the blast, but soon recovered, kicked open the half-unhinged door and rushed out, breaking through the breached outer wall – right into the waiting arms of Dominique Ponchardier!

Others, however, were not so lucky. Dr. Antonin Mans, a public health officer and prominent member of the Underground, had been among those condemned to death. He was among the first to get clear after the attack and, recovering from his initial shock, he rushed out through debris strewn on the ground floor. Suddenly he heard faint voices calling for help. The medical man within him could not refuse the heart-rending cries of the wounded, and he remained behind to tend to the wounded, German and French alike, remaining at his post of mercy and refusing to escape to freedom. With him, assisting him in his task, was a French officer, Captain André Tempez, who was later to pay for his deed of compassion with his death in a concentration camp.

While the drama unfolded below, Group Captain Pickard was circling in his Mosquito, searching the ground for escapers. He saw the clusters of dungareed prisoners emerging from the building, while Dominique Ponchardier waved at him in jubilation as he rushed his friends to safety. The German guards inside the rubble of the prison compound were still too shocked to respond, and all seemed well down there.

But aloft, another drama was developing. Pickard had sent Iredale and Smith home, while he remained to see whether the attack had been completely successful. But Priller's Luftwaffe fighter pilots were already en route, racing for the scene. Pickard, now satisfied with the job, radioed the leader of 21 Squadron to go home and Squadron Leader Ian Dale drew a breath of relief – he was quite happy to have come all this way for nothing, as he had not been looking forward to his unattractive job.

At this point Squadron Leader Alan McRitchie, leader of the second Australian section, on his way to Albert, was hit by flak which killed his navigator outright. The pilot quickly lost height and one engine was set aflame, but he managed to crash land near Albert, where he was taken prisoner. The Germans subsequently held McRitchie in solitary confinement for 40 days, threatening him with Gestapo torture unless he revealed how the RAF and the French underground cooperated, but the Australian told them nothing. Pickard saw McRitchie's Mosquito going down and set off to investigate. By now all the other aircraft had gone.

It was then that Feldwebel Wilhelm Mayer, from JG 26, appeared on the scene. Mayer was one of Priller's top aces, with 27 enemy aircraft on his scorecard. He turned right onto Pickard's trail, shot his tail end off, and the aircraft flipped over and crashed, catching fire as it came to a halt upturned on the snowy ground. Both Pickard and Broadley were killed instantly.

Air Vice Marshal Embry was devastated when he heard of the loss of England's most famous bomber pilot, which vindicated his opinion that the night bombing veteran had insufficient experience in daylight missions. This opinion was confirmed by the fact that all the rest of the attacking aircraft returned safely to Hunsdon that day, mission completed, but without their admired leader. Pickard and his loyal navigator were buried later by French patriots and a memorial erected at Amiens, in memory of a man who gave his life to save others.

Of the 258 prisoners who escaped from Amiens prison, many were later re-arrested by the Gestapo although some did manage to hide out until the British arrived to liberate Amiens a few months later. Among them were young Beaurin and the courageous Dr. Mans. Fifty prisoners were killed in the attack, together with several dozen German guards. Operation Jericho was over.

CHAPTER THIRTEEN

BLACK THURSDAY: THE SCHWEINFURT RAID

Dawn, 14 October 1943... Over the English countryside the fog lay thick; the damp, clammy morning air pervaded the dismal Nissen huts of the American bomber stations in East Anglia. The sleeping bomber crews felt it even in their sleep. But not all were asleep. Here and there a cigarette glowed, momentarily lighting up the haggard face of a youngster who had aged prematurely in the horrors of the battle over Germany. Soon the duty officer entered, and hit the wall switch, awakening the men from their fitful sleep. Another day, another mission – for many it would be their last; they would not live out that fateful day. The lucky ones might spend the rest of the war behind German prison fences. In the distance, the sound of aero engines could be heard as hundreds of bomber power-packs were tested by ground crews who had been working all night to prepare the bombers for their mission of death. The base was awakening to another day of action...

The concept of strategic bombing – the destruction of an enemy's war potential through air attack – originated in the First World War, but it could not be tested then due to the lack of suitable bomb carriers. One of the first advocates of the theory was the Italian general Giulio Douhet who prophesied that future wars would be decided by aerial bombing of enemy cities to break the willpower of the people. An American, Brigadier General Billy Mitchell, also propounded this point of view, but was sacked by his sceptical commanders when he attempted to put his theory into practice by sinking a battleship with bombs. In later years aircraft designers were instructed to come up with a bomber which could not only reach enemy territory with a destructive bomb load but also survive enemy fighters and anti-aircraft guns. When, at the beginning of the Second World War, the RAF tried to penetrate German territory in daylight attacks, the results were so disastrous that Bomber Command opted instead for the cover of darkness to evade the German defences. The same fate befell the Luftwaffe in its attempts to attack targets in England during the Battle of Britain. Due to the lack of precision instruments, neither the RAF nor the Luftwaffe were able to find their targets at night, nor could they bomb them accurately if they did. The concept of area bombing was, therefore, the only way to keep the strategic bombing offensive going.

The United States Army Air Force, on the other hand, believed in daylight bombing, with precision attacks on point targets, and *they* had the means to do it. The four-engined B-17 Flying Fortress and B-24 Liberator had been designed with such missions in mind. Both were masterpieces of the air. The 'Fort' was virtually a flying dreadnought, a giant in the sky in those days. Although its bomb carrying capacity was not great, it could defend itself with thirteen large calibre machine guns pointing in all directions. Moreover, the unique bombsight afforded such accuracy that a trained bomber crew could actually place its bomb load on target from 30,000 feet. To fight their way to the target, the Fortresses flew in sophisticated tactical formations which gave them maximum defence with their automatically controlled guns, a formidable firepower combination which soon became the scourge of the Luftwaffe fighter pilots. It is no wonder, then, that the American commanders of the US Eighth Air Force were convinced that they could outfly the Luftwaffe and succeed with their precision bombing. They did – in the end – but at a high price, a price which the young American bomber crews had to pay.

In the American bomber bases, the dawn was beginning to break, into a bleak, foggy day. High above them the drone of the last returning RAF bombers could be heard as they straggled back to their home bases. Some tired airmen – the lucky ones – were longing for a cup of tea, a cigarette and then... lovely bed, after their nightly ordeal over Germany.

But for the American youngsters who crowded the smoke-filled briefing room, it was just the beginning of their battle. This particular day came to be known as Black Thursday, a day that those who survived would never forget. At Thurleigh, home base of 306th Bomb Group, Colonel Budd Peasley was calling his crews to attention. A hush fell over the assembled men, but when he announced the target: Schweinfurt. A gasp of disbelief could be heard from the shocked veterans, some of whom had fought in the first, notorious raid over that city only two months before. The trauma of that raid was still with them – during the air battles fought with the Luftwaffe then no less than 60 Fortresses had been lost. Peasley, who was to lead the mission himself, did not mince his words. He told them that this time Schweinfurt had to be totally destroyed, so that no one would have to do the raid again. This was not much consolation to the tired young veterans, who had not wanted to go there the first time either. But they gritted their teeth and carried on, trying to fill the time with trivial jokes and small errands until take off.

Once settled in their planes, however, they had no time to ponder their fate; each man was too busy with his own job. Pilots at nineteen bomber bases checked their watches and tension mounted as they waited for Mission 115 to take off. The co-pilot called each crew member in turn over the intercom: everything set for take-off. A two-pronged green flare sputtered and gleamed up into the sky. Engines started and a deafening roar was heard as the bombers came to life and trundled

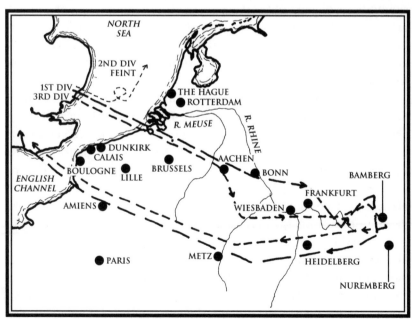

into take-off position one after the other, the ground crews waving them off. The lead bomber took up position, Colonel Peasley flying in the co-pilot's seat next to Captain James McLaughlin, the lead pilot. Nodding to McLaughlin, Peasley gave the signal to roll. Over the next 60 min-utes, some 377 heavy bombers took to the air and climbed through the thickly overcast sky until breaking into brilliant sunshine, where they formed up into combat formations. The fate of 3,000 men was in the hands of one.

Take-off went well enough, and no collisions occurred during the dangerous climb. As the groups manoeuvred into position, however, one group was seen to be missing, the leaders having strayed into another formation. Colonel Peasley had to amend his flight plan accordingly. Meanwhile the bomber formation had reached 20,000 feet and set off for the enemy coast, flying now in impeccable combat for-mation. Pilots and gunners strained their eyes to spot enemy fighters which they knew would surely come. For the time being, however, all was well and the escorting Thunderbolts, like sheepdogs herding their flocks, provided some comfort. But not for long – with the amount of fuel they could carry, they were able to accompany the bombers only as far as Aachen. Then the bombers had to fight themselves through the enemy cordon.

Not far away, in the German control centre of Luftflotte 12, Zeist, Holland, the activity of the American air armada did not long remain unnoticed. Although the target was still unclear, the controllers were certain that a major raid was on, and urgent orders were issued, putting fighter bases on high alert from the airfields of the North Sea to the Rhine bases. The Luftwaffe took to the air.

General Adolf Galland, commanding the Luftwaffe fighter arm, massed every fighter that he could muster that day. Even the nearly obsolete Stuka dive bombers were assembled, tasked to drop bombs on the bombers from above. Twin-engined Messerschmitt destroyers were there, too, armed with aerial rockets, which could be devastating weapons. JG 3 'Udet' led by Oberstleutnant Wolf-Dietrich Wilke was one of the first in position, cruising on patrol off Aachen, while the veteran JG 26 fighter wing led by Major Joseph Priller flew in the bombers' stream, waiting until the Thunderbolts turned away. Over Walcheren, two squadrons of fighters were already waiting as the great stream of bombers approached, their fuselages flashing silver in the morning sun. Flying one of the Me-109 fighters was young Leutnant Heinz Knoke, leading eleven fighters of JG 2 out of Jever. Waiting patiently, keeping out of harm's way, the Germans followed the American stream until the Thunderbolts turned away at Aachen. Only then did Knoke give the signal to attack. He chose exactly the moment when Peasley signalled the lead group to make its turn.

On the ground in Belgium, an American, Lieutenant Ted Wilson, was watching the great armada fly overhead. He had jumped to safety in August en route to Schweinfurt and, hidden by the Underground in a house near Wannebeck, saw exactly what happened as Peasley's bomber formation made its turn. Knoke's fighters moved in for their first kill. The German fighters hit first the fifteen-plane formation of Major Carl Norman's 305th Group flying in the vulnerable low position. Attacking from all directions at once, and firing rockets, they came in with devastating effect, some of them going in so close that they collided with the bombers and exploded with them. The American gunners fought back fiercely but were overwhelmed by sheer numbers. One by one the giant ships went down. Colonel Theodore Milton, commanding the wing, watched helplessly as his formation was decimated.

Colonel Peasley's formation had weathered the first shock, and was still intact. But not for long. As they reached the Rhine, the Luftwaffe came at them even more fiercely, and soon more American bombers went down, some of them exploding into huge balls of fire as their bombs exploded. For the crews it was a mercifully quick death. Others were not even that lucky. One B-17, hit by a rocket, opened like an eggshell, the right wing folded up and the stricken plane fell slowly earthward, enveloped in flames. For a moment the colonel could clearly see the pilots burning at the controls, then the giant ship dropped out of sight. No parachutes came out as it fell. One B-17 gunner was lucky: he managed to shoot away the rockets from an incoming Bf 110 just as the German was launching them. The German plane exploded. Leutnant Knoke, just behind, gritted his teeth grimly, and aimed. But at that moment he was hit by an American rear gunner. Barely controlling his stricken plane, Knoke glided earthwards and, finding a flat field, crash landed, totally exhausted by the ordeal.

Nearby, at the Luftwaffe air base at Neubiberg, the famous 'Moelders' fighter squadron was on full alert to take off and engage the bomber stream. The signal came and, once airborne, the fighter leader Hauptmann Gunther Rubell was given instructions by the ground controller to attack. Near Koblenz they could see the air armada approaching, a magnificent sight flying at 23,000 feet. Within seconds, one of the American bombers was exploding in the air, but the rest of the heavy bombers flew on, while black puffs of flak coming from Frankfurt signified how welcome these 'callers' were. Now it was time for Rubell to attack. Suddenly he and his mates were in the thick of battle, diving into the formation with their guns blazing. One bomber was set on fire and dropped, trailing smoke. A young German pilot, new to the wing, named Gunther Stedfeld found himself flying between two giant bombers. Gasping with fear, he tried to escape the fire from the American gunners, rolling from side to side. Then one of the bombers exploded next to him, blowing off his overhead bubble canopy. Shaking with fright, the young fighter pilot jumped clear and floated down, leaving the noise of battle above him.

Up in the sky, the bomber stream was closing in on Schweinfurt. Lieutenant David Williams, the lead navigator, who had also flown in the August mission, was precisely on time as he led the group into the target area. From his position up front, he could see the factories lying wide open for their attack in the midday haze. But the German defenders were waiting. Some 300 guns were ready to open fire with a withering barrage of flak covering the entire town and its surroundings. Worse, some of the German fighter pilots stuck to the bomber formation, following it right into the target in spite of getting flak from their own side. On Colonel Milton's left side, the remnants of Major Norman's 305 Group, now down to three bombers of the seventeen that had taken off that morning from Chelveston, were doggedly keeping formation. Norman had been lucky so far, and sat at his controls, grimly determined to stick it out and drop his bomb load as briefed. Still another of his dwindling force was lost just as it reached the outskirts of the city, when flak hit the right wing, and it fell off sideways, trailing flames, one of the engines dropping off. Norman, watching the stricken bomber veering towards his own, just managed to take evasive action, while his co-pilot, a new man, sat there frozen stiff with fear, eyes bulging as he stared in horror at one of the crewmen bailing out of the plane's side door – without a parachute. Turning over and over, he fell, and disappeared from view. Major Norman was an old hand, and used to disturbing sights, but this was one that would keep coming back to him as he lay sleepless in his bunk. But now he was too busy to take it in and, slapping his co-pilot, he brought him back to his senses.

The formation was now right over the city. Flak was bursting all over as the lead bombardier, Lieutenant Samuel Slayton, released his bombs, followed by the rest. High above, in his co-pilot's seat, Colonel

Budd Peasley watched the city descend into the lower levels of hell. Despite fighters, despite flak, the attack had been successful.

Less than an hour before, Schweinfurt had been enjoying a lovely autumn day. Boats were floating serenely on the river Main, war seemed very remote to these people who, since they had endured the first raid in August, had been left alone apart from a few air raid alarms. Now, suddenly, without warning the sirens were wailing once again, throwing fear into the inhabitants who hastened into their bunkers. In the ball-bearing factories, the main targets in the city, workers hurriedly left their production lines. One of the artisans working at the VKF plant, Heinrich Weichsel, hastily took some of his precious measuring tools as he left for the bunker; on his way he could already see, high above, the cluster of silver dots of the American bombers shining in the sun. Near the black puffs of oily flak, explosions were visible, but he had no time to appreciate the scene. No sooner had he opened the heavy bunker door than the first bombs started whistling down, the blast throwing him right into the arms of a terrified woman who was huddled inside. The din was horrendous, people screaming in terror as thick dust carpeted the floor and covered the bunker walls. As more and more bombs exploded, the dust intensified, while the people hiding from the blast gasped for breath. Outside the bunkers, Leo Wehner, a Kugelfischer plant employee, was in charge of a flak crew on the roof of the factory. For twenty minutes, as the attack raged, he tried to get his men to open fire but, in the ear-shattering noise, no one listened to his pleas. Dense smoke engulfed the rooftop and the men huddled fearfully behind their protective sandbags. In the end Wehner gave up and joined them.

Above, the bombers had completed their deadly work and turned to leave, leaving behind them the shell of a city. Fires raged and ruined buildings could be seen everywhere. But the battle was far from over. The surviving bombers still had to run the gauntlet of the enraged Luftwaffe on their long, arduous return trip, and many of the bomber crews would join the hapless comrades they had left littering the German countryside on the way in.

Sure enough, soon the fighters were on the attack again. Scores of them screamed into the formation with renewed fervour. The first victim was an already damaged bomber flown by Captain Ronald Sarget. His plane caught fire and exploded. No one was seen coming out as it spiralled down. Lieutenant Roger Layn was struggling with his controls trying to keep a tight formation when three fighters dived on him, firing their guns as they came. The pilot watched wide-eyed as one of the Germans, in a daring stunt, went into a roll and crossed in front of the Fort's nose upside down – so close that Layn could see the German staring into his white face. As he flew he could see two more Fortresses in the higher formation trailing smoke. Leutnant Hans Langer, a veteran fighter pilot of the crack JG 51, had already fought the big bombers in the August raid. Now he was once more in the thick of the fight, going for the stragglers which he thought would be easy meat. Diving on Layn's plane, which he saw had already been hit, he closed in, firing frontally. He could see his bullets exploding along the giant bomber's wings but, as he broke sharply away, Langer himself was hit twice. Out of ammunition, he dived to make a forced landing, managing to hold his damaged aeroplane until the exact second of landing, when the engine stopped. Way up there, Lieutenant Layn was struggling. His bomber was dying under him, slowing down, forcing him to abandon the comparative safety of the bomber formation. Leaning towards his co-pilot, Layn shouted to him to hold tight, but it was no good – he was losing control. Sweating and trembling with the effort to keep the heavy aircraft flying, the pilot turned round, only to find that the entire fuselage was filled with smoke and fire. The captain ordered the crew to abandon ship in a hurry and saw the men ejecting. But one man did not leave, a gunner who was badly hurt and in pain. The co-pilot went back to help but the man was pinned down and could not be moved, so the pilot made the fateful decision. He stuck with his crew member and sitting grimly at the controls flew the ship home. By some miracle, he made it.

But as the bombers fought their way home, more and more were going down. One formation had already lost its tenth plane. There seemed no end to the carnage that raged over Germany that day. All along the Rhine valley, pillars of black smoke indicated the death throes of crashed aeroplanes, while the few lucky men who had managed to get out of their stricken aircraft staggered about the countryside, stunned by the ordeal they had undergone. Many more of them were dead, burned beyond recognition in the shattered remains of their planes. The Luftwaffe command was jubilant: they thought that their pilots had scored a great victory, but they did not know yet that many of their own planes had been brought down by the American gunners and that many of their own men were dead.

At last the Americans came in sight of the coast, where friendly fighters, Thunderbolts and RAF Spitfires, were coming to their aid. Some of the exhausted aircrews welcomed them with loud cheers and went frantic with joy. Now it was the turn of the Luftwaffe pilots to taste some of their own medicine. As the fresh Allied fighters screamed into the fray, the German fighters, many of them worn out by the battle which had continued for hours, were no match for them and many of them were hit by the revenging guns of the bombers' 'little friends'.

Between Rheims and Soissons in northern France, the returning bombers could finally see the welcome sight of the English Channel. Black Thursday was nearing its end. For some of the crews, however, a further ordeal lay ahead, as tired pilots struggled in vain to land their badly damaged bombers. Some of them crashed, killing or maiming their crews – tragic irony for those who had survived the terrors of the great air battle over Germany.

The second Schweinfurt raid was a disaster for the Eighth Air Force. Of the 291 planes despatched that morning, 227 had survived mechanical problems and the German guns. Sixty bombers and 600 men were missing, 142 planes returned badly damaged, with dead and wounded men aboard. However, it should be said that the Luftwaffe had failed to prevent the American bomber fleet from reaching its target and fulfilling Mission 115. The damage to the ball-bearing installations was considerable, much more devastating than in August, the factories a mass of rubble and twisted metal, which took months to repair.

For the surviving American aircrews there was only a temporary respite. Many of them were soon called to go into action once more to face the horrors of the bombing offensive. Those who made it through the war in one piece physically bore the emotional scars of war for many years to come. For them Black Thursday would haunt them for ever.

CHAPTER FOURTEEN

MONTE CASSINO: THE MOUNTAIN OF DEATH

About half way between Naples and Rome lies Monte Cassino, an impressive mountain topped with a monastery, towering above the tourists who speed by nowadays on the Autostrada del Sol. Very few of these tourists, glancing up at the massive building on top of the ship-shaped ridge, know, or care, that, years ago, many thousands of people died or were lost in the muddy wastes surrounding this pretty little town.

In 1944, Cassino was a typical Italian country town of some 25,000 inhabitants. Its summers were hot and dusty, its winters harsh; the rainfall swelling the nearby river, the Rapido, into a watery marshland, making life miserable for all. In those days, Cassino's main claim to fame was the great mountain which rears up behind the town and bears its name. It was well known even in Roman times due to its strategic position, guarding the entrance into the wide, flat Liri river valley and presenting the last bastion on the way to Rome, about a hundred kilometres to the north. It was known as Casium to the Romans, who built a fort on its peak guarding the Via Casilina, one of the great highways of history, over which armies had been marching for centuries in countless military campaigns. In the sixth century the monk Benedict founded the religious order named after him and laid the foundation of the Abbey of Monte Cassino, which gained more and more importance over the next centuries.

When the Allied armies used that ancient road again for their march northwards to Rome, they found Monte Cassino and its impressive monastery towering over the valley and guarding the entrance into the valley which led to Rome. The battle for this pass would last for six terrible months and would be one of the most gruelling, harrowing and, arguably, tragic campaigns of the Second World War, taking place in biting cold, torrents of rain and lakes of mud.

The Germans had early realised the strategic importance of Monte Cassino, and it was the centrepiece of their Gustav Line, planned to block the Allied advance to Rome and from thence to the soft underbelly of Europe. The Gustav Line was perhaps the strongest fortification in Europe at that time. Using many thousands of workers brought in from all over Europe, the Germans had constructed a river defence, using concrete bunkers, stone- and earthworks, and deep underground shelters, making it an almost impregnable bastion.

The defence of the Cassino sector had been entrusted to XIV Panzer Korps commanded by Lieutenant General Fridolin von Senger und Etterlin, one of the Wehrmacht's finest and most intelligent generals. Von Senger, from an old, aristocratic German family, was as far away from the archetype of the Prussian officer as could be. Educated at Oxford, having been awarded a Rhodes scholarship in 1912, he became fluent in several languages and was more at home among intellectuals than among his brother officers. No wonder, then, that he did not take willingly to the Nazi party but, as a loyal officer, he always did his job unflinchingly, despite his growing doubts as the war went on. By the time the fight for Cassino began, von Senger was convinced that Germany's defeat was inevitable, but he had his job to do, and he set about it in his usual determined way.

Blasting emplacements into the rocky mountainside and converting the town's stone houses into fortified bunkers, he turned the entire area, and especially Monte Cassino, into an impregnable fortress. The valley itself was heavily mined on both sides of the Rapido River, with gun positions buried on its banks, and tanks placed in hull down positions, so well camouflaged as to be virtually invisible. Cassino and its mountain with the monastery atop became one of the best defended positions not only in Italy but in all of Europe.

The man who would have to fight this very professional German commander was a 47-year-old American, General Mark Clark,

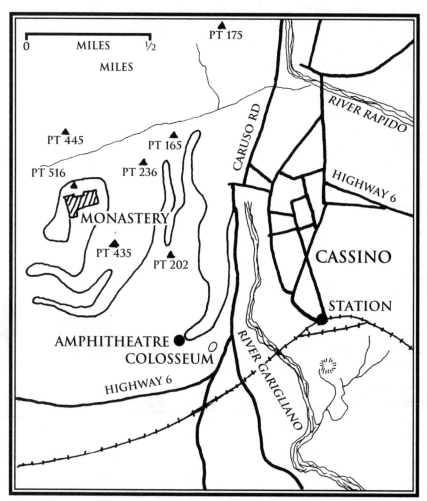

commander of US Fifth Army. Mark Wayne Clark, born in Chicago, had had a meteoric rise, becoming the youngest general in the US Army at the age of 46. His career had certainly not been harmed by his close relations with Dwight Eisenhower, with whom he had shared a room during their cadet days at West Point, but, in any case, Eisenhower had later found him to be a superb organiser when serving with him in the 3rd Infantry Division before the war. Like the British Montgomery, Clark was a brilliant showman but, unlike the austere Monty, Mark Clark cut a dashing figure. Tall and handsome, always wearing an open-collared shirt, he looked like the star of a Hollywood Western, an impression he enjoyed creating. While still at Naples, before setting off on the northward toil to Rome, he had refused one of the 1,200 rooms at Caserta Castle, and had chosen instead a modest caravan situated in the lavish gardens surrounding the Bourbon palace.

Clark and von Senger were totally opposing personalities: Fridolin von Senger's intellectual background, his sensitive face, contrasted sharply with the swashbuckling – some said swaggering – Clark. In another respect, too, they were opposites: while von Senger had seen action since the beginning of the war on all fronts, Clark had scarcely had time to gain much experience, since he had taken command of an army in Salerno only a year before. It is doubtful whether the two men would have had much in common had they met in a social setting. But that was not to be. Their meeting would become one of the hardest and most costly battles of the Second World War.

The first battle of Cassino started on 12 January 1944, and lasted for a month. The fact that it went wrong was due to the shortness of the time allowed for planning, because of the deadline imposed by the Anzio landings, which had been fixed for just one week later. The botching of both these plans was to cause six months of fighting over the Cassino area. General Clark's battle plan was for a three-pronged attack: one in the mountains north of Cassino, one a left hook across the River Garigliano, and one a thrust up the Liri Valley to link up with the Allied beachhead at Anzio, all of this facilitating the move towards Rome. It was an optimistic, ambitious plan, but it could have worked – if a worse German commander had been in place. But Clark was facing von Senger here, and von Senger had foreseen and planned for this very eventuality, and trained his forces accordingly.

On 12 January then, the French Corps under General Alfonse Juin attacked in the mountains north of Cassino, as the first prong of the attack, and advanced slowly but steadily in the appalling, wintry conditions which were nothing new to the North African troops who made up the majority of the French divisions. Trained in the Atlas mountains, these Moroccan and Algerian regiments were familiar with the hazards of both mountain combat and the cold. On the left flank of the Fifth Army, the British X Corps began its attack across the Garigliano River – the second prong – and by 18 January had ten battalions across.

General von Senger considered the British attack extremely dangerous, but awaited the main offensive at Cassino, requesting two reserve divisions to be sent to face the British until he could counter General Clark's attack and confine it with the forces he had in place further north in the Liri Valley. Field Marshal Albert Kesselring, the overall German commander, anticipating an Allied landing somewhere south of Rome, was reluctant to release his two remaining reserve divisions to von Senger, but the German intelligence reports indicated that such a landing was not imminent. German Intelligence had been tricked by Allied disinformation and, in fact, the Allied ships were already loading at Salerno, aiming for a landing at Anzio!

Kesselring therefore sent the 29th and 90th Panzergrenadier divisions to bolster the hard pressed 94th Infanterie Division heavily engaged with the British X Corps. On 21 January the two German divisions mounted a strong counter attack on the British bridgehead but the Tommies held on doggedly despite bitter fighting. The next day, two Allied divisions landed at Anzio and the two German divisions broke off and rushed to stem the new invasion threat. General Richard McCreery's troops of X Corps were saved – for a time.

So far Mark Clark had no reason to be unhappy with the battle for Cassino. The French were holding their own in the wintry mountains, while to the south the British were also entrenching across the river line. Now it was up to the Americans to settle the issue on the Cassino front. The assault over the Rapido was spearheaded by the reservists of the US 36th Texas Division. It proved a total disaster. The 141st Regiment, with two of its battalions in the lead, attempted to force a crossing north of St Angelo with its sister regiment assaulting to the south. Everything went wrong right from the start. Heavy fog hampered the approach while intense German counter fire created havoc among the advancing troops, carrying their rubber boats to the river banks. The tapes which marked cleared paths through the minefields were shot away and the men stumbled blindly about in the soggy marshes. The lead companies were reduced to a handful of men even before they neared the bank and even those who survived and managed to launch their boats sank together with their boats which were punctured by bullets. The crossing was a nightmare and, by dawn, only two understrength companies had managed to get across, trying desperately to dig in before the Germans launched their morning counter attack.

Commanders attempted to mount another assault but, since their communications had been ruptured, they had no effective information to guide them, and withering German fire blasted the infantry to shreds. Gradually the noise of battle died away as ammunition ran out and, with the exception of a few men who managed to swim the ice-cold river to safety, two regiments of the 36th Texas Division in effect ceased to exist, either dead or in captivity.

This disaster was the worst suffered by the US Army until then, although it was repeated almost a year later during the opening hours of the Battle of the Bulge in the Ardennes offensive, when two regiments of the 106th Infantry Division were encircled in the Schnee Eifel and forced to surrender. In both places the Americans put up a brave fight, but they had no chance, in this case, against General von Senger's near perfect defences.

The failure to force the Rapido made Clark decide that his next attack would be on the German flanks. By now, however, the river had flooded and become a terrible quagmire, making movement almost impossible all over the valley. Nevertheless, following some vicious fighting against stubborn German resistance, the US 34th Infantry Division had taken two vantage points by 31 January.

A daunting task now faced the Americans: to climb uphill, through masses of barbed wire and mines, to ascend Monte Cassino. In the terrible winter conditions, the Americans fought their way, inch by inch, through the rocks and boulders, managing to gain a foothold on a knoll, Point 593, which was to change hands time and again as first the Germans, and then the Americans, attacked and counter attacked in the cold and sleet. After some of the most savage close-in fighting ever known, both sides were exhausted and fought themselves to a standstill. The average fighting strength of an infantry company on that mountain amounted to no more than 30 men by the time the battle ceased!

The first battle for Cassino was over. Losses were heavy – the Americans alone lost during that one month over 10,000 men, a terrible price to pay for so very little gained.

One little known incident which took place during that month concerns a squad led by an American sergeant of 34th Division, which was ordered on 5 February to climb up the mountain from their base on Hill 445 and reconnoitre the ground uphill towards the monastery. Starting out at dawn, under cover of thick fog, the small unit set out, picking their way carefully over the rocks and bushes. But when they reached a small stream, they surprised three Germans filling their water bottles. The sergeant and his men took the Germans prisoner, sent them back downhill, and continued uphill, now in full sight of anyone who happened to be in the monastery which towered above. No one fired as they reached the winding mountain road leading up the monastery gate and soon a breach in the wall led them right up to the courtyard, when a monk looking out of his window saw them taking a number of Germans prisoner, surprised as they had emerged from a nearby cave. It was almost too good to be true and the sergeant, with about the same number of prisoners as he had men in his unit, was forced to retire. They would be the only Americans ever to set foot in the monastery.

Both sides were reorganising their forces. General Clark now realised that Cassino could not be taken in a hurried assault and that von Senger's defences were a formidable challenge which had to be tackled carefully. For his part, the German general had no illusions as to what he was facing, bearing in mind that his opponents not only fielded superior firepower but had full control over the air – a factor which would be a decisive issue when an all-out attack came. Still, he was determined to put up the best fight he could and his troops were boosted, at this time, by the arrival of Germany's crack 1st Parachute Division which took up positions inside the village and on the mountain itself.

The Allies received some first class troops as well. The newly formed New Zealand Corps brought with it two of the best fighting divisions of the war, the 2nd New Zealand and the 4th Indian, both veterans of the desert war in which they had fought so gallantly that they had acquired a sort of aura, the glamour of a corps d'élite second to none in fighting spirit. The New Zealanders were terrific fighters. Hand-picked volunteers, these highly intelligent and efficient men were self-reliant, independent soldiers who could think for themselves, ideally suited for the small unit actions to be fought in these surroundings. These no-nonsense men were led by officers of an equal stamp, who would lead by example, displaying moral courage to inspire their men. Their commander, Lieutenant General Sir Bernard Freyberg, was the best leader these fine soldiers could have hoped for. Huge, handsome, with keen grey eyes, Freyberg was the classic soldier hero. But he did not just look the part – his distinguished combat record included the VC and three DSOs during the First World War. He was just the man to lead these two fine fighting formations into the difficult and dangerous battle that was about to take place.

The second battle of Cassino began on 15 February, with a pincer attack by two divisions, the 2nd New Zealand and the 4th Indian, on the flanks of Cassino. General Freyberg's plan was, in fact, a continuation of the American attack in January. From the bridgehead clawed out of the mountain ridges, the Indians would storm the monastery hill and then sweep down towards the Liri Valley, while the New Zealanders would advance along the causeway which carried the railway line and seize the station, with its fortifications, south of the town. If the pincer succeeded Cassino would literally be pinched out of the fight and the Allied armour could burst into the Liri Valley and advance to link up with the forces at Anzio.

The bombing of the Cassino monastery which preceded the February attack has been the subject of controversy ever since and it is beyond the scope of this story to go into detail about the decision which led to the total destruction of such a valuable and historic piece of architecture. However, it should be mentioned that two German officers actually evacuated most of the invaluable art treasures from the monastery before it came within range of the fighting. Moreover, there were conflicting reports on the presence of German artillery observers inside the buildings. These reports later proved to be unfounded, since General von Senger personally instructed his troops to refrain from entering the compound proper. The building itself was inadequate from a tactical viewpoint to serve as an artillery observation post, since its windows were screened by the topographical features and no line of sight was possible. The perfect observation points were in fact on the nearby hills and it was from there that the Germans directed their fire. From a psychological and morale point of view, however, it would have been extremely difficult to convince any of the attacking commanders to leave such a prominent feature standing before an all-out assault of this kind, since it would have been hard to make the men climb a hill in view of the possibility of withering fire coming down on them from the monastery looming above.

In any case, the rest is history – From 0925 and for the next four hours on the morning of 15 February, over 200 heavy bombers of the

USAAF dropped nearly 500 tons of high explosive bombs on the monastery, pounding the famous edifice to a pile of rubble. Whatever its value as a military objective before, it became a first class fortification in its ruin, as no sooner had the building been destroyed than German paratroopers took over and within hours set up a near impregnable defence position which would, from now on, withstand all Allied attacks.

The second attack on Cassino was no more successful than the first. The German paratroopers stood fast, defending every inch of ground in spite of determined, sometimes almost suicidal, assaults by the New Zealanders and Indians. Although some ground was gained, none of the attackers reached the summit. Whenever a gain was made, the Germans immediately mounted a counter attack and dislodged the men from their hard-won positions. In this way entire units on both sides were cut to pieces. The German defenders were still holding their own when Freyberg, seeing that his troops were totally exhausted, decided to call a halt. The attack had not been a total loss, however, since most of the positions held could serve as jumping off points for the next attack.

General Freyberg was now coming under severe pressure and the prestige of his forces was at stake. His next plan was to capture Cassino and the monastery hill by frontal attack, since all other alternatives had been tried and failed. The assault was to be preceded by a strong air attack on the town of Cassino and with the majority of the defenders dead or, at least, neutralised from a fighting point of view, the infantry, supported by tanks, would enter the battered town and mop up the survivors. This was the first attempt to use bombers strategically in close support in massive numbers. The weather clamped down, delaying everything for three long days, a delay which severely tested the already frayed nerves of the infantrymen, all of whom were veterans and knew that this battle would be the toughest of them all, that many of them would die, that many more would be maimed – the added waiting was almost unbearable and by the time the weather cleared, on 15 March, the men seemed more relieved than not to be on the move.

Starting in the early morning, the town of Cassino was reduced into heaps of rubble, turning a once pretty Italian pastoral scene into something like the moon's surface. The aerial bombardment was just as terrifying to the Allied forces, shaking the ground and covering everything with thick dust that turned day into night. Not a single building was left intact, just a cloud of dust which hovered a few metres from the ground. Now the New Zealand battalions jumped off and, hoping for the best, shuffled slowly into the ruins, their tanks following behind. At first everything was silent and hopes rose – were the Germans all dead? The answer was not long in coming: suddenly, out of the rubble withering machine gun fire erupted and slammed into the advancing New Zealanders, who scurried for cover. Although half of the German 3rd Parachute Regiment had perished in the bombardment, the survivors were fighting mad. They came out of their holes, stood their ground, and fought. Into this carnage now fell the Allied artillery barrage, which further churned up the rubble into a fine powder, bringing visibility down to almost nil, while observation was impossible. Snipers were firing from every corner, men fell, some of them into waterlogged craters. To compound the misery, it started to pour again and soon the dust turned into a thick morass, while the craters filled with water. The two sides fought from building to building, with the young German paratroopers defending the lower, then the upper floors, then even walls still standing were turned into isolated bastions. They fought from ruin to ruin, friend and foe only metres apart. The noise was terrible, but most of the men soon stopped hearing it, only noticing the suffocating dust. As the men slithered along, uniforms drenched, faces covered with the white dust, they looked like demented clowns from some macabre circus.

The New Zealanders fought their way forward yard by yard, crawling through the rubble, scrambling from one bomb crater to the next, while the Sherman tanks of the New Zealand Armoured Regiment tried in vain to grind in behind the infantry, but were unable to make any significant progress. Here and there single tanks fired their guns into the apertures of bunkers held by the Germans, helping the footsloggers a bit, but not much.

However, while the two New Zealand battalions were squelching through the mud in the ruins of Cassino, a New Zealand company was climbing uphill and, in a brilliantly executed attack, captured Castle Hill, having scaled an almost vertical slope to get there.

At nightfall the rain fell in even greater intensity, while lightning flashed and thunder roared, mingling with the man-made noise. The scene became more and more like a scene from a ghost story, as the flashes of lightning lit up huddled groups of men firing at fleeting figures, not knowing whether they were friend or foe. During this cold, wet night, the fighting continued relentlessly on the slopes of Monte

Cassino. At midnight the 4th Essex Regiment lumbered up to relieve the freezing New Zealanders on Castle Hill. Two companies of the 6th Rajputana Rifles managed to get uphill over some tricky hairpin bends, and captured Point 165, but the Germans put in a strong counter attack and forced them back down to Castle Hill, which was getting very crowded by dawn. The 9th Gurkhas performed heroically, too, that night and reached a place dubbed Hangman's Hill, only a few hundred metres below the monastery! This was Point 435 – a jutting platform of rock with a sharp drop below it, a precarious place from which to fight a battle. A pylon, what remained from an unused aerial ropeway, was standing upright still, resembling a gibbet, thus accounting for the eerie name of a place which would in truth become a death trap for many men over the coming days. Colonel Nagle, the Gurkha commander, deployed his small force to defend Hangman's Hill against the counter attack which he knew would come by morning.

Down in the battered town, the battle raged on, now concentrating on two former hotels, the Continental and the Hotel des Roses, both on a slope leading uphill to the castle. These buildings had been made into virtual fortresses, with bunkers on the upper floors and tanks placed in the lobby with only their gun barrels protruding. Every attempt to rush one of these forts failed, the German defenders putting up a terrific amount of accurate fire whenever any of the New Zealanders approached.

Before dawn, the brigade commander, crouching in the confines of his forward command post, received a radio report from Colonel Nagle, confirming that his Gurkhas were holding Hangman's Hill, from which the Rajputs had been evicted earlier in the night. The commander realised that, although the colonel's force was cut off, he was clinging to an extremely important feature which, if he could hold out long enough, would enable him to reach the coveted Monastery Hill! Thus the Rajputs mounted another attack on the hairpin bend to link up with the Gurkhas, but just then the German counter attack came, sending a hail of fire from above. So, as morning came, two separate battles were raging, one in the rubble of the town, where four New Zealand battalions were fighting the 3rd Parachute Regiment, while, uphill, Castle Hill was the base for the Rajputs and Gurkhas fighting off desperate German counter attacks trying to drive them off. The battle had started on Wednesday, the 15th; it was now nearly Friday, and no end was in sight. And the fighting still went on, neither side willing to give ground, ready to fight it out to the last man.

Sunday, the 19th, was the crucial day of the battle. While the New Zealanders were still struggling through the rubble of what had once been Cassino, fighting the stubborn remnants of the German paratroopers, a great drama was about to unfold on the slopes of Monastery Hill. It was just as the Indian division was about to jump off for their attack that the German paratroops chose to launch their counter attack. For ten minutes, although it seemed like a lifetime to the defenders, the Germans came downhill covered by a paralysing hailstorm of machine gun fire which ricocheted about the rocks.

During the night the Essex battalion on Castle Hill had been relieved by the 4th Rajputs and, before dawn, Colonel Noble, commanding the Essex, gave orders for an advance to link up with Colonel Nagle and his Gurkhas, reinforced by a company of Rajputs who had climbed up and brought badly needed supplies. Two companies of the Essex had just set out on the hazardous climb uphill and the other two, with Battalion HQ, were assembling outside the castle to follow them when the German attack began – at the worst moment possible! The two forward companies were raked by withering fire, followed by mortar rounds which came raining down. Casualties mounted fast; the men scattered, some falling down the slopes. Two hundred German paratroops from 4th Parachute Regiment raced down the hillside, engulfing the Rajputs defending Point 165. Some of the Germans fought the Indians while the rest charged on towards the Castle where Major Ketteley was trying to assemble enough of his men for a rush defence. A mixed group of Essex and Rajputs took up positions on the castle walls, aiming their rifles and machine guns through the narrow slits.

The first two Essex companies, having recovered from the initial shock, resumed their way uphill, but were able to watch the battle for the castle from their vantage point below. It was an amazing sight. The German paratroops were now sweeping down the slope towards the castle walls, but the machine guns firing through the slits were reaping a terrible harvest. Still the survivors kept coming and those who made it through began to scale the castle walls, clinging on like leeches until they were blasted off with grenades or pushed off by rifle butts. But the Germans regrouped and came on again with even more vigour, shouting wildly as they advanced. Lieutenant Coghlan and Corporal Parker of the Essex rushed out of the castle to fend them off, firing their Tommy guns from the hip, but both were killed by bursts of Schmeisser fire. There was a short lull but then the paratroopers stormed the castle walls once more. A well-aimed German stick grenade penetrated into the inner chamber and killed Major Ketteley as he was telephoning brigade headquarters. Major Beckett, commanding the Essex C Company, took over and fought off some Germans clambering up the castle walls. In that mêlée Major Beckett was himself wounded, but remained in control of the action, sending a party of Rajputs to mount a counter attack on the paratroops gathering in the outer yard.

Ammunition was running low now inside the castle; the barrels of the Bren guns were red hot from continuous firing, the British had fired more than 1,500 mortar shells and some of the barrels had become bent! Sergeant Major Rose ran a gauntlet of fire to deliver bags of ammunition, and rushed in not a moment too soon, just as the Germans launched their last desperate attack on the castle walls. But their force was spent and they withdrew. Of the 200 men who had attacked, only a handful remained. Castle Hill remained in the hands of the Essex.

Down in the town the battle continued to rage, the New Zealanders desperately fighting to gain access to the hotel ruins, the German paratroopers standing their ground – and suffering heavily as a result. From time to time a single Sherman tank would manage to get in over the rubble close enough to fire shells at point blank range, but the Germans survived the terrible ordeal in their underground bunkers. They had to be winkled out, singly, one by one by bayonet.

At dawn on the last day of the battle, the New Zealand Maori battalion started an attack on the Continental Hotel in a final bid to capture it. Two-thirds of the ruins of the town were now in Allied hands, but the Germans remained firmly entrenched in the rest, guarding the uphill road to the castle and Monastery Hill. An attempt was made to try and capture the monastery from the northern flank, using tanks which used a specially prepared mountain track, allowing them to climb in single file. They managed to bypass the Indian troops clinging to one of the hill slopes halfway up then, approaching a mountain farm named Massa Albaneta, they were assaulted head on by a party of German tank killer teams which closed in on the tanks to zero range and knocked out the leading Sherman with a well-aimed bazooka round. Unable to turn around or pass, the rest of the tanks were stuck and were killed one by one by bazookas.

This killing match continued for some time, eventually petering out with each side holding on to the gains for which so much blood had been spilled. When General Richard Heidrich, the veteran commander of the 1st Parachute Division, sadly read the roll call after the battle, he found that his combat units were down to single men; nearly all the officers and NCOs had been killed or badly wounded, and the few who were left exhausted, amazed that they were still alive!

Three attempts had now been made to defeat the German paratroops and capture Monte Cassino – all to no avail. The resulting stalemate lasted until the wintry weather passed and a full-scale offensive could be launched. This time it had to succeed!

Indeed, the fourth battle for Cassino was an affair on the grandest scale – a set piece, textbook attack. Where single battalions had been employed previously, full-sized divisions would be launched, with massive firepower. General von Senger knew that his dwindling forces, now near exhaustion, could simply not withstand another major battle against fresh troops. But he was determined to make his swan song a good one, and to make a fight of it before withdrawing.

General Sir Harold Alexander now assembled two entire armies for the last attack, the British Eighth and the US Fifth, with seventeen divisions among them. Two Polish corps under General Anders, with two infantry divisions, XIII British Corps and the US II Corps were all poised to give von Senger the coup de grace. On 11 May the great day came and 1,600 guns opened fire, bombarding the rubble all over again. Then the French Expeditionary Corps under General Juin started its attack, this time doing what the French general had really wanted all the time – outflanking the entire German front through the mountains to the west of the Liri Valley. Here his North Africans were in their element and, after some vicious fighting, chased the Germans from their positions.

With this blow von Senger realised that his defence was broken. General Anders' Poles attacked on the left German flank, captured the notorious Point 593 and, at last, with the ruins of the monastery evacuated by the last handful of German paratroops, the 12th Podolski Lancers hoisted the Polish banner over the rubble of what had once been a proud edifice.

The battle of Cassino was finally over, but at a terrible price: during the six months the Allies had lost more than 11,000 dead, the Germans almost double that number. Whether it was worth it, no one will ever agree. Certainly with superior generalship and better luck much of the misery and hardship might have been avoided. As usual, it was the little men, not the generals, who had to do the fighting and dying, who had to pay the price for others' mistakes.

The town of Cassino and the monastery have been rebuilt now, mute testimony to the many who fought to their deaths in the terrible winter of 1944.

CHAPTER FIFTEEN
NIGHT JUMP: NORMANDY 1944

Lieutenant Colonel Patrick J. Cassidy, standing in the doorway of his C-47 Dakota, glanced briefly at his luminous watch: it was nearly one minute after midnight on 6 June 1944, and the 28-year-old colonel was flying to his first combat jump. Looking backwards into the dark fuselage, he saw that many of his men, crouched in the narrow and uncomfortable bucket seats, were fast asleep. Cassidy had no thoughts of sleep – in the two minutes that remained before he was to jump, he was going over his assignment for the umpteenth time. He commanded the 5th Parachute Battalion of the 101st US Airborne Division, and they had a tough job to do that night. His battalion was slated to drop in the vicinity of the beach designated 'Utah', capture and secure four causeways leading from the beach inland over a two-kilometre-wide swamp, to ensure that the 4th US Infantry Division which was to land at dawn would be able to push into the German rear zone without delay and, hopefully, without any trouble. The causeways were known to be defended, since the Germans were perfectly aware of their strategic importance in preventing a seaborne landing on that very beach, so Cassidy realised that his men would have to fight from the moment they hit the ground. This would be their first battle, and it was a first for him too.

As they flew over the coastline the anti-aircraft fire, which had been light and inaccurate over the Channel Islands, grew heavier; the Germans were firing bigger guns and the pilot started weaving slightly to avoid the flak. Cassidy could now see the ground clearly, and could see the gun flashes below. Just a few seconds to go – and then the green jump light would come on! The men, all awake now, queued up behind him, fastening their drop lines, while the jump master checked each man in turn, patting him on the back in a time-honoured gesture of reassurance.

Suddenly the view was blotted out. With less than a minute to go the Dakota had flown into cloud so thick that the colonel could not even see the wing tips and began to worry that they would have to jump blind into the night. But just as suddenly the sky became clear once more. Below him, he could now see a wide sheet of water gleaming in the moonlight, and recognised it for the swamps near which his battalion was to drop. Nearby he could see the dropping zone marker blinking in the darkness. So far, so good: his pathfinder crews seemed to be in position.

The green lamp over the doorway lit up and the colonel jumped clear, followed by his men. As he fell he thought for one split second that it was 4 July and they were watching a fireworks display: the entire sky was crisscrossed with tracer chains – quite beautiful to watch, until he realised that they were something much more deadly than fireworks! The Germans were not shooting at the paratroops, though; still unaware that the drop was on, they were aiming for what they thought were enemy night bombers!

The parachutes came open one by one as the men floated down to earth. Colonel Cassidy plunged right into a tall oak tree, but was able to cut himself free with his commando knife and drop lightly to the ground. A burst from a nearby machine gun crashed into the ground a mere three paces from where he lay, but Cassidy managed to crawl into a nearby ditch and take stock of his situation. Apart from the machine gun, all seemed quiet, but he could see none of his men. But he was lucky: at least he had hit dry ground; many of the 13,000 similar drops that had taken place that night had ended in the vast watery maze of the Normandy Cotentin peninsula.

It was the eve of D-Day, and the airborne operation which preceded the Normandy invasion was a gigantic affair, the first of that magnitude ever attempted in war. Many of the top brass had opposed it from its inception, convinced that it was too risky and unlikely to achieve its aim – namely, support of the seaborne landing. To be fair, previous experience with airborne operations had not been very impressive. First the Germans had stormed Crete in an air drop which had cost them a very heavy price. Then came the Sicily débâcle, when everything that could go wrong did go wrong: hundreds of paratroopers had drowned in the Mediterranean when inexperienced transport pilots dropped them to their deaths by inaccurate navigation. So it was natural that commanders would hesitate when it came to the planning of the Normandy invasion, fearing the worst and expecting losses of up to 70 percent! But others felt that the airborne operations could support a seaborne landing much more safely than any other method during that critical stage, and the operation went ahead.

One of the most serious problems for Operation 'Overlord' was to secure, as early as possible, a major port in order to build the vital lifeline to feed the vast number of troops essential for the job. In Normandy, the only port which suited these requirements was Cherbourg in the north of the Cotentin Peninsula. This was an area of great strategic importance, known to be held by strong German forces in key positions, on a high alert status in anticipation of the forthcoming invasion. The Allied planners, therefore, wanted to enlarge the scope of the invasion by including 'Utah' beach on the east side of the Cotentin and, once a strong bridgehead was established, to push inland, cutting off the peninsula at its base and then heading north to capture the port of Cherbourg.

Utah was isolated from the main landing beaches by the Carentan estuary, the next beach, 'Omaha', being to its east but disconnected from it. Thus the initial phase of 4th US Infantry Division's landing would be a very hazardous one, and *had* to be protected while the troops were passing through the four causeways which were defended by strong German forces. Field Marshal Erwin Rommel was in overall command of the German forces, who felt completely confident of their ability to push the Allies back into the sea.

Finally the air drop was endorsed by the Allied Supreme Commander, Dwight D. Eisenhower ('Ike' to most of the world), and his ground forces commander, General Sir Bernard Montgomery (known as 'Monty'). The original plan was for 101st US Airborne Division under Major General Maxwell Taylor to drop north of Carentan behind the Utah beach and hold open the exit causeways, preventing the Germans from blowing them. The second airborne division, the 82nd under Major General Matthew Ridgeway, was given the task of dropping further inland, cutting the vital Coutances highway and thus isolating the western half of the Cotentin from enemy reinforcements. This was a very ambitious assignment since, if the drop were successful, they would then have to depend on their own relatively light weapons and, without transport, would have to fight on foot against a fully mobile, heavily armoured enemy, familiar with the terrain and with well-established strongpoints all over the countryside. In fact, when the French Underground reported that three German divisions were deploying in this sector, the plan was changed at the very last minute and General Ridgeway was given a new drop zone nearer to the coast and west of General Maxwell's zone in the eastern sector.

The focal point for the 82nd was now to be Ste Mère Eglise, an otherwise unimportant little market town which, unluckily for its inhabitants, sat on a vital crossroads in the sector west of Utah beach. Its situation meant that it would have to be captured very early on, before the enemy could get reinforcements there.

The success of the airborne landings depended on complete surprise, but of substantial consequence would also be the part played by the French Underground, by sabotaging important enemy communications, bridges and other vital installations, all of which had to coincide with the Allied attack; so timing was all-important.

In Normandy, it was a night without stars. Major Friedrich Hayn, intelligence officer of the 84th German Corps, stepped out of his office at the headquarters in St Lô and looked up at the sky. It was completely black and rain clouds scudded across the surface of the moon. Shivering inside his greatcoat, he went back inside; at any rate, he thought, it would be a quiet night; no one would start an invasion in this weather!

But at that very moment a giant armada of the air was taking off from scores of airfields all across England. Two US airborne divisions, some 13,000 men in all, were loaded into 822 transport planes which roared off the wet runways in carefully planned series to fly to the French Cotentin Peninsula and their designated drop zones. The time and place of the invasion caught the Germans totally by surprise. It was not as if there had been no indications – in fact, the German counter intelligence force had managed to get hold of the Allied code announcing the invasion to the French Underground. Too many Frenchmen were in the know and one of them, on the German payroll, betrayed his friends and gave the Germans the information days before the invasion. But the German commanders ignored the warning, finding it hard to believe that the invasion would take place in Normandy, even preceded by a massive airdrop on the Cotentin. They were convinced that this was just a red herring and that the 'real' invasion would take place somewhere further east in the English Channel.

Still, Major Hayn was uneasy; he had seen reports of increased air activity earlier that night and, although the RAF had been very busy lately, this somehow had a different feel to it. Looking out over the lush pastures and orchards which surrounded his headquarters building, he could hear the beat of the heavy engines of a British bomber roaring low over the river. From a nearby flak position 20mm tracer shells streaked into the night sky, some going straight into the giant bomber, which burst into flames and crashed. Then, the twelve strokes of midnight tolled solemnly from the cathedral – almost an omen for the Germans, if they had heeded it, of what was to come in just one hour.

While Major Hayn brooded, Leutnant Arthur Jahnke was relaxing in his bunk in a bunker west of Ste Mère Eglise. A responsible man, the officer had done his inspection tour in the pouring rain an hour before and was now getting ready to sleep peacefully until dawn.

Oberstleutnant Hoffman, commanding the German 919th Infanterie Regiment, was at his post in St Floxel east of Montebourg; as the drone of many aircraft was heard above he looked at his watch: it was forty minutes past midnight. He stepped outside; the moon had just broken through the clouds and he watched some parachutes drifting earthward. At first he thought it was the crew of a damaged bomber bailing out, but suddenly he realised that they were paratroops descending! The colonel ran to his telephone and sounded the alarm. The men in his headquarters scrambled their clothes on and rushed outside with their weapons. The long-dreaded invasion had begun and the enemy were on their way.

Above, in the leading plane of the 82nd Airborne Division, the green light flashed on and Brigadier General James Gavin, the deputy division commander, looked down, and jumped. His parachute jerked open and the young general floated down into the darkness, together with thousands of others parachuting alongside him right into the centre of the French Cotentin Peninsula. Some 100 kilometres to the east, at exactly the same time, the British airborne drop was starting – the greatest air drop in history was about to begin.

The chaos and carnage that ensued would be remembered by men on both sides for as long as they lived – those who did live.

Not far from Colonel Hoffman's command post two German soldiers were crouching in their foxholes, shivering in the rain and complaining, as soldiers have done since war began. Private Friedrich Busch was a schoolmaster from Dresden; his friend Erwin Mueller was a reservist who had been living in Copenhagen until being called up. Both of them agreed that being a soldier was no picnic, and that the waiting was the worst. But tonight they did not have long to wait. Suddenly their platoon commander shouted to them to get out of their foxhole and march to Azeville, one kilometre to the north. No one told them that this was not an exercise and the men still had blank cartridges in their magazines. But when they were shot at, going through the local churchyard, it was not with blanks! It was the real thing. The platoon dropped as one man into the roadside ditches, digging into their pouches for the live ammunition, and reloaded their rifles. Then, scrambling from grave to grave, they crawled towards the church.

Mueller could see dark figures running between them, while carbines barked in the dark and parachutes floated down from above, shot at by tracer bullets from a machine gun. It was a scene worthy of the Brothers Grimm. Mueller and Busch crawled side by side, trying to identify friend from foe. It was impossible – everyone was firing wildly at everyone else. As they crawled between the gravestones, Mueller touched something soft and pulled back his hand in horror as he realised it was the body of an American paratrooper. Pulling himself together, he signalled Bush to follow him into a nearby garden where they found cover behind the garden gate, but not for long; from the village street they saw a platoon of Americans advancing. Mueller and Busch took aim and fired, and two Americans fell, but from the other side a tremendous volley of automatic fire burst into the gate. Mueller managed to escape into the bushes, but the little schoolteacher from Dresden died. When Mueller emerged from hiding, he found himself totally alone and, although the firing had died down as suddenly as it had started, the village seemed completely empty; it was as if he was alone on the planet.

Not far away another drama was about to unfold. James R. Blue, a farmer's boy from North Carolina, was about to jump from his Dakota into his first battle. As he floated down, red tracer bullets seared by him, lighting up with their brilliance the countryside below. It was nothing like the map he had been briefed with in England. He was surprised that the ground was coming up faster than he had expected. The Dakota pilots had been instructed to drop their loads at 180 metres but, attempting to avoid the thickening flak, they had gone much lower and dropped them from less than 90 metres – much too low for comfort. So within seconds, Private Blue was watching the ground come up; he was prepared for a bump, but what he got was a *splash*! Expecting solid earth, he fell into swampland one metre deep – he fell over, dragged down by the weight of his equipment, and the stinking water closed over his head. He struggled with his lines and felt the muddy bottom, but luckily he was an exceptionally strong man; he managed to flounder to the surface, dragging his parachute behind him, and crawled onto dry land. There was no one in sight; the only sound to be heard was the croaking of some frogs in the swamp – just like home!

Getting rid of his parachute and picking up his carbine, Blue set off to search for some of his friends. Suddenly, his farmer's instinct told him that some one was approaching. Releasing the safety catch, Blue clicked his toy cricket, which had been issued for mutual identification, and waited tensely for the reply. It came – right behind him – and as he turned he stood face-to-face with General Jim Gavin, the man young Blue admired most in all the world, who was leading a bunch of stragglers.

General Gavin was thirty-six years old, but a veteran paratroop commander. Having already jumped in Sicily, he was the most experienced of all the men there, but even he, who was familiar with the most detailed elements of the plan, had at that moment no idea where he was! He was puzzled by the water but, seeing a flashing light on the other side of the swamp, he sent an officer to try and establish contact. The officer came wading back after 30 minutes, and reported that he had found a railway embankment. Peering at the map with the general's flashlight, they thought they were in the Merderet Valley just north of Ste Mère Eglise, but the swamps had not been mentioned in the pre-mission briefing. In fact the Merderet Valley had been flooded for over a year! Since the summer of 1943 the water had been rising from the La Barquette Lock until it flooded the entire area. However, the water had been covered by thick grass and so, on the many aerial photographs taken by reconnaissance aircraft, the ground appeared quite solid from the air. It was only as the first men dropped that they could see the water shimmering in the moonlight. This was to spell disaster for hundreds of American paratroopers who, dragged down into the swamps by their heavy equipment, drowned, unable to stand up even though the water was quite shallow.

Most of the airdrops of General Ridgeway's 82nd Airborne Division went completely wrong, the frightened, confused transport pilots scattering their men all over the peninsula. However, one of the division's missions was carried out according to the original plan: this was the capture of Ste Mère Eglise. This success was due to an exceptionally good drop of the 505th Parachute Infantry north-west of the town. Here, although most of the planes were initially scattered by enemy flak, just like the rest, the pilots were able to circle back on track and release the paratroops over the assigned drop zone, clearly marked by the pathfinders. In addition, one battalion, the 3rd, commanded by Lieutenant Colonel Edward C. Krause, actually came down in relatively good order in an area apparently devoid of enemy troops. But even here there were snags.

At about midnight a fire broke out in a building in the little town square of Ste Mère Eglise. Many of the citizens were helping out, handing buckets from hand to hand, and no one was paying any attention to the sound of aeroplanes, to which they had long grown accustomed.

Some Germans from the anti-aircraft battery, roused by the hubbub of the fire-fighters, had come out too, carrying their Schmeisser submachine guns, and were standing around watching the fun. Suddenly, the church bell rang. The mayor, M. Alexandre Renaud, looked up and gasped! Sweeping low across the square, almost in silence, came a host of aircraft, their navigation lights twinkling, wings and fuselages black against the moon. For a moment firefighters and Germans alike were transfixed by the sight, while parachutes drifted down from on high, silhouetted against the brilliant light of the fire. Then the German gunners recovered from their initial shock and, within seconds, the entire square was alive with the staccato rat-tat of the bullets and the deadly tracers winged their way up into the sky. As the Frenchmen watched in horror one man fell right onto the blazing building, crashing through the roof in a volley of sparks as his hand grenades exploded. Another body hung from a tree, his parachute draped over the branches like a shroud. One American drifted straight for the square, firing his own machine gun at the Germans, but was killed as he dropped onto the ground. The church bell was still pealing, while more and more aircraft passed over, and the German town commander rushed around trying to clear the square of Frenchmen. More paratroops were falling, but most of them, seeing what had happened to their unfortunate comrades, struggled with their parachute lines so that they would drop outside the town square.

The excitement died down as suddenly as it had started. The Germans, seeing no more targets in the square, held their fire and waited, quite pleased with their first contest with the invading forces. In fact, it was only a small and unlucky fraction of the 505th which had dropped inside the town square, and the remainder landed in the drop zone as planned.

Lieutenant Colonel Krause, an American officer of German origin, serving with the 3rd Battalion, was one of the lucky ones that night. From his doorway in the low flying Dakota, he could clearly see the green light twinkling in the dark, indicating the drop zone which the pathfinders had prepared for his battalion. He made a soft landing on firm ground and, before he had even got rid of his parachute harness, he had almost a platoon of his men around him in the meadows. He organised four combat patrols and sent them to look for further members of the battalion; within less than an hour he had managed to assemble over a company of fully equipped paratroops. Then a Frenchman stumbled into Krause's temporary command post established next to a roadside hedge. He was drunk – but not too drunk to report that there was only a company of second-rate German troops in the town garrison. The locally deployed infantry battalion had left the day before! The colonel was delighted by the news, and wanted to exploit the situation by capturing the town immediately before the Germans could send in their rapid reaction forces. The Frenchman turned out to be an extremely worthwhile ally: he agreed to guide Colonel Krause into the town by a path which he knew to be unguarded. Two companies were quickly formed and the force set out – precisely 90 minutes after the initial drop – and half an hour later Colonel Krause's battalion was firmly established in Ste Mère Eglise. The jubilant mayor, himself a veteran warrior of the First World War, embraced Colonel Krause warmly – he had the honour of being mayor of the first liberated town in France! Not a shot had been fired and the amazed Germans, who had only a short time before slaughtered the paratroopers in the square, were now prisoners and were ordered to cut the bodies from the trees without delay. One man, Private John Steele, had been hanging from the church steeple with a bullet through his heel; swinging from his harness he had watched in horror as his comrades were shot to pieces all around him. The Germans had taken him for dead, and left him dangling, but now he shouted to his friends to cut him loose. He and Pfc Ernest Blanchard were the only survivors of the unlucky drop into the town square of Ste Mère Eglise that night.

Colonel Krause went straight to the German communication centre and cut all the telephone cables. Then he organised his men, who had by now been joined by several other units, to establish an all-round defence, blocking the approach roads and especially the main road to Montebourg and Carentan, both of them known to house strong enemy reinforcements.

As Krause was organising his force, not far away another colonel was searching for his objective. This was Lieutenant Colonel Benjamin Vandervoort, a jovial, swashbuckling paratrooper, commanding the 2nd Battalion of the 505th, who had been assigned the job of capturing and holding the northern approaches to the town, blocking any reinforcements from Montebourg where the German 919th Regiment under Colonel Hoffman was known to be. Vandervoort had broken his ankle when he jumped and was in great pain, limping along and cursing his bad luck. But he was not one to let such a trivial matter stop him! His battalion surgeon found him sitting against a hedge studying his map by flashlight. He ordered the doctor to bandage him and replace the jump boot, gritting his teeth as he laced it tight. Then he got up and signalled his men to follow him to his assigned position. He had just reached it when an urgent radio call from his regiment told him to join Krause inside Ste Mère Eglise. By now Vandervoort had commandeered a baggage cart and had two of his men wheel him to the town, but not before detaching a strong force, commanded by Lieutenant Turner Turnbull, to establish a blocking position in the small hamlet of Neuville to fend off any German forces coming from the north. Then he linked up with Colonel Krause inside the town.

It was not until dawn that Turnbull encountered the Germans at Neuville, but by then he had established his men in good defensive positions. The Germans had been receiving only scattered reports of isolated clashes, and had no idea that two full Allied airborne divisions had actually jumped into the Cotentin Peninsula. But Colonel Hoffman at his headquarters near Montebourg was worried. He had received a short, unclear message from Ste Mère Eglise indicating that strong forces were attacking the town but then the telephone lines had been cut and, although his communications officer tried desperately to raise the local commander on the radio, it was to no avail. The colonel therefore decided to act – and sent out a battalion force towards Neuville.

They got there soon after Lieutenant Turnbull's men had taken up their positions on both sides of the road in some well covered copses. Turnbull could see the German column approach from 400 metres away. He did not lose his nerve: his position was excellent for an ambush, but he sent a strong patrol with a bazooka team to outflank the Germans from the west, moving through a thick orchard which provided good cover. The German commander had seen the move, though; he deployed his own men into the ditches by the side of the road and opened fire. Turnbull could see that the Germans were attempting two encircling movements to outflank his positions, so he called back his patrol and set up a strong roadblock at the exit from the village. The Germans attacked, storming from the two flanks with withering machine gun fire, followed by a heavy artillery barrage which smashed into Turnbull's force, causing several casualties with the first salvo. Some 200 of the enemy were now converging on Turnbull's 40 men, of which a third had already been killed or wounded.

For eight long hours, which seemed like days, Lieutenant Turnbull held his position, fighting off several German attacks, his bazooka teams destroying three German tanks and assault guns. At noon

Colonel Vandervoort sent strong reinforcements and some fighter bombers also screamed across the sky to give support, forcing the Germans to call off their attacks, and Turnbull led the few survivors of his forces into Ste Mère Eglise. Unfortunately Lieutenant Turnbull – a very brave young commander – was killed a few days later in another action in Normandy.

In another place, the 508th Regiment was in deep trouble: still scattered over a wide area of swampland, hundreds of men in small groups were trying to reach their assigned objectives, but most of them had got completely lost during the night, and kept stumbling into equally confused German patrols sent out without clear instructions by agitated commanders. Men fired at each other without any clear knowledge of who was friend or foe. This was no way to run an invasion, but, until they could raise sufficient forces and organise them into coherent combat formations, there could be no question of an organised battle. Fortunately the American paratroops had been thoroughly trained for such combat conditions and eventually most of the men rallied into small groups under leaders of some kind and moved into their assigned assembly areas. It was a night of chaos and confusion, but one good thing emerged from it – they had confused the Germans even more, no small success during this critical period when the main seaborne assault was gathering offshore, ready to go in at dawn.

Lieutenant Colonel Thomas Shanley, commanding the 508th, watched the bundle with the signal light drop like a stone into the swamp. Its parachute had failed to open. But when he hurried over to it he saw the signal lamp was still working. Wading into the shallow water, he plucked it from its container and ordered a man to tie it to a nearby tree, adding a few flashlights on the branches until it looked like a Christmas tree. Guided by the signal, isolated men stumbled to it and within half an hour some 100 men had assembled. Shanley organised an all-round defence and set out for what he believed to be an isolated farm near Hill 30 which was his objective. He was devoid of heavy weapons and only a single machine gun had been salvaged from a container protruding from the swamp. Suddenly help came from out of the sky! A glider swept low over the water and crashed. From it emerged a lone pilot – somewhat dazed but very welcome – he had brought a small bulldozer with him. He joined Shanley's force and they set out for the farm. On the way an officer managed to recover another container from which he drew a bazooka with ammunition, and a radio, which seemed to be working.

It was near dawn as the men deployed along the causeway near the farm. A bridge was taken and secured – no trouble so far. But it would not be quiet for long. To the west, Oberleutnant Franz Hubert, commanding a platoon of infantry and two Mk IV tanks, noticed some movement on the Picauville road. Within minutes a firefight began, both sides firing aimlessly, without being able to see each other as yet. Hubert contacted his company commander and asked for a tank company to come forward while he moved his own men into position. Within 30 minutes the entire German force mounted a company attack on Hill 30 while the tanks advanced slowly along the causeway. Colonel Shanley's small force was now threatened by a double flanking move. Sending his only bazooka team to hide in the roadside brush, the colonel concentrated the remainder of his men on the hill. Just as all seemed lost, news came over the radio that one of his patrols had encountered a company of paratroopers 1,500 metres to the north and sent them hurrying to the rescue. Meanwhile the bazooka team had fired one of its rockets into the lead tank, which was hit below the turret. As the tank commander peered out from his turret, he was shot dead by a rifleman crouching nearby. Two men rushed the tank and blew it up with two grenades into the turret, but were killed by fire from the second tank. The bazooka team now fired its last round at the second tank, but missed, and withdrew.

It was time to go, thought the colonel, and he organised an orderly withdrawal. But all the escape routes were under German fire. Losses were mounting. The only way out appeared to be through a narrow alley between two thick hedges, but even this was blocked by the crashed glider and the 'dozer. The colonel realised that his men must actually go *through* the glider and, sending two men to pry open the side doors, he ordered them to run for it, under cover from his single machine gun which sprayed the front long enough to get most of them through. Last to jump through the glider doors was Shanley himself, with the Germans in hot pursuit only metres away. Shanley and his men soon made contact with the company of paratroopers who had nearly reached the hill, just too late.

A few kilometres to the east, a battle was raging over the causeways leading to Utah beach. Here Lieutenant Colonel Patrick Cassidy was leading the men of his 1st Battalion, 502nd Parachute Regiment of the 101st Airborne Division from Drop Zone A. To his east were the swamps, to his north-east the village of St Martin, known to house a strong German contingent and nearby was a coastal artillery position, which his force was to neutralise. Having collected a company of his men, the colonel set out for the village, collecting more men as he went. In one field, they encountered another colonel, Robert Strayer of the 506th, who had hurt his leg in the drop and was limping badly. More men from various battalions were assembling nearby and Cassidy took charge, leading what now amounted to two companies towards the road junction where he established a secure ring and went forward to reconnoitre. In the distance he could hear small arms fire, and he ordered some of his men to follow him in the direction of the village. As they entered the main street a volley of hand grenades fell on them from the upper windows of the corner house, followed by machine gun fire, which was returned by the Allied forces. Two men fell, wounded, and were drawn to cover. The colonel radioed for reinforcements, and a bazooka team crawled forward and sent two rounds into the building. This silenced the Germans; some came out with their hands raised and were sent to the east. Colonel Cassidy took his men to the gun battery that they had heard, and found it abandoned. The rest of the battalion entered the village and rounded up dozens of Germans. By 0800 the village was secure, and Cassidy paused and took stock.

So far his battalion was intact. But his primary task was still to seize the causeways leading to Utah beach in advance of the main landing. Time was pressing, and he was just organising his men to move out when a messenger rushed in, gasping that a large German force had assembled for a counter attack in the artillery barracks south of the village, which they had thought abandoned. These barracks were only a few hundred metres from the village, hidden from view by some thick brush. Cassidy detailed Staff Sergeant Harrison Summers, a quiet youngster from Virginia, to lead a motley collection of paratroopers to rout the Germans from their barracks. The fifteen men who followed Summers unwillingly along the brush covered track were strangers to one another and lacked that sense of camaraderie which men who have trained and battled together possess. Summers set out rapidly and, when the barracks came in sight, signalled the men to take cover in a ditch, and sallied forth himself to observe his objective. He had reached a point some 40 metres from the first buildings when the Germans started firing from all the windows at once. As Summers charged forward firing his submachine gun at the windows, no one followed him – he was fighting alone! He saw some of the Germans escaping from the rear door and threw some hand grenades after them. He shouted to his men to join him, but realised that no one did. So again he charged alone, gun blazing, into the next barracks, further down the road. The Germans fired at him, but Summers managed to avoid them, zig-zagging from side to side. Reaching the door, he kicked it in and hurled two hand grenades into the room, jumping backwards to escape the blast. Several Germans died and two ran out with their hands up. Now help did come, from Pfc Burt, who set up his light machine gun to fire at the windows of the next barracks, forcing the Germans to duck. Summers was just getting ready to storm the third barracks when Lieutenant Brandenberger from his battalion rushed to join him, but, as the two men charged, the officer was hit in the shoulder and fell. Six Germans were firing from the windows, but Summers and Burt killed them before they could hit anyone. Summers was nearly exhausted now, but his men still cowered in the ditch, until one man, seeing the officer fall wounded and Summers fight alone, summoned up sufficient courage to get up and join the sergeant in his lonely fight. Private Camin rushed forward and joined Summers near the fourth barracks and they both stormed it, one hurling grenades, the other charging with his gun blazing. So they went on, storming five of the remaining buildings until, after some heavy fighting, a German officer led the survivors from the last building. Sergeant Summers had fought almost single-handed against an entire company of German infantry – and won! His outstanding action did not go unnoticed: he was highly decorated and, what is more, he survived the war.

The situation at St Martin had now stabilised and Colonel Cassidy sent out strong forces to secure the causeways leading towards Utah beach. The Germans in the outposts overlooking the beach had been fighting hard for some hours to try and stop the seaborne invasion which was gaining ground, and the paratroop attack from the rear broke their spirit to some extent, but they put up a stiff fight.

The Germans were recovering from the initial shock of the airborne landing by early morning when the situation became clearer. 84th Corps had already sent two strong counter attacks to try to recapture Ste Mère Eglise, sending a mixed combat group from 709th Division towards Neuville, which was blocked by Colonels Krause and Vandervoort's men, while elements from the crack 6th Parachute Infantry, led by the veteran Friedrich von der Heydte, pushed along the Carentan highway north towards the coast. But German resistance faltered under the two-sided American pressure, although isolated outposts still fought back desperately and had to be stormed one by one, with heavy losses on both sides.

Then, about four hours after he had waded ashore, Captain George Mabry of the 8th Infantry, 4th US Infantry Division, was advancing along one of the causeways when from behind a sand dune appeared some yellow flags indicating the link up between the 505th Airborne and the 4th US Infantry had been successfully accomplished. The paratroops who had survived some never-to-be-forgotten experiences through that long night looked at Captain Mabry and his men as if they were beings from another planet. The time was 1105. The day was 6 June. For many of the men the day ahead was to be their longest day.

CHAPTER SIXTEEN

THE JEWISH BRIGADE GROUP IN ACTION ON THE SENIO

The full story of the soldiers of the Jewish Brigade Group in the Second World War has never been told and history books rarely even mention their role in the Italian campaign.

The Jewish people of Palestine, less than half a million strong in 1939, immediately offered to serve with the British forces, but were rejected as combat troops due to the shortsightedness of British colonial officials, who only reluctantly allowed the Jews to serve even in rear units far from the fighting. Only a few resourceful individuals managed to talk their way through the bureaucracy and gain entrance into commando and other front line forces, where they soon made their names, British commanders being quite happy to include them in their ranks.

Three infantry battalions were eventually formed consisting of Jewish volunteers from Palestine, but it took nearly five frustrating years – and a specific order from Winston Churchill – until the Jewish Brigade Group came into being in 1944. By this time news of the Holocaust had leaked out, giving enormous impetus to the hunger of the Jews to join in the fighting against their mortal Nazi enemies. On 19 September 1944, therefore, the Jewish Brigade Group, totalling 5,500 men, was officially formed and declared by Churchill, to a cheering House of Commons, to be in operation a few days later.

Chosen to lead them was a British Jewish brigadier, the 44-year-old Levi Benjamin, a regular officer who served in the Royal Engineers and was currently commanding the Central Training School in Italy. The brigade was to contain the three infantry battalions, 1st, 2nd and 3rd, two field artillery regiments and support troops. The troops assembled at Fiuggi near Rome, where they underwent a speedy but tough battle training period under difficult conditions. The men reached a fighting peak within a few weeks, since they were eager to get into action as soon as possible, before the end of the war deprived them of their chance.

At the beginning of March, they set out from Fiuggi for the front, and Rome was witness to a proud and historic moment: the vehicles of the Jewish Brigade, adorned with their blue and white insignia plus a yellow Star of David, passed through the Gate of Titus where, nearly 2,000 years before, the survivors of the destruction of Jerusalem had been paraded as Roman slaves. Leaving Rome, the men headed for the front line at Cervia, near Faenza, on the Adriatic coast, where they deployed into a vast assembly area, shared by thousands of Allied troops from all over the British Empire who were gathering for the final assault, which was expected soon.

After a short period of reorganisation, the three regiments went forward to take up their combat positions in the line. The brigade was to relieve elements of the 2nd New Zealand and 1st Canadian Divisions, who were quite glad to be relieved and get some rest on the nearby beaches. A group of selected officers and NCOs had already been sent forward and were acclimatising themselves to the routine at the front line, pending the takeover, which was always regarded as a difficult period. The New Zealanders and Canadians, however, proved to be very helpful.

At 0400 on 4 March 1945, in total darkness, the 2nd Battalion left the assembly area and, driving through the sleepy town of Ravenna, approached its assigned frontal sector at Mazzano-Alfonsino. Gunfire could be heard and the smell of battle was in the air; ambulances could be seen racing in the opposite direction, while the dark hulks of Churchill tanks stood by the roadside. Tension rose – the men knew that their first battle testing was at hand. The battalion was met at a road junction by an officer waving his flashlight, who directed them to drive into cover in a small wood near the roadside. Here the company commanders assembled their men and briefed them on where to proceed into the line, each platoon being led by a guide.

The regiment in line was a crack British armoured regiment, the 9th Queen's Royal Lancers, holding the sector under command of the 8th Indian Infantry Division, which would also be in command of the Jewish Brigade. Here they were joined by the officers and men who had gone ahead with the Canadians and New Zealanders, who had gone to another sector. Although the Jewish Brigade was fully trained and the men keen to go into action, General Sir Richard McCreery, commanding the Eighth Army, realised that few of the troops had undergone their baptism of fire, so he decided to let them spend some time in a relatively quiet front sector, opposed by second rate enemy troops, before sending them to face the crack German divisions holding a sector on the Senio river.

The Alfonsino sector into which the Jewish troops now deployed was fairly flat open country, criss-crossed by several canals. Two of the battalions deployed along the Fosso Vetro canal, in front of a no-man's-land where some isolated farm houses offered good observation posts, some occupied by Germans and others by Allied troops. The enemy force was made up of two components. The 362nd Infanterie Division consisted mostly of Austrian troops who, having barely survived the horrors of the Russian front, were exhausted and morally spent. They had already fought some ferocious battles near the Anzio bridgehead and had had enough. But their command echelon was still of a high standard, and their commander, General Reinhardt, was a dedicated Nazi, even at this late stage in the war.

The 42nd Jaeger Division, commanded by General Karl Jost, was quite an inexperienced unit. Having mainly fought against Yugoslav partisans and in Hungary, they had not seen much action on the Italian front. Most of the men were elderly conscripts from Austria and Alsace, and their motivation to fight in a war that they considered already lost was not very high.

The Germans, however, were well dug into fortified positions; every farmhouse was bunkered with concrete. They were supported by heavy artillery and mortars, but lacked air support, which the Allied forces had in abundance from nearby air bases. Where the Germans excelled was in night patrols, and mines were the main source of concern for the Allies, which the Jewish Brigade was soon – and painfully – to learn.

The first days in the line were spent in combat patrols, and on 6 March the brigade suffered their first casualties. Two men from the 1st Battalion were badly wounded by German mortar fire, and an officer and two men were hurt by a booby-trapped mine which they were trying to lift. In consequence, the brigadier ordered every patrol to work with sappers who would clear mines for them. On 16 March, a night ambush led by Lieutenant Bob Hendler confronted a German patrol and killed several of them. The following morning the Germans tried to evacuate their wounded under a Red Cross flag and covering fire but, in the meantime, the 3rd Battalion mounted a company attack on the Fosso Vetro canal and managed to cross over in some rubber boats. They met no resistance, as the 42nd Jaegers were busy recovering their wounded, but later that day the Germans retaliated with a strong barrage of Nebelwerfer fire which wounded some of the men. The Germans seemed more nervous than usual that night, and shot off a magnificent display of rockets which lit up the sky, enabling brigade patrols to discover that a few of the German forward positions had been evacuated.

19 March saw the first real battle for the Jewish Brigade. Two of the frontal battalions, the 2nd and 3rd, were ordered to send out fighting patrols in daylight into no-man's-land. In the 2nd Battalion sector, the patrols advanced up to the Fosso Vetro canal, some 800 metres from the first line positions. 'C' Company patrol, led by Sergeant Yehuda Harrari, set out at 1000 hours, carefully searching for mines, and at noon reached an elevated earthen dam parallel to the canal. Following them was Lieutenant Meir Sarudinski's platoon, keeping in close touch by radio. As Harrari stopped to look for a way to cross the water, his squad came under heavy fire from Spandaus located in the houses facing the Fosso Veccio canal to the north. The machine gun was soon followed by mortars, which caused some casualties among Harrari's patrol and, while searching for a way to outflank the German gunners, the squad stepped into an uncharted minefield and had to withdraw. Through his binoculars Harrari spotted the German gunners firing from an upper window of one of the houses, and directed his Bren gunner to silence them.

Moving on, the squad arrived at a railway junction where they saw an abandoned German Spandau position, its aperture on the dam wall. Below on the water line lay the girders of a demolished bridge, still a few inches above the water. Harrari thought this a perfect way to cross, but when he radioed his officer, he was ordered to await the arrival of Sarudinski and his men. As they kept lookout, Sarudinski's platoon could be seen coming in, crouching low and scanning the terrain ahead. Just as Harrari was signalling the enemy positions to him, the entire force came under withering fire, first from small arms, then dense mortar fire – very accurate, as the Germans had ranged this exact position.

Harrari now attempted to lead his squad through the aperture of the deserted Spandau position, cross the canal over the girders, and engage the enemy from the other side but, just as he was crawling through, he was pulled back by two strong hands. Turning round, he saw sapper Sergeant Motti Sharoni yelling at him to let him pass through first. And it was lucky that he did, because he soon detected a dense minefield along the water line, on which Harrari would surely have stepped! To clear a path, Sharoni lifted sixteen anti-personnel mines within minutes, using his probe, disposing of them in the canal. The second he signalled the men that it was safe to advance, Harrari came forward and, lying low, almost immediately detected a German sniper at some 50 metres distance, Mauser rifle at the ready, coming straight at him. He waited till the German got to a mere five metres and then stood up, fired a burst from his submachine gun, and saw him topple into the grass.

At the water line, the entire platoon was pinned down by a heavy mortar barrage, and casualties mounted steadily. Sarudinski tried to move one of his squads to the right, but they came upon a minefield which Sharoni, under heavy fire, was unable to clear. By 1400 the situation was critical, and battalion headquarters ordered 'B' Company, led by Captain James Rabinovicz, to engage the enemy. Without artillery support, this was no easy matter and soon the entire company came under heavy fire from the hamlet of La Giorgetta, whose houses faced the parallel canal, Fosso Veccio. With no support they were pinned down and unable to move. A dozen men were hit within minutes and, under these circumstances, withdrawal was inevitable.

Lieutenant Sarudinski and his men covered 'B' Company's withdrawal and managed to pin down the Germans firing from one of the abandoned houses. He noticed that the German mortar commander was a methodical man who, in an attempt to save ammunition, fired in salvos of six rounds, pausing in between. Sarudinski timed his salvos and effected the withdrawal in the intervals. But evacuating the wounded under fire was a problem and a courageous medic, Corporal Moshe Silberberg, volunteered to carry some of them on his back, dodging bullets as he went. On his third sortie, the Red Cross flag which he waved was ignored by the enemy, and he was killed by a sniper's bullet which pierced his heart.

The abortive attack on the Fosso Vetro canal failed mainly because of lack of support and the brigadier rightly blamed the colonel in command. He was sacked and his deputy, Major Gash, took over. Lieutenant Sarudinski was awarded the Military Cross, while Sergeant Harrari and the medic, Corporal Silberberg, won the Military Medal, the first won by the brigade – but not the last.

Another patrol from the 3rd Battalion set out that day, led by Lieutenant Anthony Van Gelder, an English Jew, 22-years-old, who had volunteered to leave his own crack regiment, the Sherwood Foresters, to serve with the people of his own faith in the Jewish Brigade. Van Gelder was a remarkable man; although young, he was a born leader of men and had already had 'a good war'. He had seen action at Cassino, so this sector was for him almost a holiday. On that afternoon he led his patrol to capture three German outposts near La Giorgetta. When they took over one of the houses, the young officer found an abandoned Spandau still in position, just where the German crew had left it as they departed in a hurry. Taking the gun, he rejoined his men waiting outside and led them towards a gully where, to their surprise, they found several Germans chatting and eating their rations, with no one on guard! Van Gelder ordered his men to attack and Sergeant Reinhold, ironically a German-born Jew, threw some grenades; very soon twelve sheepish Germans came out with their hands raised. It turned out that they were a squad from 1st Jaeger Regiment, most of them either elderly men or mere children – at this stage of the war, Germany was really scraping the bottom of the barrel as regards manpower. The Germans had no idea who had captured them and, when Reinhold told them in perfect German that he was a Jew from Palestine, the prisoners went white with fear. However, military discipline was observed by the Jewish soldiers and the prisoners marched safely into the company compound, arms raised above their heads. Certainly they fared better than the helpless Jews who were being exterminated all over Europe.

A sad postscript to this affair was that Lieutenant Anthony Van Gelder was killed a few days later at his post when an explosive charge went off by accident.

As a consequence of this incident, news leaked through to the Germans of the existence of the Jewish Brigade Group and, wishing to obtain information, the German headquarters sent three English-speaking soldiers in British uniform through the lines. Unfortunately for them, the first place they approached was a 2nd Battalion outpost manned by Corporal Israel Tal and a few men from Captain Chaim Laskov's Support Company. Tal, always very alert, confronted the 'Englishmen', who identified themselves as field security sergeants on a special mission. Keeping them at gun point, he ordered one of his men to examine them closely and, to his surprise, discovered swastikas inside their berets. Tal sent them to the rear where, after a thorough interrogation, they were executed.

On 20 March the brigade mounted a full scale ground assault on 40th Regiment, 42nd Jaeger Division in the La Giorgetta region. Captain Jochanan Peltz commanding a company of 3rd Battalion was ordered to attack a German bunker complex situated in a group of farmhouses near the village, supported this time by a troop of Churchill tanks from the North Irish Horse and with air support flown by two squadrons of Spitfires from 8 Wing, South African Air Force (SAAF). This was the brigade's first combined attack and special care was taken with coordination so as to get it right first time.

Between the brigade's lines and the enemy position there were several minefields which needed clearing. Peltz went out the night before the attack by himself and cleared a narrow path, lifting the mines out one by one. Then, with the aid of two of his men, the path was widened until it reached four metres, just enough for the Churchills to pass. Peltz crawled along the path until he reached a point fifty metres from the Germans where he lay and listened to them talking and singing 'Lili Marlene', No. 1 on the Germans' hit parade during the war. He then returned with sufficient information for the morning's briefing, which was held at brigade headquarters. Present were the brigadier and senior officers from 8th Indian Division, together with the North Irish Horse troop commander and Colonel Daniel Human, DSO, the Jewish commander of 8 Wing, detailed to give Spitfire support.

At 1000 hours Peltz set out for La Giorgetta leading his company in battle order, with the tanks moving with them through the cleared minefield, four sappers running in front of each tank to show them the way. Human's Spitfires were strafing and bombing the German positions, which were already engulfed by flame and smoke. Obviously the Germans were already on full alert and returned fire, hitting the company as it advanced through the minefield. One man was killed, but the others stormed on, supported by the tanks, which fired point blank into the bunker slits, directed by their tank commanders standing upright in their turrets. One after another the Spandaus were silenced, but the heavy mortar fire still fell.

By this time Peltz had reached his start line and, ordering bayonets fixed, signalled the charge to the farmhouse. The troopers stormed into the lower floor of the building, clearing it with grenades and rapid bursts from their Tommy guns. Within fifteen minutes the battle was over and the sappers came in, setting demolition charges to blow the bunker complex, which went up in a blast of fire and smoke. Not one German survived in the farm buildings. On their return, Captain Peltz and his men received an accolade from the British tank crews, who stood on their tanks to cheer them as they passed.

A few days later Captain Chaim Laskov, commanding the Vickers Machine Gun and Carrier Platoon in 2nd Battalion Support Company, was on the front line when a German fighting patrol managed to infiltrate through the outposts and approach a nearby company headquarters. Immediate action was called for to prevent the Germans storming the company bunker. The duty officer, RSM Carmi, did not lose his nerve: a former commando in the desert fighting, Carmi was the very man to deal with such an emergency. Rushing out, Tommy gun blazing, he shouted to Laskov to set up his Vickers and open fire. Laskov jumped into a slit trench and manhandled two of his heavy guns into position. But he soon realised that the Germans were positioned right along the line of sight over the company's outposts so that the Jewish gunners – in the prevailing darkness – would be hitting their own men! But Laskov, a man of ideas as well as courage, called to Carmi to radio the men in the outposts to crouch low in their foxholes and lift up their steel helmets on their rifles over their heads. Then he opened fire and the machine gun bullets pinged as they hit the helmets! His idea worked, and the Germans were hit, some of them killed and the rest captured by Carmi and his men. One German who had been hiding in the brush surrendered to Carmi, who received him in perfect German.

This was the last event of the brigade's stay in a relatively quiet sector. Now they moved to their new assignment – they were to take part in the great spring offensive, culminating in the crossing of the River Senio as part of Operation 'Playmate'. This was one of the war's last great contests. The Allied commanders, US General Mark Clark, commanding the Fifteenth Army Group and Field Marshal Sir Harold Alexander, Supreme Allied Commander, knew that the Germans had to be beaten and chased right to the Swiss frontier, and 'Playmate' was to be the opening gambit in achieving this objective.

The new brigade sector was near the village of Brisighella. In contrast to the open ground of Alfonsino, this one leant on a mountain ridge in the eastern Apennines, with the River Senio winding through a narrow gorge below. The northern bank, held by the Germans, dominated the southern one where the Jewish Brigade deployed. On the German side isolated houses had been turned into well defended fortified bunkers from which the Germans could fire at will at anything moving below.

The brigade was now joined by its field artillery regiment and was now considered at full complement, although its units were still under strength at combat level. The opposing side was quite the opposite! Entrenched on the other bank were the crack German 4th Parachute Division, under its commander General Heinz Trettner, a young, vigorous fighting leader, with great combat experience in France, Russia and Italy. In contrast to the two German divisions which the brigade had confronted at Alfonsino, Trettner's paratroopers were, like their leader, young, vigorous and full of motivation. They knew who they were facing and having been indoctrinated with Nazi propaganda, they felt an extra zest in the prospect of killing Jews. They were well trained and equipped with the best weapons, including a newly introduced P-642 assault rifle, Panzerfausts, Nebelwerfers, and guns. To fight these Germans would be a real challenge!

On the right of the Jewish Brigade were Major General Bohusz-Syszko's 2nd Polish Corps, on their left the Italian Friuly Group under Brigadier Clemente Primiere. The Jewish battalions had relieved the 43rd Gurkhas – who had earned every moment of their rest.

General McCreery's Eighth Army, of which the Jewish Brigade Group was part, was assigned to penetrate the German lines through the Argenta Gap, across the River Po, where the Germans were expected to make their last stand in Italy. In order to give the Eighth Army a clear run, the Americans in the western sector were given the task of staging a massive deception manoeuvre, to prevent the German commander, General von Vietinghof, from establishing the exact direction of the Allied offensive.

Prior to the great offensive, General McCreery assembled all his officers from battalion commander upwards in a cinema at Cesena for a briefing. It was to be a spectacular affair! Playmate would start off with the US Fifth Army staging its diversion to the west of the city of Bologna, which was the key of the German defence. Then the Eighth Army would jump off on two major axes – one along Route 16 leading from Ravenna towards the Po Valley, and one over Route 9, the main Cesena–Bologna highway. The Jewish Brigade was deployed on the south-west of the latter axis.

In that sector the main thrust of the attack would be made by the 2nd Polish Corps, who had withstood a terrible ordeal at Cassino and were now eager to take their revenge on the Germans. The Jewish Brigade's task was twofold: to stage a tactical diversion at Cuffiano, on the bend of the Senio, and later to occupy a German stronghold at Fantaguzzi to the north. Then, once a bridgehead was secured, the entire brigade would take part in the advance towards the high ground and, if all went well, to Bologna itself, the coveted prize!

The preliminary air bombardment was a spectacular one. It began at 1330 on 9 April when 700 15th US Army Air Force bombers thundered into the target area north of the Senio and pounded the entire German front line with nearly 200,000 fragmentation bombs. The aim was to destroy defensive installations without causing widespread devastation as had happened in Normandy a year before, leaving a charred and burned landscape like the surface of the moon. All did not go well, however: one American lead navigator was off mark and the lead bombardier mistook the bomb line; as a result, 21 Liberators dropped short, killing nearly half a Polish battalion in its assembly area.

The bombers were followed by fighter bombers which strafed and bombed the enemy positions at low level and, as they left, a great artillery barrage opened up. The forward elements of the brigade watched in awe as the earth shook and dust covered the entire area. Overhead, in the bomb aimer's position in one of the Liberators of No. 31 SAAF Squadron, crouched Flight Sergeant Hans Weisbrod – one of the few Palestinians who had managed to wangle his way into an aircrew – acutely aware that he was supporting the attack of his own countrymen: his squadron was dropping its bombs only 2,000 metres from the Jewish Brigade Group.

In the brigade sector, Major Uri Shugurinsky's 'D' Company led off 2nd Battalion's attack over the river and was the first to cross over. They then dug in and awaited the preliminary bombardment. Brigadier Benjamin was with Colonel Kash in the forward command post overlooking the river, following the action closely.

At 0430 on 10 April, the Poles jumped off, under cover of a tremendous barrage by 1,500 guns with the aid of searchlights and flares which lit up the entire front like a particularly good Guy Fawkes' display, while colourful rockets joined the thunder of the guns. The Poles began to cross the Senio, overcoming the heavy resistance with the aid of flamethrower Churchills which came forward with the infantry as they burned out enemy bunkers.

While the Poles were making good progress towards with their objectives – Castel Bolognese and Imola – the Friuly Group on the initial Italian bridgehead suffered a severe setback from the German paratroops who were in a dominating position from which they could not be dislodged. They covered the Italians with withering fire, causing the two lead battalions to withdraw, having lost a third of their men.

This mishap threatened the left flank of the Jewish Brigade, which was by now crossing over into Shugurinsky's small bridgehead at Fantaguzzi. Benjamin therefore, having consulted with the Italian brigadier, ordered the crossing of 3rd Battalion to be accelerated and Cuffiano to be captured forthwith, before the Germans could reorganise and try to roll up the Polish flank as well as the Italian. Within an hour the 3rd was over, but, arriving at the German strongpoints, they found them empty, as the Germans had already withdrawn.

By now two of the Jewish Brigade's infantry battalions were in the bridgehead, although they were much harassed by sniper fire and mortar shelling, causing a growing amount of casualties. The engineer company was working at breakneck speed – also under heavy sniper and mortar fire – to construct a temporary pontoon bridge over which the heavier equipment could be moved. Shugurinsky sent a fighting patrol up the slope to silence the snipers who were hiding in buildings and dugouts. One by one they fell silent – for a while: the young German paratroops were not giving in easily and soon others stole into their dead comrades' places and opened fire in their stead. On their way to cope with this new threat, one Jewish Brigade patrol stepped on a hastily laid minefield and two men were killed, others being badly wounded, and they had to be evacuated.

The lead company of 3rd Battalion now began to climb the steep mountain slope towards Monte Gabio, from which the Germans were firing rapid Spandau and mortar rounds, constantly changing position so as to make it harder to find them. One squad clashed with some Germans in a fortified house and disposed of them, taking one young German prisoner. He belonged to the seasoned 12th Sturm Regiment, and his information on what the paratroops were up to was of the greatest importance in the events of the next morning.

Another patrol which was sent to dislodge a German position did not fare so well. Creeping up the slope was Sergeant Major Eli Hershkovicz, a courageous leader. As he jumped through the front door of one fortified building, throwing a grenade as he entered, another soldier, Corporal Wechsler, was killed by a German sniper firing from the attic above, the bullet missing Hershkovicz by inches! Racing up the stairs he killed the sniper, who was still looking out of the window, with a quick burst. Sadly, Hershkovicz himself was killed soon after, but was awarded a well deserved Military Medal for his action.

Until the remaining German bunkers were rooted out with the aid of some tank destroyers crewed by British soldiers, casualties had reached dangerous proportions. The brigade had suffered almost 60 dead and more than 150 wounded – a substantial amount in view of the fact that they had started below strength in the first place.

Lieutenant Meir Sarudinski, the only officer left in his company, led 3rd Battalion over extremely difficult terrain, constantly clearing enemy strongholds which, more than once, he stormed himself. Due to his excellent leadership the battalion suffered hardly any casualties while he was in command.

During the advance, two jeeps containing Captain Ormrod and eight men from a Jewish battery had got as far as four kilometres from Bologna, where they were directing fire on the outskirts, when they received orders to return to base! But the captain decided he had not come this far for nothing. Determined to get a view of the city, he shut down his radio and drove on. Passing some detachments which were waiting to make an official entrance, the British officer and his two jeeps entered the town, proudly displaying the Jewish emblem on their vehicles. They were thus the first Allied troops to enter Bologna and were engulfed by a jubilant crowd!

The activities of the Jewish Brigade came to an end the following day, since the Eighth Army had made faster progress, bringing the brigade sector to the rear of the advance. Following Playmate, the Jewish Brigade Group spent several weeks of inactivity, moving up to northern Italy when the war ended in Europe. The next year was spent by the Jewish Brigade Group, now stationed in Austria and Holland, in saving as many Jewish Holocaust survivors as possible, feeding them, clothing them and sending them to Palestine to begin a new life.

Some of the men who had served in the brigade reached high rank later in the Israeli Defence Forces, two of them, Majors Makleff and Laskov, becoming Chief of Staff, while Sarudinski became a major general, a fitting tribute to these men who represented all that was best in the men who served in the Jewish Brigade.

CHAPTER SEVENTEEN

THE EPIC STRUGGLE FOR CALVARY HILL

To the west of Caen the little Odon river wanders through its valley, eventually merging with the larger Orne south of the city. Along its southern bank is a low ridge, at the eastern end of which the ground rises fairly steeply to the flat-topped summit of a feature which, in the summer of 1944, was marked on British maps as Hill 112. At a nearby crossing stood a wayside shrine of the Calvary, which was to become a significant feature in the battle codenamed 'Epsom'. Hill 112 would become for both British and Germans a symbol for the most bitter fighting of the entire war, with both sides grimly determined to capture and hold that hill at all costs.

Having created a bridgehead on the Normandy beaches in June 1944, General Montgomery now wished to enlarge it sufficiently to make enough space for the massive build-up which would follow. On his left flank, where British divisions were located, it was anticipated that the fighting would be tough, dogged and slow, but the British commander-in-chief wanted to draw the bulk of his armour into this sector so that on his right flank the Americans, whose temperament was thought more suited to fast-moving operations, could break out and pursue the enemy, outflanking the entire German forces, and thus unhinge the front in a wide, wheeling manoeuvre.

On the German side, Field Marshal Rommel was well aware of what was at stake. He knew Montgomery well from the battle of El Alamein and therefore wanted to pre-empt his old rival, striking as soon as possible with a massive armoured thrust before Montgomery could concentrate sufficient forces in the bridgehead.

Allied airpower was a decisive factor here: the Germans, constantly hampered by fighter bombers which dominated the skies, were slow in getting their armoured reserves to the front line. What the airmen did not achieve was completed by the French resistance fighters, who disrupted railway lines and blew important bridges.

When Montgomery learned of the impending German counter attack, he decided to act quickly and forestall the move with his own offensive. In his path, however, lay a major stumbling block: the city of Caen, which should have already been in Allied hands by D-Day, but was still stubbornly held by the Germans. Operation 'Epsom' was planned to lever the Germans from Caen, to secure the crossing of the Rivers Odon and Orne, and to establish a strong hold on the high ground south-west of the city, from where an attempt to break out to the south could be initiated.

Operational responsibility for 'Epsom' was delegated to VIII Corps, commanded by General Sir Richard O'Connor, the man who had won a spectacular victory in the desert in Operation 'Compass' and who had later achieved an equally remarkable feat by escaping from a prisoner-of-war camp in Italy. Detailed as main fighting elements were

11th Armoured Division under 37-year-old 'Pip' Roberts, the youngest –
but the most experienced – British armoured commander, and 15th
Scottish Division, the best infantry formation, which had fought every-

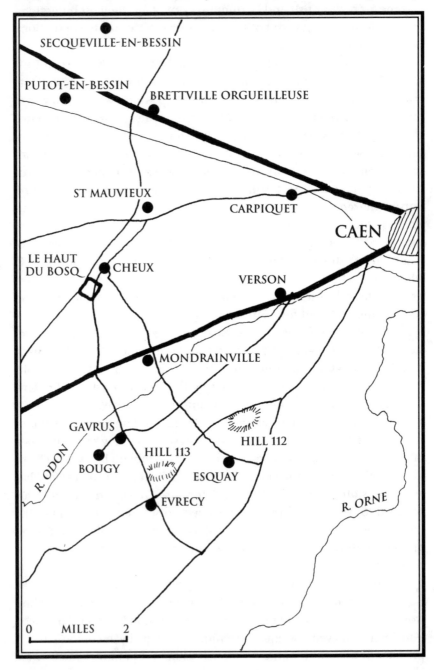

where with remarkable success, backed up by 43rd Wessex Division. Both infantry divisions were to be supported by the new Churchill tanks of 31st Tank Brigade. As much of the route over which the corps would be advancing was dominated by high ground on its right, 49th Infantry Division with 8th Armoured Brigade in support was to launch an attack and capture the village of Fontenay.

On 25 June, less than three weeks after the landing, the attack began. But the enemy was expecting it. The Germans had deployed some of their toughest troops in the sector, mostly youngsters, of the crack 12th SS Panzer Division, commanded by one of their best officers, Kurt Meyer, as well as elements of the 21st and Panzer Lehr Divisions, all of which had held that very sector for over three weeks and were familiar with every nook and cranny. Positions had been carefully chosen and manned by determined men, ready to fight for every inch of ground.

A vicious thunder started the attack and the men went forward into the chest-high corn. The whole area was infested by machine gun nests and snipers. A young German in a camouflaged uniform rose up from the field and a Scottish Sten gunner, reacting instinctively, shot him down. As they passed the still writhing body, the Scotsmen saw that the German was only a boy. But this boy was a member of the crack 12th SS Panzer Division, one of the best and most highly motivated units formed by the Hitler Youth to fight here in Normandy.

Rain was falling now, pouring into the cornfield and turning it into a soggy mess. Machine guns opened up at the leading companies which, shocked by the suddenness of it, went to ground. The noise was deafening, and the men lay there, their skin quivering from the impact. The artillery barrage was ordered to move forward and the officers rose, signalling their men to follow. A last cigarette hanging from their lips, deafened by the noise, blinded by the rain, the men disappeared into the dust and smoke billowing up behind the barrage. Cranking slowly behind were the Churchill tanks, their machine guns clattering as they sent tracer towards the German positions.

Only a handful of the Hitler Jugend teenagers were defending the field, with rifles, Schmeisser machine pistols and Panzerfausts. A German mortar crew had sheltered from the artillery barrage in their deep bunker. When they ventured out they found that their position had already been surrounded by some Scotsmen bearing grenades. These lucky men were rounded up and sent to the rear; but some of the Scots were not so fortunate. The German panzergrenadiers had been well hidden in their camouflaged dugouts, so well that the Scottish troopers had passed without detecting them. The Germans waited and then shot at them from their vulnerable rear, gunning them down at point blank range to the last man.

Inside the villages, which by now were only dusty rubble, the fighting was vicious, too. Sergeant Roger Green of the Highland Light Infantry just poked his head round the side of Cheux church, where he was hiding with his platoon, when he saw a giant Tiger tank aiming its gun right at him. A shot followed, together with a terrific blast as the big tank round ricochetted off the church wall, covering the men with dust. They froze for a second, but no one was seriously hurt and, as soon as their legs stopped shaking, they made off in a hurry!

As the British troops advanced they were met by withering fire from well-hidden German 88s. The effect was devastating: within minutes several of the heavy Churchills were knocked out while others, still out of range, received volleys of air burst which forced tank commanders to close down, limiting their ability to see. The open-topped Sherman tank destroyers with their more powerful guns fared even worse. Especially heavy fire came from the high ground where 49th Division were still battling but unable to make progress.

A squadron of Churchill tanks from 7th Royal Tank Regiment under Major Richard Joscelyne waddled through the streets of Cheux, amidst gutted and burning houses, making for the open ground beyond. At first there was little opposition as the Germans were concentrating all their efforts against the infantry. As the squadron moved uphill, however, it came under heavy fire from Spandaus and snipers who held up the supporting infantry. As the advance neared the crest, a crack was heard, well-known to all of them. Luckily it missed, but it was only the prelude to a grisly game of hide and seek, with the Churchills on the slope and a group of German Panthers on the crest. But the British guns were more effective, this time, and soon one of the enemy tanks was knocked out. Lieutenant Barret's tank was destroyed almost immediately after, however, while Captain Webb's was hit by a high explosive shell on the turret which blinded both him and his gunner, the crew just managing to bail out seconds before an armour-piercing shot followed.

The fighting became more and more ferocious. The commander of 12th SS Division, Kurt Meyer, one of the youngest division commanders in the German Army, was also one of the most experienced combat leaders, with years of ceaseless combat to his credit. He had earned the nickname 'Panzermeyer' for his personal courage in Russia, but here in Normandy he was to reach the zenith of his career. He was visiting his sector, having received pleas for help from his 3rd Battalion, under heavy pressure near Fontenay. As he was conferring with the battalion commander, a massive artillery burst on the Hitler Youth front sent Meyer flying for cover into the nearest ditch.

The British were attacking. Through a hollow path in the underbrush, two giant Churchills edged forward, firing their machine guns. A youngster with a Panzerfaust stood in their way but was gunned down; another raced over and took his place, aimed, fired – and halted the tank. Meyer raced back to his headquarters at Verson where he was confronted with more shattering news: an entire regiment had been overrun, all guns destroyed, British tanks smashing through the bunker line. The 12th SS Panzer Division front was collapsing and help was urgently needed to stop the crisis from becoming a catastrophe.

Meanwhile, on the British side, advance became a matter of urgency. If the tanks of 11th Armoured Division were to have any hope of reaching Hill 112 before dark, they must move now. This meant that they would have to fight their way out of the 'Scottish' corridor, a narrow defile. If the tanks failed to get out into the open there would be a terrible traffic snarl-up behind and Pip Roberts with his 400 tanks would have to be launched into the enemy rear, with incalculable results.

As they started to move, the division suffered its first casualty – the general's Sherman command tank ran over a mine and lost a track. The Cromwells of the Northamptonshires, the divisional reconnaissance regiment, picked their way through the rubble that was all that remained of the streets of Cheux, passing some previously knocked out Churchills whose crews cheered when they saw the armour going to continue what they themselves had started. Tank commanders stood up in their turrets, the only way they could find their way through the mess. Here and there snipers were still shooting; one tank commander used his pistol to shoot a determined German who had climbed on his tank to fix a magnetic mine.

As they cleared the village, however, the lead tanks were confronted by panzers, and a sharp gun duel ensued. On the German side a tank was hit; its commander, Sergeant Bucholz, who was standing up, had his head torn off by a direct hit. As the Cromwells drove on, the rest of the division followed, led by the Fife and Forfar Regiment with their Shermans. A company of Panzer IVs from the 12th SS Hitler Youth Division raced across the valley from Rauray to bar the way, but were held up by deep sunken ditches, and were too late.

As Lieutenant Don Hall took his Sherman troop around the edge of a wood there was a terrific flash, a roar, and his lead tank dissolved into smoke and flame, the second going up seconds later. The tanks behind laid smoke and searched for cover, while their colonel urged them to advance, in vain. The Germans were defending with determination, and time was running out. Night fell over the front line without the British having captured the hill.

Nightfall came – bringing increased misery to the exhausted infantrymen. The battle had slowed down a bit, but snipers still lurked in every corner waiting to pounce on any target that moved. And targets in plenty they found among the men risking their lives to get supplies forward. Many died that night in a desperate effort to get food and ammunition to the combat troops and evacuate the wounded on their way back.

As the 12th SS Panzer Division tried to reorganise, officers huddling together against the rain, supplies arrived, but their joy was interrupted by a sudden burst of automatic fire. Dark figures pounced on the leaguer, firing Sten guns from the hip. The Germans fought back; one of the officers leapt on an attacker and grappled with him, while from nearby tanks crews fired machine guns. For a while there was pandemonium then, as suddenly as they had appeared, the attackers disappeared, and a ghostly silence fell on the scene.

As the first light of dawn came, the earth was still steaming with moisture from the rains of the previous night as the tired German grenadiers huddled under their tarpaulins in their slit trenches, awaiting the attack which they knew would come any moment.

Then the first enemy shells screamed over, announcing the attack. Fountains of earth were gouged from the earth and spat upwards; trees were uprooted bodily by the tornado of fire, while low-flying Typhoons came over the hills, firing their rockets to add to the din. Then the tanks came. It seemed to the grenadiers as if hundreds of them were grinding through the mud at them, their engines thundering. But the young Germans were not ready to give up the fight! As the British infantry emerged out of the morning mist, they were hit by a tremendous volley of fire from hundreds of defensive positions. The leading troops were caught in a heavy barrage which caused heavy casualties, and the heartrending cries of the wounded could be heard all over the battlefield. But the Jocks struggled on, determined to close with the enemy, only to be cut to pieces by a company of Panther tanks firing at close range. The survivors went to ground, clawing out the ground and digging in as best they could to escape the withering fire.

But there seemed no end to the inferno. Mortars plastered the field, the Sherman tanks coming under fire too, their 75mm guns no match for the lethal high velocity guns that the Panthers mounted, let alone the murderous fire from the giant 88mm Tiger guns which were right behind the Panthers. Tanks exploded one after the other, boiling black smoke signalling the death throes of the British tank crews who tried desperately to manoeuvre around the Germans, but became bogged down by the deep, rain-soaked earth – sitting ducks for the German guns.

But sheer numbers won out as the day wore on. The fighter bombers created havoc among the German panzers and the toll of attrition favoured the British, who could field ten tanks to replace every one destroyed or damaged, whereas the 12th SS Panzer Division had no reserves at all, so that every tank killed was a total loss for Meyer, and he knew it.

At dawn the next day the British attack resumed, the commanders determined to reach the summit of Hill 112 this time. The weather had improved as the Shermans of the 23rd Hussars climbed the lower slopes, accompanied by the 8th Battalion the Rifle Brigade. The broad summit was cleared of its last defenders and the hill secured. As the tank commanders raised their heads above their turrets they could see over the entire area, from the beaches to Caen. It was indeed a highly strategic place they had captured.

The Germans, however, were not willing to let it go that easily. Just as the 3rd RTR was coming up to replace the Hussars, the entire hill came under tremendous artillery and rocket fire. On the southern slope some Tigers moved into position and started sniping at the Shermans with their powerful guns and II SS Panzer Corps was moving into the line.

The British infantrymen were utterly exhausted by now, but so were what remained of the Hitler Jugend, both sides struggling numbly on, determined to fight to the death. A flame-throwing Churchill tank waddled through the brush and halted, hissing and smoking, as it aimed for a German bunker indicated by an infantry officer located at the rear. Suddenly, it blew into pieces: a German, just a teenager, armed with a Panzerfaust, had crawled out of his hiding place, stood up right in front of the fire-spitting steel monster and shot his rocket right below the turret ring! The brave youngster did not live long enough to enjoy his victory: he was shot dead by a short Sten gun burst from a British trooper.

General O'Connor was becoming concerned about the concentration of German power: elements of no less than six panzer divisions were now converging on the bulge which the British had created north of the Odon river. General Roberts attempted to improve his position by ordering the veteran 44th Royal Tank Regiment to take Hill 113. As they climbed it, however, they were engaged by German tanks and, after a fierce fight, had to withdraw.

The German pressure on Hill 112 was growing. Although it had seemed that the Panzergrenadiers had nothing left to fight with, still more fresh Tigers were rushing up the hill. The British, on top, had masked themselves with thick smoke when they saw the giant Tigers coming into view, the company commander in the lead, his 88mm gun belching smoke as he confronted the Shermans. Some British anti-tank guns fired back and two Tigers were hit, but another knocked out two Shermans one after the other. The fight on the hill went on for the rest of the day, growing in ferocity, and for many days to come. The bloody saga of Hill 112 ended not with a bang but with a whimper. On 25 July the Americans started their breakout and made excellent progress. The Germans had to react fast and their last Tigers descended the battered southern slopes of the Hill of Calvary and ground away into the darkness. But all who had fought here bore the scars of battle for the rest of their lives.

CHAPTER EIGHTEEN

DIVINE WIND: THE KAMIKAZE FIGHTERS

It was 0750 Pacific Time on 25 October 1944 and Lieutenant Yukio Seki's Mitsubishi Zero fighter was ready for take-off from Mabalacat airfield on the island of Luzon, in the Philippines. It was a fine morning, and the lieutenant's eyes were shining with anticipation as he pushed the throttle control lever to maximum power. The big radial engine began to cough, then thundered as great blasts of black smoke blew from its exhaust. The propeller spun faster and faster until the aeroplane was straining at its brakes, vibrating with power, like a tiger on a leash. Seki held it down then, as a coloured flare shot up from the shabby flight hut, he waved his arm and set the aeroplane in motion.

The Zero lunged forward and Seki watched the airspeed indicator rise until it reached take-off speed; the tail came up and he watched the 20-metre cliff at the end of the runway fall away as he rose into the air. As Seki flew on, holding the bucking aeroplane down with deft touches on the rudder, he heard the satisfying thud of the wheels locking in, and he settled down to cruising speed watching for his wingmen to fall into place.

So far it had been a normal take-off, one of many thousands that had already occurred and would occur again, around the world at war in 1944. But this one was different – Lieutenant Seki and his fellow pilots had just taken off on their last flight, one from which – as they all knew – none of them would return. The first kamikaze raid was on its way to the US Navy off Leyte, and to its final destiny.

Lieutenant Yukio Seki was neither a bloodthirsty killer nor a nationalistic fanatic. In fact he was a very ordinary young man, tall, handsome and quiet spoken. Seki, a trained carrier bomber pilot who had flown many missions against the Americans, had recently been reassigned to Commander Asaichi Takeda's 201st Air Group from Formosa. A few days before he had been roused from his sleep and told to report to his superior officer, by whom he was informed that he had been chosen to lead the first 'Sho' operation – a last resort offensive to stem the American assault on the Philippines, which was only a short step away from the Japanese homeland. The strategy was, quite simply, suicide; this was the Japanese Imperial Navy's last desperate attempt to stop the overwhelming American war machine which had already rumbled through Midway, the Marianas and New Guinea.

The concept of suicide attacks in war, known as 'kamikaze' or 'divine wind' had its origins in age-old Japanese tradition. According to legend, in 1282 the invasion fleet of Kubla Khan had been destroyed by a terrifying typhoon off the Japanese coast which sank most of the Mongol ships and saved the Japanese islands from occupation. Now, 700 years later, the human 'divine wind' – the pilots – were called on to save their homeland through their own sacrifice.

Seki flew on, scanning the sea below, searching for a sight of some enemy ships. Suddenly, coming out of some cloud at 1010 through light rainfall, he saw it! An American fleet was heading north under a combat air patrol of Hellcats. It was Admiral Thomas Sprague's Task Force 77, returning from their morning strike wave. The first aircraft were circling round the carriers, waiting in turn to be recovered on the decks, while crews feverishly rearmed and refuelled the aircraft which had landed. Abruptly, sirens began to wail and horns tooted loudly as the Zeros were spotted. Lieutenant Seki signalled his pilots and, one after another, they banked and plunged. The first, seemingly out of control, plummeted down steeply, came out of a cloud, and crashed onto the deck of the light carrier *Santee*. The 'plane went right through the flight and hangar decks and exploded, causing a horrifying conflagration, and a nearby stack of bombs was just about to explode when an officer and several men rushed in, disregarding their own danger, and started hosing out the blaze. They had hardly brought this crisis under control when another explosion rocked the ship – this time it was a Japanese torpedo from a low-flying bomber which had penetrated the American flak.

Meanwhile Seki's own kamikaze attack was underway. Swerving to escape the heavy gunfire from the ships, he went for his prey. As he dived down to evade an American fighter which had drawn up behind him, he saw one of his wingmen plunge right into a carrier at an almost vertical angle. Determined to do his bit, too, he plunged to sea level, zoomed up again, and then plunged for an American carrier, *St Lo*, aiming for the aft elevator, the most vulnerable point. Seki was functioning like a robot, his piloting skills telling him not to make his final dive too steep, as this could throw his aircraft off course, the increase in gravity making it swerve at the last moment. He felt no fear, only elation at dying for his country, within seconds he would die his honourable death... High above, Chief Warrant Officer Hiroyoshi Nishizawa watched as Seki's plane plunged right onto the aft elevator he had aimed for, striking squarely into the carrier. Seconds later, his wingman hit too, in the identical spot where Seki had crashed.

On the carrier *Santee* there was wild confusion, as explosions erupted everywhere, to be followed by blazing fires, while fire fighting parties desperately tried to extinguish the flames. The *St Lo* was listing dangerously to port; then minor explosions below decks culminated in a massive detonation at 1058 which ruptured the carrier amidships, spewing 230-metre jets of boiling water, flames and debris. Within minutes the ship rolled over and sank, taking half the crew with her, as well as Lieutenant Seki and his wingman.

On the *Santee* the fires were still raging fiercely, although the ship's gunners battled on, the skies around the ships darkening from the fleet's anti-aircraft fire, while soot and grease rained down. Gunfire from the ship had already downed two incoming Zeros, although one had managed to swerve at the last second and tore through *Santee*, blasting a big hole in the hangar and starting a blaze which detonated several aircraft stored below. However, the damage control crews showed great ability and within three hours the carrier was ready to launch its planned strike wave.

Two more of Seki's Zeros tried to attack but the inexperienced pilots were shot down, one by a fighter and the other by ships' guns as they dived for the USS *Fanshaw Bay*. Another went for the carrier USS *White Plains*, only to be met by a storm of 40mm cannon fire which tore into the attacker, shattering the cockpit and wounding the pilot. But he kept his head and went for the carrier as he plummeted down steeply; he aimed for the bridge but missed the deck by inches, exploding instead in the water, showering the carrier deck with debris and fragments of the pilot's body.

The last of Seki's Zeros tried for the same carrier but swerved away at the last moment and went for another ship, tearing through the deck and breaking it in two. Thus ended the first kamikaze attack. Seki and his men had achieved a major success and died a hero's death in the old Samurai tradition.

The kamikaze idea originated out of the despair engendered when Japan realised for the first time that defeat was inevitable. The battle in the Pacific was clearly turning in the United States' favour in 1944, but surrender was an unthinkable concept to the Japanese soldier, to whom death was preferable, in fact the most honourable course of action, as in the Samurai tradition. Thus kamikaze was not regarded as all that out of the way by the Japanese high command when they saw that American industrial superiority left them no chance of winning the war. In that case, they felt, just like the Biblical Samson, they would take as many of their enemies with them as they could before the sun finally set on the Nippon Empire.

The name most closely associated with the kamikaze concept is that of Admiral Takijiro Onishi. However, the suicide attack concept as such evolved with the junior pilots themselves, who had realised by the summer of 1944 that for all practical purposes they could consider themselves as living on borrowed time. Following the terrible losses in the great naval battles when the US Navy carrier task forces had clearly gained the upper hand with superior combat aircraft as well as improved fighter direction tactics, advanced radar and other modern equipment, the losses of the relatively small Japanese Imperial Navy air force were becoming unbearable. From the outset the Japanese Navy had chosen to create an elite force rather than build a vast reserve of combat pilots as did the RAF, the USAAF and the Navy. Thus, following the battles in the Pacific, the number of highly trained Japanese pilots dwindled sharply, to be replaced as time went by with ill-trained, inexperienced aircrews, no match for the better trained Americans.

However, single suicide attacks had begun much earlier. The first is believed to be when Captain Colin P. Kelly Jr of the USAAF crash-dived his Flying Fortress into the Japanese battleship *Haruna* in December, 1941 sailing at Luzon, exactly where Lieutenant Seki flew his last mission. Kelly's bomber had been badly damaged by a Zero fighter while returning from an attack on a Japanese transport. Kelly sacrificed his life by remaining at the controls of his blazing bomber to hold it steady while his crew parachuted to safety; then he crashed to the deck of the enemy ship, sinking it. A number of such suicide attacks were also flown by RAF pilots when they saw no chance of saving their stricken aircraft.

It was Ensign Mitsuo Ohta, later to propose the basic design for the Ohka rocket-propelled manned suicide missile, who was one of the leading proponents of the kamikaze concept; his enthusiasm infected a senior officer, Captain Eiichiro Jyo, who at that time commanded the light carrier *Chiyoda*. Jyo hoped that these tactics would not only hold up the American attack, but would give Japan time to recover and rebuild some of the war resources which would enable them to fight on. Jyo finally convinced his superior officers that his ideas had some weight at this crucial time.

Rear Admiral Masafumi Arima, commanding the 26th Air Flotilla at Nichols Field, gave the supreme example of the kamikaze concept. On 21 September 1944, after his forces had beaten off a strong American air assault on Manila, the admiral led an attacking force against the US carrier force, scoring five direct hits on Task Force 38. The admiral was a veteran, over 50 years old, taciturn, dignified, and a fine scholar. He was certainly no fire-eater. But he led up front, never asking his young pilots to do what he did not do himself first. A man of frugal lifestyle, quite unusual for a senior officer of his day (and, possibly, of ours!) Arima was a sailor's sailor – a true samurai. On 15 October 1944, he stripped off all his rank badges then, boarding the lead plane, Arima took the controls, in spite of his staff officer's protest. He lifted the heavily laden aircraft off the ground – and flew off to die. Some 240 miles from Manila, he spotted the enemy fleet and signalled all his planes to attack. His own plane led the way, and was last seen plunging downwards, streaming smoke, as he crash-dived into the USS *Franklin*, which was damaged but did not sink from the blast. Admiral Arima's gesture is difficult to understand for those of us not imbued with the samurai tradition. Perhaps he believed that, in asking his pilots to fly their one-way attacks, it was only fair and right that he should lead them on their final mission into death. Whatever the rights and wrongs of it, Admiral Arima's sacrifice prepared the way for Admiral Onishi to form the Special Attack Units which would bear the brunt of the savage fighting a few months later off Leyte Gulf.

Admiral Takijiro Onishi was a remarkable naval officer. Highly intelligent, inquisitive and open-minded, he had been the pioneer of Japan's paratroop forces in the 1930s and gained a high reputation during the fighting in China. At first an opponent of Admiral Isoruki Yamamoto's Pearl Harbor plan, he had been convinced by his mentor of its value and had become an enthusiastic proponent of the idea. A man of fierce enthusiasms, Onishi was the perfect choice to command the kamikaze special units to be formed in the Philippines.

Onishi was sent from Tokyo to assume command of the First Air Fleet at Clark Airbase near Manila on 17 October 1944 and, as soon as he had taken over from his predecessor, he met with the officers of 201st Air Group at Mabalacat on Luzon to discuss the operational aspects of the newly created Special Attack Group. During an evening session in Commander Asaichi Tamai's headquarters shed, the admiral came straight to the point. He stressed the urgent need to destroy, or at least neutralise, the American carriers, thus delaying the otherwise inevitable capture of the islands. The fate of the empire, he said, would depend on the resolution of the pilots to succeed in their mission. As he spoke, he scanned the bright young faces of the men sitting around him, seeing the meaning of his words sink in. When he finished, no one spoke for a time. Everyone there knew what he meant – it was a one-way ticket to oblivion...

Then Commander Tamai spoke, and seeing their own boss acquiesce, the men began to cheer, and, to a man, the 201st Air Group volunteered to fly and die for their emperor! The kamikaze Special Attack Unit came into being. The 'divine wind' of centuries before had been reborn.

In Japan, as word began to filter out of the first kamikaze sorties, the media made sure that support and encouragement for the heroic airmen rose to fever pitch. Lieutenant Yukio Seki's epic ride on 25 October was widely publicised and he himself was honoured as a national hero. Many more followed suit, and volunteers flocked to the attack units which were quickly formed and trained. From the Naval Academy in Japan hundreds volunteered, although commanders in the field were reluctant to accept these youngsters, however eager, in view of the mere 40 flying hours in their operational logbooks. But as losses rose, there was little choice but to accept them and hope for the best.

The climax of the kamikaze offensive came with the United States' invasion of Okinawa, the last stop before the Japanese islands. This threat to the homeland brought about new tactics, in which conventional air attacks were combined with kamikaze crash-dives on target ships. The battle raged for weeks, both sides fighting for their lives with terrifying fury and venom. From March to August 1945, out of a total of 6,300 Japanese sorties, half were kamikaze attacks but, even with these tremendous losses, there was still no shortage of new volunteers. Nearly 300 Allied ships were sunk or badly damaged, with the losses of US sailors rising by the hour. The effect was even more damaging from the point of view of morale. The fear of the kamikaze was tremendous; men lost their nerve as soon as a warning of impending attack was given and officers had their hands full keeping them at battle stations and functioning.

In early April 1945 the Americans had already landed on Okinawa; Commander Tadashi Nakajima was sent to join Captain Motoharu Okamura's Special Attack Group at Kanoya Airbase on Kyushu. Nakajima was one of the most experienced airmen still alive by this time, and his presence was an important morale booster to the newly formed group at this crucial time.

The beginning of April saw the largest mass attacks by Japanese kamikazes on American ships off Okinawa. In spite of an early interdiction strike on the Kyushu airfields by US carrier aircraft, some 400 Japanese planes took off on the afternoon of 6 April. One of the fiercest – and most macabre – air battles of the war was about to take place. At 1753 the USS *Leutze* sighted an enemy plane and immediately opened fire. Within a few moments the sky was filled with bursts from all the ship's guns, sprouting red balls of fire, while shortfalls fell into the sea, raising huge sprays of grey-green water. About twelve Japanese planes swooped down, roaring and screaming, some of them trailing smoke as they came. Others skimmed the water at zero height, hopping over the waves; one plane was seen crashing in one of the giant sprays of water, its propeller churning the sea into a milky froth.

The *Leutze* bore the brunt of the first attack. A kamikaze crashed straight into her amidships, gouging deep into the bowels of the destroyer and causing a tremendous explosion. The ship listed hard, belching oily black smoke. All power was cut off; both engine rooms were just a mass of wreckage. The bodies of the dead were strewn around, while the wounded screamed for help. Commander Edward McMillan saw another plane coming for the stricken ship from the port side, grabbed a 40mm quad battery whose gunner was in shock and unable to function, and opened fire on the attacker. He hit home, but too late... it crashed into the forward stack, spraying debris everywhere. The entire ship was now aflame, the fire shooting up hundreds of feet into the air, while a thick pall of smoke covered the destroyer from stern to bow.

The destroyer *Newcombe* was coming close to try and help, when another kamikaze, skimming the sea's surface, closed in fast and crashed into the ship, but the captain continued to close in on the stricken *Leutze* in a last minute effort to save what could be saved. They were just starting to pick up survivors when another kamikaze was seen heading for the bridge of the *Newcombe*. One of the 5-inch guns managed to hit it, tilting it and sending it crashing onto the *Leutze*'s fantail, already under water. Meanwhile, on *Newcombe*, the damage control crews were now fighting for their own ship. While the gun crews continued to fire at incoming enemy aircraft, the fires were brought under control and, with power restored, the ship was once again underway, although in a terrible state. Fire-scored, half-wrecked, the destroyer stumbled on at half speed, trying to manoeuvre just enough to escape further attacks. She was listing heavily, her decks abaft the superstructure buckled into the shape of a roller coaster and her fantail only inches above the water, while part of a Japanese kamikaze plane could be seen in its final resting place on the shattered deck. But the ship was still afloat...

The destroyer USS *Bush* fared much worse that afternoon. Her crew had shot two kamikazes out of the sky just before 1500, when another was sighted by a lookout, coming in low under a squall of spray. The plane jinked and wove sharply trying to escape the withering fire from the *Bush*, where every gun was blazing away. But the pilot kept on coming, and crashed right between the two stacks. The bomb exploded in the forward engine room, killing the entire crew. Water poured in and the ship started to list heavily. As men stumbled about in the dark, an officer went down and started the auxiliary generator, restoring some power. Some of the crew were using hand pumps to stop the flooding, while medics dragged the wounded on deck.

Another kamikaze came in, missing by inches and crashing into the sea. Another was shot clear out of the sky and splashed into the sea, its port wing aflame. Commander Wilson, the skipper, watched another plane heading straight for his bridge but, at the last second, managed to drag his ship into a turn and evade it. But the plane hit the main deck below and killed the gun crew which had been firing at him. The *Bush* was in deep trouble, but Wilson was determined to save his ship. He beat off five attacks within fifteen minutes; then – two more kamikazes were seen coming in as a pair. The gunnery officer kept his presence of mind and fired his 5-inch guns point blank in quick succession; one plane was shot out of the sky, but the other managed to evade and crashed into them, blowing a great hole below the waterline and stopping the destroyer dead in the water, a sitting target for the next attack.

The kamikaze attacks continued throughout the summer of 1945, but petered out as losses grew and the war drew to its end. As a last gesture of defiance, Admiral Matome Ugaki flew the last kamikaze sortie with his men, in spite of the attempts made by both his superiors and his loyal staff to prevent him from flying to his death. But the admiral who had sent so many men to their own untimely deaths decided that he could not face the inevitable defeat and surrender and remain alive himself. On 15 August 1945, Admiral Ugaki went out to the airfield, stripped off all his insignia, retaining only the sword given him by Admiral Yamamoto, the commander of the combined fleets. On the runway stood eleven aeroplanes, their engines roaring, their crews ready. Thanking each man personally, the admiral took his seat beside the observer and signalled the take off. Shortly before crashing onto an American ship, the admiral was heard, through heavy static, passing his farewell message. Then – only silence. The last kamikaze had flown to his death, bringing to an end a bizarre chapter in the annals of military history.

CHAPTER NINETEEN

THE BLOODY SANDS OF IWO JIMA

As a piece of real estate, Iwo Jima would hardly seem worth fighting for. This egg-shaped island formed of volcanic rock is only four kilometres wide and eight long, and has only one dominating feature – an extinct volcano, the 150 metres high Mount Suribachi, at its southern end. The rest is a desolate waste of black, volcanic sand and rock, huddled together as a plateau of ridges and gorges, which makes up the northern half of the island. But – in 1945 at least – Iwo Jima had great strategic importance, both to the Japanese, who had gained control of the island in 1891, and to the Americans, who needed it for their bombing offensive against the Japanese mainland. Thus, Iwo Jima was to have its moment of fame – or notoriety – as one of the most costly and savage battles in the annals of the US Marine Corps.

The Japanese had constructed two airfields there, from which their fighters could intercept the American bomber fleets on their way to Tokyo – two and a half hours' flying time away – and, worse, harass the American bombers on their return trip, when many of them would be sitting ducks as they limped home damaged by flak and with crews exhausted after the long flight.

By 1945 General Douglas MacArthur's forces had brought the war nearer to the Japanese mainland. The Pacific islands of Saipan, Guam and Tinian had been captured after savage fighting, and new bases were constructed on them for the specially designed B-29 four-engined heavy bombers, which could fly their bomb loads non-stop from the Marianas to Tokyo. The first raid was flown by the USAAF on 22 November 1944. These long range raids, which became known as the Great Fire Raids, would eventually destroy most of the cities of Japan even before Hiroshima and Nagasaki were devastated by the atom bomb in August 1945. The B-29 bomber attacks were one of the top strategic assets of the American war machine in the Pacific theatre and it was only with their backing that most of the combined sea and land assaults were mounted in the late stages of the war.

But the US bomber offensive on Japan was a costly affair. Until a base for fighter escorts could be secured within effective range, the 5,600 kilometre round trip from the Marianas to Japan was extremely dangerous. Iwo Jima, situated halfway between the two, and with the bonus of two completed airfields, would be an excellent base for fighters to escort the bombing parties. There was an additional plus to the capture of the island: as a traditional Japanese territory, administered directly by Tokyo, its conquest would send a severe psychological shock to the Japanese in their homeland, lowering their morale as well as denying them a strategic outpost. For all these reasons the island had to be taken.

The Japanese High Command was also well aware of the island's strategic value, and put its defence at the top of its list of priorities. For several months, indeed years, the Japanese had been turning Iwo Jima into a virtually impregnable fortress. No less than twenty kilometres of underground tunnels had been excavated into the basalt rock connecting one end of the island with the other in a warren of burrows which led to well-situated fire positions, whose apertures were so low and well camouflaged that they could be seen only when the attackers were right on top of them! Command posts and communication facilities were placed in bombproof underground shelters hewn 30 metres deep and protected by three-metre thick reinforced concrete walls. Hundreds of concrete blockhouses, bunkers, and gun and machine gun emplacements were placed around the island, with masses of them covering the beaches.

Commanding the island was Lieutenant General Tadamichi Kuribayashi, a cavalry officer who had graduated with distinction from the prestigious Military Academy and War College. He was very cosmopolitan for a Japanese of that time, having served for several years as military attaché in the USA and Canada and travelled widely. Having seen the vast American industrial capacity at first hand, he was under no illusions as to the eventual outcome of the war, but was determined to fight this, his last battle, to the bitter end and at the highest cost to his enemy.

Kuribayashi did his homework well. He assessed every American attack in their island-hopping campaign, especially the costly struggles for Tarawa and Peleliu. His style of defence would differ from the traditional banzai charges, which actually played into the Americans' hands, as they were costly, ineffective, and easily quelled by the superior American firepower. Kuribayashi determined to fight on Iwo Jima not for victory but to use attrition and delaying tactics to achieve his goal. Instead of trying to defend the beaches and throw the invaders back into the sea, his forces would conduct a disciplined position defence, fighting over every inch of ground from well placed and protected shelters. The men in every position would fight their own battle and, when overrun, the survivors would move through their interconnecting burrows to another position from which they could start fighting again.

To support his underground defence complex the Japanese general had no less than 700 heavy and medium, and thousands of light guns, a formidable array. His 109th Infantry Division, almost 14,000 strong, was augmented by some 7,500 crack Navy troops, 24 tanks and 70 superheavy rocket launchers. The underground storage depots were filled to the brim with huge quantities of ammunition, food and water which could serve the defenders comfortably for a three-month siege. Any way you looked at it, Iwo Jima was a deathtrap, an impregnable fortress, perhaps the strongest the American forces would ever have to face.

The American commanders had been gathering information for months about the defences on Iwo Jima. In September 1944 their military intelligence had published a full-sized book on the Japanese Army, indicating in the minutest detail the various operational facilities which the Japanese had used on the island. In addition their reconnaissance aircraft had taken hundreds of aerial photographs.

What the Americans did not know about, however, was the extensive honeycomb of tunnels on Iwo Jima, and this ignorance was to cost the marines dearly once they landed.

Admiral Chester Nimitz, the United States' overall naval commander, had placed the operation to take Iwo Jima in the hands of Lieutenant General Holland M. Smith (nicknamed 'Howling Mad' Smith), a leading exponent of amphibious warfare and commander of all the US Marines in the Pacific. The operation was to be carried out by the 5th Corps. Three Marine divisions were earmarked for the invasion. The 3rd, commanded by Major General G. B. Erskine, was a veteran unit which had already seen action on Guam; the 4th, led by Major General C. B. Cates, was also battle hardened on Saipan and Tinian; only the 5th, whose commander was Major General K. E. Rockey, was a new and untried unit, with seasoned veterans making up about half of its numbers.

Once the target had been selected, the marines began a rigorous training programme on Maui, in Hawaii, where some volcanic terrain could be used to simulate the conditions on Iwo Jima. The operation was codenamed 'Detachment' and some very lavish naval and air support was planned to get the Marine divisions ashore.

D-Day was scheduled for the morning of 19 February 1945. Three days earlier a tremendous naval bombardment opened up from the giant guns of six battleships hurling their heavy ordnance at the Japanese bunkers known to be defending the landing sites. But the Japanese defenders on the island, hiding snugly in their deep underground shelters, felt very little – apart from the noise.

D-Day... The leading wave of the LVTs (Landing Vehicles Tracked) hit the beach at precisely 0902, north-east of Mount Suribachi; these landing beaches had been chosen because they were the narrowest point in the south of the island, which the attackers hoped to be able to cut off from the north. First ashore were the men of Colonel Harry B. Liversedge's 28th Marine Regiment. Their job was to capture Mount Suribachi, so as to remove the Japanese observers from the mountain top, a position from which the entire battle could be controlled. The landing was surprisingly easy! Not a shot was fired as the men emerged from the landing craft and scrambled onto the beach. Some of the veterans could hardly believe their luck. They had faced the withering fire on Tarawa where even a slight movement could mean certain death. This seemed like a school outing in contrast. But, as they left the hard-packed beach, they ran into trouble. Trying to move forward on the loose, black volcanic sand was impossible – it was like running on the spot, or climbing a waterfall. As the men tried to crawl uphill, they could see the mass of Mount Suribachi glowering down on them. A few minutes passed, then suddenly the morning silence was exploded by the shattering thunder of the Japanese defence barrage. The Marines were hit by crossfire from hidden bunkers which none of them could locate. Colonel Liversedge dropped down beside his men, panting heavily from the effort. But this burly man of six foot four was not about to take any nonsense from Japanese gunners. He signalled to his operations officers, who were still wading through the surf, and the two officers crawled up the shifting sands and set up a command post near the top from which the colonel hoped to control his attack.

The scene was one of confusion. Men were emerging from the landing craft and trying to come inland; some fell straight into the surf, others into the black sands, while medics rushed about trying to tend to the wounded. The naval barrage added to the noise. The ships' guns were trying without avail to silence the Japanese gun positions, but they were not only well hidden but protected under thick walls of concrete which no shells could penetrate. If anyone could lead his men through this chaos it was Harry Liversedge. He and his executive officer, Lieutenant Colonel Robert Williams, were absolute opposites in demeanour and character, but together they made a perfect team. They had both been highly decorated for valour, but here on Iwo Jima the pair would face their toughest challenge yet. Mortar shells and machine gun fire were falling faster, the wounded were moaning, the dead lay where they had fallen and their number grew by the minute; this was no place to stay.

The colonel stood up and waded uphill, ignoring the bullets which pinged and whined around him, signalling the men to follow him inland. Iwo Jima was alive, the volcano spitting fire as if the mountain slopes were alight. The entire mountain seemed to be on fire! It was a tremendous sight, but too dangerous for comfort for those who were there.

General Kuribayashi had instructed his local commander, Colonel Atsuji, to fight and delay the American attack as long as possible, causing them as many casualties as he could in their attempt to take the mountain. And that is precisely what he did. As they struggled up the western slopes of Mount Suribachi, the Marines were temporarily paralysed by the intensity of the defensive fire. The bunkers were barely visible, hewn as they were into the volcanic rock, with only the narrow slits of the apertures at ground level spitting terrifying showers of machine gun fire. Some of the men who had survived the horrors of Tarawa cursed that Iwo was the worst yet. Little did they know that this was only the beginning of a 36-day struggle for this barren piece of rock, a struggle which many of them would not live through.

Somebody had to get up and go forward, though. If not, they would all die here on these desolate slopes. And one did: Second Lieutenant Norman D. Brueggman, a youngster in his first combat, yelled and rose to rush uphill, his submachine gun blazing at one of the apertures. A moment later he was dead. Another officer, Lieutenant Colonel Chandler W. Johnson, commanding the 2nd Battalion, had better luck – for a while. Ignoring the enemy fire the colonel rose and by the sheer force of his courage, carried his men with him into the inferno. His luck was to last for another two weeks. Then he, too, was killed, by a direct hit from an explosive shell.

While the ships in the lagoon continued to pump shells into the Japanese positions, the 28th Marines clawed their way through the shifting sands onto the slopes. Pfc Tony Stein, a small, slightly built young Jew from Ohio, had already been through three campaigns in the Solomon Islands and seemed to lead a charmed life. He had guts, this youngster: having designed his own special weapon, a hand-held Browning machine gun, salvaged from a wrecked navy fighter, he had teamed up with two demolition men, and all three were blazing away, knocking out one Japanese pillbox after the other. Soon he ran out of ammunition, but that did not stop him. Taking off his boots, he ran towards the beach through a hail of fire and filled up his helmet with enough bullets to continue his private war! He was still going strong as evening fell, despite having had his gun shot out of his hands twice by Japanese snipers!

By nightfall some 30,000 Marines were ashore, digging in despite withering Japanese fire which turned the beaches into a scene of carnage. Some 1,300 marines were already casualties and the figures were rising by the hour. But, on the slopes of Mount Suribachi the 28th was fighting its way to the top. Colonel Harry Liversedge was in the thick of battle all the time, in a makeshift command post inside a destroyed enemy bunker, and well ahead of his three battalions – not a healthy place to be in a battle, but the best from which to urge his men on. He was receiving urgent calls from 'Howling Mad' Smith to get up to the top of Mount Suribachi so that the marines below could push inland and cut the island in half, prior to the main effort in the north. But Suribachi was a formidable obstacle; every step uphill was costly, since every couple of metres fire was spitting out from concrete bunkers and caves. In addition, with so many men in such a confined space, it was difficult to move at all, a fact of which the Japanese forces took full advantage, holding their fire and opening up only when the marines had passed them. Sometimes the hapless Americans came under from above *and* below – a real nightmare. One grisly example of true hand to hand fighting came when Pfc Leo Jez, rushing towards a pillbox, was confronted by a Japanese officer swinging a giant sword straight at him. Jez caught the blow with his outstretched arm, wrenched the sword away from his enemy and chopped off his head with a single stroke! All he suffered was a severed finger!

According to the initial plan the 28th were to capture Suribachi in twelve hours, but it took nearly four days; the casualties mounted, reaching 900 men, until, following a final air strike by 40 carrier planes which turned the mountain top into a blazing inferno, a patrol led by Lieutenant Harold G. Shirer reached the top, and hoisted a small, makeshift, Stars and Stripes, cheered by the men watching below. Shortly afterwards a larger flag was obtained from one of the ships, brought uphill, and hoisted by six men who had to struggle to drive the flagpole into the hard volcanic soil. This photograph has become a classic of the Second World War, as well as a symbol of the devotion and dedication of the US Marine Corps.

But the epic battle for Mount Suribachi, though it was long and costly, was only the beginning of a terrible struggle for the northern part of the island, which General Tadamichi Kuribayashi had prepared for in such detail and with such ingenuity. The battle began on the morning of the 24th, after a preliminary two-hour naval bombardment, a massive air strike and support from the divisional artillery. The Sherman tanks led the way, skirting the airfield which was heavily defended by a maze of bunkers and pillboxes, but no sooner had the tanks left the airfield area than they were hit by a terrific volley from well-hidden anti-tank guns, followed by huge 320mm mortars – three times bigger than anything the Americans could field – which smashed into the advancing ranks, causing horrible casualties with their fragmentation pattern. The marines called these shells 'garbage cans', they were so big. As if this was not bad enough, soon 16-inch rockets came screaming in from mobile folding chutes. The damage from these two combined caused nearly ten percent of all the casualties who would later die from their wounds, even if they were still alive when they reached the hospital ships. The massive American bombardment seemed to make

no dent in the Japanese bunker positions, even when they were identified. The Japanese seemed virtually impregnable to fire. This time there
were no costly banzai charges for the Americans to destroy with their
overwhelming firepower. Instead, General Kuribayashi kept his men
snug in their underground shelters, and let the Americans pay for every
inch of ground.

The marine commanders, realising they would have to rout the
Japanese out from their hiding places, changed their tactics too. Instead
of charging behind a barrage of fire, they would have to go in close to
the bunkers, blind the apertures with smoke, burn them with
flamethrowers and, finally, blast them with explosive demolition
charges. These tactics cost many lives and a bitter joke went around
among the Marines: 'Iwo Jima – no better place to die young!'

While the marines moved cautiously behind the Sherman tanks
whose flamethrowers sprayed the located bunkers with searing flame,
the Japanese, using their hidden underground passages, emerged actually behind the attackers! In one night attack alone, over 500 Japanese
soldiers were killed who had infiltrated into the rear in an attempt to hit
the logistical build-up on the beaches, days after the battle had moved
inland. There was no safe place on Iwo Jima!

The American flamethrower tanks turned out to be a godsend.
Originally the idea had been to replace the 75mm gun with a modified
flame gun, but the change in silhouette made the tank instantly recognisable and therefore extremely vulnerable to enemy fire. It was accordingly redesigned so as to fit the flame gun into the gun tube, and this
worked out better. But working with the flamethrower tank remained a
distinctly hazardous job: not only was there the usual danger of being
hit by the enemy, but, sitting on nearly 300 gallons of highly inflam-
mable fuel, the crew had little chance to survive if an explosion followed a hit. Strangely, although such tanks were hit on several
occasions, the fuel tanks did not explode, thanks partly to the fact that
they were protected by layers of concrete.

While the battle raged on the island, another drama was unfolding offshore. The Japanese naval commander had shifted his attention
to the ships in the lagoon, to intervene against the so far relatively
unopposed fire support by the American naval guns. A specially
equipped fleet of submarines was sent to the area in order to launch
manned suicide Kaiten torpedoes from the submerged craft. Three submarines were mustered to carry the Kaitens to Iwo Jima. Leading the
suicide torpedo group was Ensign Itaru Okayama, a former instructor

from the Kaiten school at Hikari. He had under his command no less than fourteen Kaiten torpedoes, all manned by zealous youngsters who were ready to die for their emperor. But the US Navy was by now well prepared for this type of attack. Hunter-killer groups were constantly on the alert, roaming the surrounding lagoon in a search for infiltrators of any sort. Captain G. C. Montgomery, commanding the escort carrier *Anzio*, and his light escort destroyers were all experienced submarine hunters. On 27 February 1945 the *Anzio* group located their first Japanese submarine and sank her with well-placed depth charges before Lieutenant Commander Mituteru Irisawa could launch his Kaiten torpedoes; all went down with their ship and no survivors were seen after the explosion. One submarine claimed a hit on one of the American ships, but the attacker was located by sonar from the destroyer *Finnigan* south of Iwo Jima which closed in and began a four-hour hunt, terminating in an underwater explosion which indicated a kill. The remaining submarine, commanded by the veteran Lieutenant Commander Genbei Kawaguchi, reached the area somewhat later, but found it difficult to penetrate the protective web of US patrol craft. He escaped detection by skilful manoeuvring, but was unable to come up to sufficient depth to launch his Kaitens, and had to remain low in the water for a dreadful 46 hours until his crew were on the verge of suffocation from lack of air. He abandoned his mission and brought his men home to an angry admiral – humiliated, but alive!

The battle for Iwo Jima raged on, with no quarter given or taken on either side. Into the second week, the Marines were confronting General Kuribayashi's main defences in the central part of the island, an area of cliffs, crevices, gorges and ravines. An advance through such jagged natural obstacles would have been difficult enough in normal times, but here hundreds of excellently camouflaged caves, bunkers and dugouts covered all possible avenues of approach in overlapping fields of fire. This region, known as the Motoyama plateau, was surrounding by sulphur pits whose acrid stink added to the misery of the men. Here, Colonel Harry Liversedge's 28th Marines suffered over 240 casualties in just three days. They were fighting for the notorious Hill 362, not much of a feature in itself, but a nightmare when defended by a bunch of savage Japanese soldiers who fought like madmen and seemed to come out from nowhere all at the same time.

Corporal Tony Stein, the little toolmaker from Ohio, was still on his feet. Although he had a painful shrapnel wound in his shoulder, he refused to be evacuated and, with all the officers dead or wounded, he led twenty men in a charge onto a Japanese bunker complex on the hill. Only seven men survived the charge; Stein was not one of them. His luck had finally run out. But the Japanese position was demolished, with not one defender left alive.

Pushing north, the regiment hit Nisi ridge, a jagged volcanic outcrop running towards the shore. It took three days of savage fighting to clear the well-hidden enemy positions which had to be taken out one by one in hand to hand fighting. Every metre of ground took its toll and numbers dwindled fast. It was here that Sergeant William G. Harell, a tough Texan, won the coveted Medal of Honor. Having lost his left hand to a grenade he fought on undaunted until his other hand was torn off by an exploding shell. But he was not alone – no fewer than 24 of these rarely awarded medals were won the hard way on Iwo Jima!

Of all the men fighting on the island, some of the most exposed were the combat engineers. These men had to blaze the trail for the tanks which, if unprotected, were soon knocked out by Japanese anti-tank fire or by suicide tank killer teams. On one such occasion, a Sherman tank was stopped by a Japanese private, Gondo by name, who emerged from his hideout, shot the tank commander with his rifle and then climbed onto the top of the tank to throw a grenade into the turret before being shot down by a marine.

Pfc Larry Rogers of the 3rd Combat Marine Battalion was even more courageous. Having rescued a buddy under intense enemy machine gun fire, he crawled forward to the enemy bunker aperture and hurled a satchel charge, with a five second delay fuse, into the slit. But the Japanese defenders were ready and promptly threw the charge back out. Rogers rushed back and returned the charge; it exploded, killing the Japanese and sealing the bunker for good. But that was not the end of the story. Finding another of his buddies groaning in pain, he carried him back under withering fire, then assaulted the position and fired into the bunker's aperture; this time, however, his luck ran out and he was mortally wounded.

Offshore, the ships of the US Navy were facing great danger as Japanese kamikaze fighters appeared on the scene. Most of these attacks failed to sink any major vessels and only one escort carrier had been lost in this manner. Then, however, the Japanese mounted one of their most determined suicide attacks and the fleet carrier USS *Saratoga* took five hits from a wave of six kamikaze Zeros inside three minutes. Just as she was listing badly and on fire, one more hit came from a group of five kamikazes. 123 of her crew were killed and nearly 200 wounded, but the ship did not sink; she survived her ordeal, returning to the United States for repairs.

As soon as the first airstrip was secured, although still under sporadic fire, the first crippled B-29 landed on its return trip from Honshu. The tired, haggard crewmen were cheered by the equally exhausted marines who thronged around them. But the fighting was not over yet and the bomber took off once more for Saipan, waved on by the marines who returned to their own battle. All around the airfield lay hundreds of shattered, burnt out enemy fortifications and in them, buried for ever, the charred bodies of their defenders. The severity of the fighting had turned the island into a mass of holes and craters, covered with dust, looking like the surface of the moon, so that the maps and aerial photographs which had been handed out prior to the invasion were no longer of any use for combat control. Officers had to direct their men by visual means, pointing out features as they came into view.

By this stage of the battle, there were not many officers left, anyway. Twelve battalion commanders were wounded and five dead. Many of the men who were left were on the verge of exhaustion, momentarily expecting death, which most of them regarded as a welcome alternative to the mutilation they all dreaded. The combination of mines, mortars and rockets, as well as the face-to-face combat with savage Japanese fighters ready to die, was a horrifying experience and one which would haunt the survivors to the end of their days.

The number of cases of combat fatigue, otherwise known as shell shock, grew alarmingly, since men who are surrounded by filth, stink, and the incessant battle noise often become fatalistic, helpless and numb. Some, although not all, of the officers coped better. Their preoccupation with responsibility left them with too little time to worry about themselves during the heat of battle. Captain David Severance, a company commander in the 28th, had lost 71 dead and 167 wounded. All his platoon leaders had been killed, a replacement lieutenant lasting but fifteen minutes. Dead tired, blackened by soot and wounded, he went on commanding his dwindling force with a corporal and a pfc. But, by some miracle, he survived, fighting without pause for three weeks, his spirit clearly indestructible.

The final battle for Iwo Jima took place at its northern end on a ridge overlooking Kitano Point. Here General Kuribayashi had deployed his best unit, the 145th Infantry Regiment, who were holed up along the ridge in a warren of fortified caves. It was to take another week of fighting, with a marine dying for every yard gained, until this last hurdle was finally overcome.

The battle for Iwo Jima lasted for 35 days and nights, a time of terror, hunger and thirst. In these killing fields, time seemed to slow down, and no other way of life, no possibility of a future, could be seen – only the incessant noise, the hunger and thirst, the fear, and the blood.

General Kuribayashi knew that the battle was lost. In his candlelit bunker, he and his loyal staff listened with tears in their eyes to a special song broadcast from Tokyo for them, the defenders of Iwo Jima, over the radio whose batteries were fading fast. Then the general sent his last message to Major Horie on Chichi Jima island, informing him that he would lead one last banzai personally, as all was lost.

On 24 March, 35 days after the first US Marines had set foot on the island, the enemy resistance officially ended. But at dawn the next morning the Japanese mounted a final, desperate banzai charge against the northern airfield, on which the American Seabees were preparing the runway at breakneck speed to receive some returning bombers.

No one knows if General Kuribayashi himself was leading the remnants of his 145th Regiment in their final charge, but the question is academic. For the American marines were up and ready as the first shots fell and, rallied by 1st Lieutenant Harry Martin, they took a terrible toll of the attackers, killing every single one in that last, desperate fight. 223 Japanese bodies were found, among them at least 60 officers with their Samurai swords. American losses were 53 killed and double that number wounded. General Kuribayashi's body was not identified, as the gallant Japanese commander had removed all his badges of rank and distinction to fight beside his men to the end.

Although the battle for Iwo Jima was finally won, there remained over a thousand enemy soldiers alive, still hiding in the hundreds of underground dugouts, who had to be tracked down and killed by the island's garrison. Strange as it sounds, in 1948, *three years* after all the Americans had long gone from Iwo Jima, two Japanese soldiers were dug out alive. They were the only survivors, apart from 216 prisoners-of-war, out of the original 22,000 defenders of Iwo Jima. But for the Americans, too, the price had been terrible. Nearly 6,000 American marines were dead and 17,373 wounded, by the end of this nightmare ordeal.

But the two airfields were in action soon after the fighting stopped. 2,500 bombers returning from Japan were able to make emergency landings on Iwo Jima's airstrips, saving thousands of American airmen from a certain watery grave in the endless wastes of the Pacific.

Colonel Harry Liversedge survived, but of his gallant regiment only 600 men of the original 3,900 remained on their feet when the battle was over. They, and many thousands more, paid an appalling price for the capture of just two bomber bases. But, strangely, as they marched towards the ships that would take them, morale was high. They had destroyed a skilled, highly motivated force and had overcome a fortress stronger than anything the US Marine Corps had ever visualised, let alone confronted!

One final question nagged at the senior Pacific commanders after Iwo Jima. If it had taken 72 days of air bombardment, three days of naval hammering and a full 36 days of savage fighting to conquer such a tiny island, and this with the best that the US Marine Corps could put in the field, what would it take to overwhelm the Japanese mainland? The answer came only with the atomic bombs on Hiroshima and Nagasaki.

CHAPTER TWENTY

SIXTEEN HOURS OF HELL: ST SIMON MONASTERY

In the spring of 1948 the Jewish population of Jerusalem numbered about 100,000, twice that of the Arabs. But the Jewish majority was facing starvation. Under the British Mandate the lifeline of the city was a winding asphalt road which for almost all of its length ran through hostile Arab dominated territory, some of it traversing dangerous mountain passes over which every single convoy had to fight its way through a gauntlet of fire. In Jerusalem itself, most of the Jewish quarters were quite isolated from each other, with Arab areas dominating the heights. Some of the Jewish quarters were totally cut off from the city centre, defended only by a handful of young fighters equipped with obsolete rifles and hand grenades. The city was close to starvation. The supply of water, which came from pumping stations located in the hills, some of them already in Arab hands, was running short. Since the British Army was occupied with its planned evacuation of Palestine, and was anyway firmly enclaved in fortress-like installations in the city centre and in camps, the situation for the besieged Jewish population was desperate.

The situation in the narrow coastal strip was not much better. A makeshift army, based on former underground forces, was fighting desperately to gain control of the small territory which would come into being as Israel, once the British relinquished their hold and left. But thousands of Arabs, both volunteers and regular armies, were waiting on the borders to bolster the local Arab elements already fighting the Jews over every inch of ground of the tiny region. The War of Independence of 1948/49 would be a matter truly of life and death for Israel and Jerusalem, with its religious, historical and emotional connotations for both Jews and Arabs, would become the focal point of that struggle. For the Jews the loss of the city was not to be thought of if the fledgling state was to have any meaning at all. And April 1948 would be a crucial month in the fight for that city.

The Hagana (the Jewish underground army, which would become ZAHAL, the Israel defence forces, one month later) decided to rally all its available forces in the plains and open the lifeline to Jerusalem once and for all. Operation 'Nachshon', as it was called, was launched during the night of 5/6 April with a successful battalion raid against the main Arab headquarters in the Jerusalem area. A number of abandoned British Army camps and two Arab villages were also captured after some sharp battles although one of these, which was too close to the British force guarding the Latrun police station – a vantage point on the Jerusalem road – had to be evacuated, as British armoured cars were threatening to open fire on the attackers. In the end, in spite of the initial success (partly due to a clandestine arms supply airlifted from Czechoslovakia into an ex-RAF airfield), the road to Jerusalem remained closed and was still dominated by the Arabs positioned on the cliffs towering above it.

The situation in the besieged city deteriorated daily and in order to keep up the morale of its inhabitants, the Hagana decided to mount another offensive action, using for the task its crack Palmach troops. The Palmach, or Shock Troops, were raised during the Second World War, when General Erwin Rommel's Afrika Korps was gaining ground fast in Egypt. At that time the British were actually planning to evacuate not only the strategic Canal Zone but also their rear supply zone in Palestine, which would mean abandoning the entire Middle East base of the British Empire. For the small Jewish population, less than half a million in number, this would mean certain death, as the local Arabs, whose population was nearly twice that, joyfully cooperating with Hitler in his aim for a 'Final Solution', were eagerly waiting for Rommel's panzers to arrive in the Holy Land and take over from the hated British. It was only then that, for the first time, the British authorities agreed to allow the creation of a Jewish military force, to train it, and to arm it with light weapons hoping that the Jews could fight a partisan-type warfare against the German occupiers, during which time the British Army would reorganise and, perhaps, return later. However, once Rommel was beaten at El Alamein, the volatile relations between the Jews and the British authorities took another turn for the worse, and the Palmach was forced underground to wait. But the training they had obtained enabled them to become the nucleus and cornerstone of the Israel Defence Forces.

By 1947 a few thousand men and women had been trained as an elite fighting force, highly motivated and full of the desire to fight for Israel. What they did not have, though, was enough, or suitable,

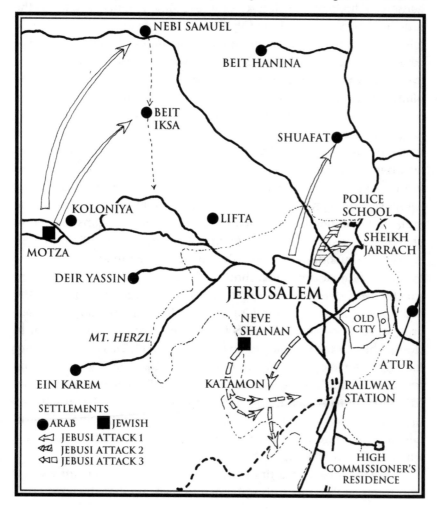

weapons to fight with. The Arabs had plenty of arms, smuggled over the borders under the noses of the British patrols, who were not very vigilant in stopping the flow. For the Jews, it was not so easy. There were strict regulations prohibiting the carrying of arms of any kind, not to mention storing them. Underground caches, usually stored in kibbutzim, were frequently discovered by British forces on surprise search raids and taken away, and the painstaking process of building up another stockpile would begin. The Jews used the utmost ingenuity in thinking up hiding places for their tiny stocks of arms, and the British demonstrated dogged determination in trying to find them. While this cat and mouse game went on, the Arabs' arms inventory was constantly growing.

So in April, 1948, when the Palmach's Harel Brigade ran the gauntlet of fire along the tortuous route leading to Jerusalem, it was the final hope of saving the Holy City. If the Palmach failed, the city would fall and, with it, any dream of an independent Jewish State. Even if the youngsters of the Harel Brigade had known what lay in store for them over the next few weeks, most of them would not have flinched for one minute, knowing the cause for which they were fighting.

Commanding the Harel Brigade was twenty-six-year-old Yitzhak Rabin, already one of the most experienced commanders in the Palmach. It was a brigade in name only. Its two battalions each numbered only a few hundred men, and the entire brigade was just under a thousand – and that included girl soldiers and non-combatants. It was equipped with light weapons only – locally produced Sten submachine guns and a handful of assorted rifles, light machine guns and hand grenades. Some 81mm mortars (with not enough ammunition) were in reserve for support, to be used only if the going got rough.

In contrast, the Arabs had a plentiful supply of ammunition, which flowed in constantly despite the British neutrality. Moreover, the Arabs, natural snipers, familiar with their weapons and with their ground, could outshoot the Jews four times in range, forcing them to close right in if they wanted to do any harm at all. This entailed a very high price for the Jewish forces in every engagement and, during the savage fire fights on the Jerusalem route, the Palmach suffered heavy casualties, units sometimes losing half their members. The result was that Palmach commanders preferred to fight at night, using the darkness as cover, and using their superior eyesight to outfight the Arabs, who fought rather badly in the dark.

Jewish intelligence units, listening in to the British Army's network, learned that the British planned to speed up the scheduled evacuation of Jerusalem, originally set for mid-May, 1948. This placed the Jewish High Command in a serious dilemma. If the reports were true and the British were to evacuate the strategic installations before the Hagana could take them over, then the fate of Jerusalem would be settled finally in favour of the Arabs who, with the consent of the British, had the Arab Legion already standing by to take over. On the other hand, the British withdrawal would give the Jews an opportunity, albeit an uncertain one, to change the situation in Jerusalem for the better.

In order to mount a decisive battle, however, there were not enough forces available in Jerusalem. The only viable force there was a 500-odd infantry battalion, the Moria, short of everything – weapons, ammunition, even food. There were another thousand elderly men, equipped with obsolete rifles and a handful of ammunition, and on the verge of starvation, manning the winding city borders. This was hardly a force which could fight an ongoing offensive battle! Thus the decision was made to bring the Harel Brigade into the city for this onerous task.

The operation, codenamed 'Jebussi', after the biblical name for Jerusalem, was a daring and ambitious one. Two Palmach battalions and the Moria battalion were to mount a series of independent attacks in the Jerusalem area, with three major objectives being defined. The first was to open the route to the Jewish quarters in the north of the city by assaulting an Arab stronghold at Nebi Samuel (named after the prophet who is believed to be buried there), the second to open the route to the besieged Mount Scopus by capturing the Arab district of Sheikh Jarrah and, the third – to link up with the isolated Jewish districts in the south, mainly Mekor Haim which, under total siege for several months, was on the verge of starvation. This last goal was to be achieved by the capture of Katamon, one of the most beautiful and prestigious Arab areas of the city, where the VIPs of the Arab world lived.

The first two attacks went wrong. At Nebi Samuel, the element of surprise was lost and the vanguard company was caught by a well-placed ambush, which held its fire until the Palmach fighters were nearly on it. The company commander was among the first killed; his deputy took over but became disoriented in the dark and a badly organised withdrawal caused havoc among the troops. Thirty men were killed and many more wounded. The battalion commander was too far away to intervene and by the time reinforcements, rushed to the scene by makeshift armoured cars, arrived from a nearby kibbutz, it was too late.

The failure to capture Nebi Samuel was bad enough. But even worse was to come when Rabin's Palmach youngsters attacked the

Sheikh Jarrah quarter two days later. At first everything went well. They managed to capture most of their assigned objectives in a short night attack and settled into a four-storey building dominating the road which led to Mount Scopus. However, as luck would have it this time the British decided to intervene. Brigadier Jones, the British city commandant, had chosen this very route for the oncoming evacuation route and the presence of the Jews was definitely not part of his plans. Soon after midnight an officer appeared and ordered the Palmach commander to withdraw. An English-speaking girl soldier tried to persuade him otherwise, but the captain was not to be moved. The brigadier was not bluffing: at precisely 0600 on the morning of 27 April, a force of the Highland Light Infantry, supported by a troop of Comets from the 4th Royal Tank Regiment and some 25-pounder field guns, started to move into position ready to open fire. The Palmach group decided to call it a day.

In order to accomplish at least something of Operation Jebussi, the Palmach set out to capture Katamon on 29 April. The main objective in the quarter which was spread on a mountain slope was the dominating feature, the Greek Orthodox Monastery of St Simon, which had lately been occupied by a force of Iraqi volunteers who had joined the Arab Liberation Army – some 300 well-armed and trained men. The Palmach's hope was that once the monastery and its compound had been secured, the southern Jewish district would be safe and a wedge driven between Arab-held Jerusalem and the outlying villages in the west. The safest and most convenient approach route towards the monastery was by way of Neve Shaanan and a small Jewish outpost on the northern ridge. The climb would be difficult at night, and the men, heavily loaded with equipment and demolition charges, would have a hard time reaching the jump-off line unobserved. Still, it had to be tried. A first attempt failed against heavy fire, and the attacking force withdrew, with only one single house remaining in their hands, held by a small force.

Next day the 4th Palmach Battalion tried again. It was made up of two infantry companies, the already badly-depleted B Company led by Motke Ben-Porat (there were no military ranks at that time; these came in May, when ZAHAL was officially established). The other company, commanded by the Berlin-born Uri Banner, was in better shape, but it had also suffered considerably during the latest battles, and was tired and spent. It was planned that the attack would be supported by two lone 3-inch mortars, with only enough ammunition to send an opening barrage of a few rounds before the attackers struck. A single armoured car, which had been 'requisitioned' by some resourceful men a few nights before from a British Army garage, was there to give fire support with its two-pounder gun, but the little Humber, impressive though it was to show the flag, would be very limited in an uphill attack; moreover, it had only the ammunition that was in the turret. So the Palmach fighters had not much more than their guts and determination with which to fight.

For the Arab side, in Katamon, things looked much brighter. The quarter was defended by several hundred highly motivated men, one group being partisans of the Grand Mufti, some of them actually trained by elite SS Commandos during the Second World War. Another group was made up of volunteers from the Iraqi and Syrian armies seconded to assist the local Arabs in their campaign against the hated Jews which was planned to start as soon as the British left Palestine. The local commander was a former shepherd, Ibrahim Abu Dayieh, a resolute fighter and natural leader, firmly determined to fight it out to the end. He and his men wanted revenge for a severe blow to their prestige which they had received early in January that year, when a Hagana commando team had blown up their headquarters in the Hotel Semiramis, killing some of their prominent leaders. Abu Dayieh and his men were in fortified positions under the guidance of the Iraqi commander. The solid stone villas of that district were perfect for defence and the Arabs were using them well. Banner and Ben-Porat had a tough nut to crack.

Just before midnight the two-company force assembled at the former British military court building in Rehavia, awaiting the signal to move. They all knew that this was their last try, they were too exhausted to attempt another attack on Jerusalem. Huddled in their torn, flimsy greatcoats, wet from the rain, most of them just teenagers, they listened to their commander's final briefing. They trusted him. A commander in the Palmach held no special privileges; there were no badges of rank, there was no officer's mess to relax in – just the heavy responsibility for your men, who trusted you all the way. They knew that you would be right there with them when the going got rough. The loss rate among Palmach commanders was truly appalling. As an example, Uri Banner's company mounted no less than 65 attacks in three months' fighting in Jerusalem and, when they finally got down from the mountains, only 15 men of the original 200 who went up returned unhurt: 85 were dead, and a hundred in hospital.

Then, suddenly, the order was given and the long column set out, slinging their weapons over their shoulders as they plodded through the soggy ground towards the dark mountain slope ahead. As they climbed the steep, rocky hill, they could see the shadowy silhouette of the massive monastery looming at the top. The lanky figure of 23-year-old Uri Banner led up front, a reassuring sight to the men following him. Banner stopped for a moment and peered into the darkness through his binoculars. All was quiet, but it was a deceptive calm. He knew that the Iraqis were alert, searching the ground for what they knew was coming, although they did not know exactly where. Waving his arm for the men to follow, Banner continued uphill past trees bent by the wind. Some of the men stumbled in the darkness on the rocks which strewed their path, and were helped to their feet by their comrades. As was the tradition in the Palmach, the platoon and section leaders were carrying most of the load. These men were carefully chosen for courage, skill and physique.

The advance was still undetected when Banner's column reached some stone walls about a hundred metres from the monastery wall. Up ahead, eerily gleaming in the dark night, was the cross on top of the slender tower.

The monastery compound consisted of a large stone building surrounded by a stone wall, with two buildings on its southern side, and a green-shuttered, three-storey house to its north, known to house a strong Arab position with heavy machine guns. The compound was surrounded by a large area of brambles, trees and low stone walls, giving excellent scope for counter-attacks, once the monastery itself was taken. Inside the monastery there was a platoon-sized force of Iraqis manning the defences with machine guns and light infantry weapons. In addition, some armoured cars were known to be in reserve somewhere on the hill.

Ibrahim Abu Dayieh was sitting in his headquarters building at Claridges Pension, listening to reports from his superior in the city. At that moment he was a happy man. Just the night before he had managed to beat off an attack on his district without too much effort and he was confident that he could repeat this success if the Jews were foolish enough to try again. The reports he was receiving from Emile Ghory, the overall commander in Jerusalem, were reassuring: the Jews had suffered nothing but reverses in their ambitious Operation Jebussi. Time was running out for them, since soon the Arab Legion would enter the fray and Jerusalem would be Arab. Then, suddenly, a messenger arrived, panting heavily, and gasped that figures had been seen approaching from the valley below the monastery.

Uri Banner looked at his watch: exactly 0200. Two explosions ripped through the pastoral silence and seconds later Motke Ben-Porat's voice could be heard shouting to his company to follow him into the charge. Banner followed their progress with his binoculars. Two buildings were on fire, lighting up the dark night. Ben-Porat's company was less than 80 men strong, and they were coming under withering fire from the buildings and the monastery on top of the hill. Hand grenades exploded and men crumpled to the earth like rag dolls. But the charge went on, troops firing their submachine guns and lobbing grenades. The fire intensified and losses mounted; frantic calls for medics could be heard everywhere. But the battle went on and some of the men disappeared into the burning buildings.

It was now that Banner gave the order to rush up toward the outer gate of the monastery. They managed to reach the outer gate safely – the Arabs were too busy with the other company to observe Banner's approach – and they crouched there, waiting for the demolition team to blow the wall. The fire lit up the scene so that they could see the gate in detail. As another group, led by an officer, rushed through the narrow alley between the monastery and the burning houses, the Arabs saw them and covered the alley with machine gun fire. The officer fell, and one man rushed over to drag him clear, but fell too. The company commander watched in frustration: his natural instinct told him to rush over and help, but he drove the thought out of his mind – his mission was to capture the monastery, and from that aim he must not be deflected. His men, crouching near the wall, nearly went crazy as, for what seemed like an eternity, the Arabs went on firing at the two bodies, which were writhing and jumping from the impact of the bullets as if they were still alive. It was too much for one man to bear and he crawled over to drag the body of his friend away from the firing. The officer had to be left there; it was too risky to drag him too.

Finally the time came when Banner and his men could move. They rushed towards the main gate which fortunately was not under enemy observation. Firing a burst of submachine gun fire into the lock, he pushed the door open. The vanguard stormed into the dark compound, crossed the courtyard and entered the building itself. They advanced from room to room, shooting short bursts and exploding grenades. Here and there some Iraqis fought back, and were killed or wounded. A stairway led up towards the roof and Banner, followed by a few of his party, rushed upstairs, throwing grenades as they came into the open. The battle was a short and bloody one, no prisoners were taken but some of the Iraqi survivors jumped over the stone wall and escaped, the others were killed. It was all over within minutes and Banner began to reorganise his force for the all-round defence of the compound. The company had lost two men killed and several had been wounded, most of them lightly, who, after receiving attention from medics, returned to their posts.

But the situation of Ben-Porat's company was far from good. More than half of the company, which had been small when it started the charge, was dead or wounded and, under cover from Banner's company, the wounded were rushed through the terrifying gauntlet of fire into the monastery building where the medics had set up shop inside one of the rooms, while bullets pinged on the walls.

The deputy battalion commander came in with the last of the wounded and set up a local command post in one of the rooms. There was not much to command with, since all the radios – and there had only been three to start with – were out of action. Two had been shot to pieces and one was out of order, with the signaller working on it. After some time he managed to repair it and a message was sent to the rear that the monastery had been secured, although losses were high. A short briefing session led to the general agreement that the battle would start only in the morning, when the Arabs would counter attack.

The defence was organised accordingly. One platoon, led by Rafael Eitan, a twenty-year-old farmer who had already fought alongside Banner several times, was sent to defend the two burning buildings. The rest of the force was directed by Uri Banner to take up positions inside the monastery compound. The few machine guns, most of which were newly arrived Czech-made, ex-Wehrmacht MG 34 Spandaus, were divided up among all vantage positions. That was all there was to stop an all-out attack by superior forces with mortars and heavy machine guns. It was 0450. There had not been time to rest, and there was nothing to eat, as the men had preferred carrying additional ammunition rather than food, a decision they would regret as hunger and thirst nagged at them.

Abu Dayieh was worried. He had heard during the night that the monastery and nearby buildings had fallen into enemy hands. King Abdullah in Amman received word from his Jerusalem commander, Colonel Abdullah Tel, that Katamon was on the verge of being captured and he pleaded with the king to send his Arab Legion armour to evict the Jews from such a strategic position. But the king hesitated – the British were still in the city and he was not willing to risk a full scale war with the Jews so early. So Tel acted on his own and sent, without authorisation, three armoured cars and a number of Legion soldiers dressed as civilians to answer Abu Dayieh's urgent calls for help. During the night his mortars and machine guns had been pounding the walls and windows of the monastery relentlessly while he got his men ready for their dawn attack. A resourceful leader, he had ordered his men to manhandle four 3-inch mortars on donkeys up the mountain and set them into position to bolster his smaller weapons for the morning attack.

Dawn was breaking as Uri Banner scanned the outer perimeter in the direction of the green-shuttered building a few hundred metres to the north. It was still dark enough to watch the red tracer bullets speeding towards the monastery building; he could even pinpoint the firing positions, but had nothing with which to counter at that range. He looked around, and spotted a small loft in the roof, where he ordered a machine gun crew to take up position.

Around the two burnt out buildings another drama was unfolding. Rafael (known as Raful) Eitan was holding off a small group of Arabs nearing his position. Leading a small party, he raced forward, firing his Sten gun. A nearby gunner with a Spandau had his fingers shot off by a bullet and Raful ran to take over, but was stopped in his tracks by an Arab who was pointing his rifle right at him, for what seemed an eternity. Then both men fired simultaneously: Raful was hit in the head, then one of his men killed the Arab with a short burst, and dragged his leader to safety. Raful was lucky; the wound looked worse than it was and soon, head bandaged, he was back in action. He sat on a stool by a table inside the monastery, firing at the Arabs as they attempted to approach.

On the rooftop, Uri Banner was waiting for the Arabs too while the machine gun in the loft fired away. But mortar shells began to explode on the rooftop, with stones and splinters flying everywhere. The number of wounded was growing constantly, but still they held on. Men who could still walk were bandaged and went back to their positions. Some of the Arabs rushed the gate and Uri Banner, standing behind the stone wall, lobbed hand grenades at them, killing them in droves. No one survived his grenades and made it to the gate.

The first morning attack had been beaten off and the Arabs withdrew. But not for long. Banner took stock of the situation. It was not very encouraging. Two men had been killed in the loft position, the most dangerous in the building, but had been replaced. All they could do was hold on for the next attack. It was not long in coming. An hour later, two hundred Arab villagers, led by their 21-year-old sheikh, charged again. Among the cypress trees and brambles around the monastery they fell and lay motionless, patches of blue, red and white of their kaffiyes attesting to the high price that Banner's men were exacting. But still they came. Inside the monastery there was not a single safe place. Due to the windows being placed high in the stone walls, the defenders had to drag tables and other furniture to the walls, on which they stood in order to shoot from the window sills. The Arab snipers were extremely good and, as soon as they detected a gun appearing on a window sill, they shot at point blank range, with deadly effect. As the morning advanced more and more defenders died until almost 70 percent of the force were casualties. The stench inside the cramped rooms was horrible. Men lay on the floor, wounded and dead mingled together. Some of the more lightly wounded struggled to their feet to join the dwindling force, which was near exhaustion by noon. Reserves could not be sent; they were occupied elsewhere.

Just as it seemed that things could not get worse, the Arab armoured cars appeared. Uri Banner, who had just beaten off another attack, handed over to one of his deputies on the roof and rushed over to the platoon besieged in the burnt out houses on the other side of the alley. Realising that much of the enemy fire came from a nearby armoured car, he ordered smoke grenades to be thrown in front of the car and, under cover of the smoke, he crawled over into the doorway of one of the houses. He and the platoon commander who had replaced Raful decided that they had to blow up the armoured car, and this was done by a courageous demolition party which crawled right under it to place their charges!

But the situation in the monastery was now desperate. A decision had to be taken either to withdraw or to fight to the end, and the commanders realised that it would be impossible to evacuate so many wounded under fire – there simply were not enough men left standing to carry them and to fight the retreat. As they discussed the impossible options, a lookout on the roof shouted that another attack was about to be made from the house with the green shutters. Banner ran out and called one of his few remaining platoon commanders to take some of his men to a stone wall outside the fence and set an ambush to catch the attackers from the flank. He himself rushed back to his position on the roof to give his men fire cover. David Elazar, a youngster born in

Yugoslavia, led his men to the stone wall and signalled Banner that he was in position.

A few minutes later the first onrush of Arabs came. They shouted wildly as they charged right towards the building, little knowing what awaited them from the flank. As they came within range Elazar and his men opened fire from close range and the Arabs fell in scores, some of them spreadeagled against the very wall behind which Elazar's men crouched. Others retreated in terror. Those who made it to the gate were blown to pieces by Banner's grenades. Another charge had been beaten off.

By now even the courageous Abu Dayieh had reached the end of his resources. He had lost hundreds of his men and the desperate cries of the wounded still trapped inside the cypress grove was heartrending, but no one dared to go and fetch them out, or even tend to them. He picked up his telephone and, sobbing over the line, told his superior that he could no longer hold out; with only a handful of men still unwounded, the battle for Katamon was lost. Emile Ghory, who had Colonel Tel with him in the room, tried to calm him and told him that several armoured cars were on their way to help him out. But the little shepherd would no longer listen to promises. So far he had held out alone, and he had done more than was humanly possible. Since dawn, his men had mounted no less than six all-out charges against the monastery. He could do no more.

Inside the monastery, hope was fading. The radio had broken down again, there was no contact with the outside world and the commanders resigned themselves to die with their men here. On no account would they leave the wounded behind at the mercy of the Arabs. They knew they would not take prisoners. The demolition party was ordered to lay their remaining charges around the room in which the wounded lay. Each man who could still hold one requested, and was given, a hand grenade to blow himself up if the monastery was taken.

Then, at the last minute, the radio came to life again. The deputy commander was called to the set – and told that the Arabs were withdrawing! This report resulted from an intelligence radio monitor who had been party to the frantic conversation between Abu Dayieh and Emile Ghory, as well as a lookout on the water tower of Mekor Haim who had seen Arabs coming back down the slopes. This was the first good news that the besieged defenders of St Simon Monastery had had for sixteen terrible hours.

As the day was ending, the first reinforcements came in, followed later by a convoy of armoured cars, which managed to lumber uphill and start taking off the wounded. Of the 150 who had defended the monastery, including two girls, less than 30 could stand on their feet as they started downhill that evening. But their terrible ordeal had ended and they were safe, for the moment at least – but not for long. Several more months of continuous fighting was in store for many of them, and only a handful would live to see the end of the war.

For Jerusalem, at least, the capture of Katamon was a joyful occasion. The besieged quarters were safe and Jerusalem reunited. But, with the evacuation of the British in May that same year and the entrance of two brigades of fully equipped Jordanian Arab Legion troops, the city was once more divided and it was only in 1967, when the Israel Defence Force paratroops of Colonel Motta Gur captured the Old City, that Jerusalem became one again.

Several survivors of the St Simon drama rose to high rank in the IDF. Raful Eitan and David Elazar both served as chief of staff, while Uri Banner later became a brigadier, commanding armoured brigades in two wars, in 1956 capturing central Sinai with the crack 7th Armoured Brigade and in 1967, in a reserve armoured brigade – by chance the successor of the Palmach's Harel Brigade, he was not only to capture the notorious Radar position, but would also help capture Jerusalem from the north, assisting Gur's paratroopers on Ammunition Hill. But that is another story...

CHAPTER TWENTY-ONE

THE WIRE CUTTERS IN ACTION

One of the most unusual air combat missions ever performed took place in the Middle East, shortly before the 1956 Sinai Campaign.

This top secret assignment started with a simple little telegram sent during the summer of 1956 to the Israel Defence Forces Engineering Department. But its contents sent the department into a whirlwind of enquiries and a frenzy of activity. It contained instructions to tear down Egyptian telephone lines in the Sinai Peninsula from the air to disrupt Egyptian communications in the event of war. It soon became clear that the telephone lines in question consisted of five copper cables strung between posts five metres apart – not exactly the Israeli standard. It was also apparent that the aircraft to be used must be very reliable, fast and able to remain steady at extremely low levels. The obvious choice at the time was the P-51 Mustang, the 'Wild Horses' squadron, which had been in service since the end of 1948 when it flew its first operational sortie with the fledgling IAF. An operational test facility, consisting of four telephone poles with copper cables strung between them, was soon established at an abandoned airfield near Quastina in the northern Negev desert. Curious civilians working in the fields nearby were told that the Postal Authority was trying out new automatic dialling systems!

Meanwhile, strange things were occurring in other places too. Israel's Ekron air base was witness to a most peculiar scene one day. A pick-up truck loaded with a considerable length of thick cable was moving slowly up to the end of the runway. Two men in stained work clothes took this cable, attached it to the truck's double hook and stretched it along the tarmac. Then the truck zoomed at high speed down the runway, the cable twisting and whipping behind it like a live thing. The officers watching were satisfied.

The next trial was in the air. One Mustang, mounting a specially designed cable-cutting device, took off with a fairly worried man – the squadron's senior pilot – at the controls. The aeroplane headed for the test facility, trailing the cable and its studded weight behind. The plan was to cut the copper cable by sheer weight as the airborne cable wound itself, it was hoped, over the telephone wires between the poles. On the first trial run the Mustang pilot headed for the gap between the poles at a speed of 200mph, barely skimming the ground at 60 feet. It seemed to the spectators that, even at that low level, the plane was flying too high; and, in fact, the airborne cable leapt over the telephone lines instead of tearing through them. Another pass followed, even lower, and this time the cable tore through the copper lines like a knife through butter. The officers on the ground were jubilant, but the pilot, climbing sharply to gain altitude, had little time to be proud of his manoeuvre. He realised that the cable had been detached from its hook by the shock of impact. Clearly something would have to be done about this, otherwise each wire cutter would have only one go at the target when flying the actual operation! The engineering department, however, were not entirely discouraged by the results of the test run, despite the detached cable; they were gratified to see that the basic concept actually worked. The necessary modifications soon followed and by early October the squadron was ready for action.

On Saturday, 27 October 1956 Squadron Leader Zachik Livne was called to a squadron leaders' briefing at Air Force HQ. All senior commanders were present as the Air Force chief, General Dan Tolkovski, issued his orders. Livne now heard for the first time that a member of his own squadron had been practising the art of wire cutting for several months, so well had the secret been kept! He realised that more than one of his aircraft would be flying these missions deep inside Sinai behind the enemy lines.

While the squadron leader was attending the briefing his deputy, Captain Harry Krassenstein, had not been idle. He and several pilots were on their way to another Mustang squadron, a conversion unit at Ramat David Air Force base in the north of Israel, to see if they could 'borrow' a few aircraft. This, however, turned out to be unnecessary: Air Force HQ had already ordered the new Mustangs to be flown to Livne's squadron, and they arrived right on time.

An intensive training programme now took place to familiarise the other pilots with the new technique, and soon the test facility was swarming with activity – generally unsuccessful, unfortunately, as most of the pilots trailing the cutter cable for the first time tore the hooks on their first pass, losing the cable, some lost the cable by contact with the ground as they approached the poles, while even those who managed to cut through the copper wires lost their cables afterwards. Something had to be done – and fast. An order was issued to manufacture ten new cables, each strung with 25 lead weights. In order to carry out this task, however, the engineers had to find some lead, not an easy task in Israel at that time. After they visited several junk dealers all over the country, the lead was found in an abandoned ex-British surplus dump and rushed to the IAF depot.

After several days of nerve-racking waiting, the day for action finally arrived: 29 October 1956 – a fateful date. The day before, four pilots scheduled to take part in the line-cutting operation were summoned to a special briefing. There, in top secret conditions, they were informed that within 24 hours Israel would be at war with Egypt and their mission would be the first and one of the most decisive for the success of the entire campaign. While the airborne drop at Mitla was taking place, the 'Wild Horses' would take out the Egyptian telephone communications along the main routes in the peninsula thus, hopefully, cutting off the command and control infrastructure during its most critical period.

While the ground crews worked feverishly to prepare the aircraft, fitting the cables and testing the other devices, the pilots underwent a detailed briefing. The line-cutting teams were finally selected on the morning of 29 October. Two pairs of Mustangs would go first. Major Zachik Livne would lead his wingman, Lieutenant Hasson Amitai, nicknamed 'Rabbit', while the second pair, led by Captain Harry Krassen-stein with Arie Zeitlin as his wingman, would follow. Krassenstein, a veteran pilot sporting a great RAF-type moustache, was to be called later 'Harry the cutter' by those in the know as a result of his exploits in this action. To many people this name was something of an enigma, as the mission was kept secret even in the IAF, which in itself was quite an achievement!

The four pilots were carefully briefed with the latest intelligence updates. They were to fly towards their target areas at 100 feet – high enough to avoid dragging their airborne cables on the ground, but low enough to avoid being spotted by the Egyptian radars. One pair was assigned to a target some ten kilometres east of Suez city, and the other to a spot 30 kilometres east of the Mitla Pass, the objective of the Israeli airborne drop. Navigation would be through the configuration of the shaped desert hills, easily recognisable from the altitude at which they were flying, so full radio silence would be observed.

Shortly after briefing, the four aircraft were instructed to take off. Each pilot was issued the standard IAF survival kit: a service revolver, a Mae West life jacket, a heliograph and combat rations. All documents except their international pilot's licence were left behind. The pilots strode to their aircraft, mentally preparing themselves for their first combat operation of the war; tension mounted, but dissolved into laughter when they tried to settle into their cramped cockpits, only to discover that the water-filled seat cushions, designed to block the shock of the cable impact, had heated up in the sunlight and were nearly at boiling point!

After cooling down, the pilots started their engines and rolled to the checkpoint. There they were met by a truck bearing the cutter cables. Two teams now attached the cables to each aircraft's hooks and, when they were secure, signalled the leader, who gave the thumbs up sign and took off. As the first pair raced down the runway and lifted into the air, the cables tossed and twisted behind, but there were no problems. Now it was Harry's turn. Down the runway he roared, engine at full take-off power but, as he lifted off, he was astonished to find that the cable had torn off and remained on the runway. Making as tight a turn as he was able, he landed alongside his cable and it was re-attached; this time he made it safely off the ground trailing his cable behind. As the second pair thundered down the runway, the pilots could see on the far side of the airfield the paratroopers assembling near their transport planes, ready for their battle jump. It looked as if the war was really on.

Major Livne and his wingman parted from Harry Krassenstein and his partner, each pair flying to their designated target. It would be a steaming hot flight for the next 150 minutes, far away from home, with no hope of rescue were they forced to land in the barren, lifeless desert. But the leaders had no time to worry about their own welfare; they were too busy worrying about finding ground sights to point the way and keeping their precious cables trailing behind.

The ground streamed away under the Mustangs. Harry flashed the thumbs-up signal to his wingman, who responded in kind – both cables still intact, they nodded to each other. The pair was now cruising at some 200mph, slowed by the trailing cables to 50mph below the Mustang's normal air speed. Suddenly Harry waggled his wings and pointed to Zeitlin's plane: the cable had snapped clear! Their chances of success had been literally cut in half, but there was no time to go back; they were already deep inside Sinai. Nearing their assigned destination, the pair climbed to 3,000 feet, skimming along the stream-beds between the hilltops. Suddenly the landscape opened up as if by magic and the plains of the Suez Canal spread out below them, with the Gulf gleaming in the sunshine 20 kilometres away. But there was little time to enjoy the scenery; the two Mustangs dropped down to a bare 100 feet.

Within minutes their target was below them. They were in the heart of enemy territory, hundreds of kilometres from home and only minutes from three Egyptian air bases, well stocked with Russian MiGs and their alert pilots. But now the telephone poles were in sight, virtually inviting the pilots to have a go. As his wingman had lost his cable, Harry was determined to do the job by himself. As he approached the target from the north-east it was nearly sunset, and the setting sun nearly blinded the pilot as he flew right into the glare. Signalling Zeitlin to follow him in, Harry went into a trial run to identify the exact spot where he would start cutting. Then, climbing sharply, he returned and dived into his attack pass. The telephone poles seemed to rush up at him faster and faster as the Mustang gathered speed. As he dived straight into the sun's glare, he could hardly see the poles, but kept his line of flight, then headed sharply right into the gap between them. He thought that he was low enough as he tore through, but soon realised that his cable had torn off. Now neither of the pilots had a cable and, as Harry passed low over the gap between the poles, he could see that the copper wires were still intact. It looked hopeless, but Harry was not a man to give up easily. Neither was his wingman. Glancing at each other, the two pilots read each other's thoughts. Both were recalling an

210

incident which had made the rounds in the IAF some months before, when a Stearman from the flight school had inadvertently passed too close to some electricity high-tension cables, cutting through them with its propeller. The Stearman had landed safely, but the entire area had an electricity blackout. Now, Harry thought to himself, what an old junk heap of a Stearman could do, a wild horse like the Mustang could certainly do better! So, waggling his wings, the leader swooped down once again and headed for the telephone line, took aim, and attacked, with Zeitlin right alongside to watch how it turned out. But, as he rushed for the cables at 200mph, instinct took over and, instead of tearing through the lines, at the last moment the Mustang jerked up and sailed overhead. Refusing to give up, however, Harry went in for another pass: this time he stayed low and, using his propeller as a pair of pliers, cut right through the cables, the copper strings spraying his windshield with a fine fog of metal. He felt a slight jolt, but that was all.

Not wanting to be outdone by his leader, Zeitlin gritted his teeth and went in for his own ride. Picking a spot between two poles to the south of the gap created by Harry, Zeitlin quickly duplicated his feat. As they turned and headed for their next assignment, the pilots could see the cut copper lines lying on the ground. As they flew off to cut the wires some kilometres to the north, they already felt like old hands, cutting the cables to ribbons. Any fears the pair might have had as to possible engine failure or other damage proved groundless: the engines roared on comfortingly and the propeller discs gleamed bright in the setting sun. After their unorthodox, to say the least, combat mission, the return flight was virtually uneventful and, when they landed at Ekron air base, the Mustangs were still functioning perfectly.

The other pair, Zachik and Amitai, for their part passed over the crack 7th Armoured Brigade deployed near the Egyptian border, continuing their flight for a further 45 minutes to the eastern end of the Mitla pass where they spotted their target exactly as planned. Zachik immediately dropped to less than 100 feet, a manoeuvre which proved fatal to both their line-cutting devices. First Zachik and then Rabbit felt the shock of impact as their cables hit the ground and tore off. The leader had misjudged the ground altitude. But they too remembered the Stearman incident, and decided to have a go with the propellers. Just like the first pair, on their first pass they instinctively lifted the planes at the last moment as they passed the wires. That would not do. So they tried again, forcing their fighters as low as they dared without touching the ground – and roared over the desert sand glimmering in the evening sun, tearing right through the wires. Only a slight jolt was felt as the wires snapped. Another three passes followed, and that part of their mission was completed. But there was another area to be attacked. Passing west of Temed, they reached their last assignment. This time it was young Rabbit who tried out one of his own ideas. Signalling his leader to let him go, he aimed for the gap between the two poles and, at the last minute, swung on one wing, going right for the wires! But he was too low and, as the major watched anxiously, he saw his wingman go right *under* the wires like a crop duster. Then he went in for another try: dipping his wings as he went, this time he cut right through the copper wires with no effort at all. Later, on his return to base, the fitters were shocked to hear what Amitai had done, but apart from a few marks there was no evidence of any substantial damage – the Mustang proved to be a much more reliable aeroplane than its designers at North American had imagined when they produced the airframe.

Mission fulfilled, the second pair set course for home as it was getting dark. The Sinai Campaign was on and, as they flew north, they could see the Dakotas with the paratroopers already beginning their jumps.

The cutting of the telephone communications seems to have been very successful and the Egyptian command system was disrupted, although not entirely. The Egyptian commanders switched to alternative circuits and radio communications as soon as they realised that their land-lines had been cut, and could be heard passing messages by the Israeli intelligence monitors. Still, some precious time was gained, as the paratroops were landed without mishap before nightfall.

For Major Livne and his squadron pilots, the war had only begun. Over the next few days they roamed over the Sinai front, flying countless combat missions against a growing danger from extremely accurate enemy ground fire. Shlomo Gilbert, one of the Mustang pilots, was the first man to destroy an Egyptian tank. Flying with a wingman nicknamed 'Cheetah', he spotted a tank down below, and was just making a pass to fire on it when Cheetah spotted an enemy anti-aircraft gun firing at them from a nearby sand dune, and swooped down at the same time. One second, and both tank and gun were knocked out by accurate shots, while close by an ammunition truck exploded into a ball of fire. The force of the explosion, however, threw Cheetah's Mustang off course, almost into collision with Gilbert, who managed to veer away at the last minute thanks to his training and the speed of his reflexes. Having recovered from the shock, they flew off to find some more targets – and there were many.

Others, however, were not so lucky that day. One Mustang made a forced landing near Bir Hamma on the central high road; its pilot had to hide in some desert scrub until he was rescued by a daring Piper Cub pilot who landed beside him. One man was killed when his Mustang crashed, hit by ground fire.

The next morning the Wild Horses were back on the job. But by now the Egyptian anti-aircraft gunners were on full alert and, moreover, they knew where to aim. The Mustang's wide radiator and glycol hoses were perfect targets for the Egyptians' automatic cannon and, without a cooling system operating, the Mustang was dead meat in the hot desert climate. Both Gilbert and Cheetah were shot down in this way in central Sinai. While the latter managed to land his aircraft out of harm's way, Gilbert was unlucky; he had to force land right in the middle of a fierce armoured battle. While the rest of the Mustang formation cruised overhead, trying to keep off the Egyptian tanks, an Israeli command car daringly burst into the area and rescued the wounded pilot. To round off that gloomy day, one pilot limped home, his Mustang collapsing as it came in to land on the runway.

Throughout the entire Sinai Campaign, the Mustang squadron proved most effective in flying close support missions to the ground forces operating in the desert. But the price was high. Being relatively unstable aircraft, their propeller-driven platform made them much less suitable for accurate firing than the new jets which had entered service shortly before the war. Nevertheless, their pilots proved their resourcefulness and devised some unique combat tactics which won the day for them in spite of the nearly obsolete fighters they flew.

After the Sinai Campaign ended, the Wild Horse Squadron lost its remaining Mustangs and re-equipped with jets. But the venerable Mustang has its place in the historical flight of the IAF Museum, where it retains a place of honour.

CHAPTER TWENTY-TWO

COMPANY 'C' AGAINST THE EGYPTIAN MARINES

Yom Kippur (the Day of Atonement) is the holiest day of the year for Jews all over the world – a day of fasting, prayer, reflecting on one's sins and how to atone for them. On that day in 1973 – 6 October, the Egyptian army managed to surprise the Israelis completely. Five Egyptian divisions crossed the 200-metre wide Suez Canal, and gained a substantial foothold in bridgeheads on the eastern bank along a 160-kilometre line stretching from the Mediterranean Sea to Suez City. By the time the Israelis, hastily recalled from their synagogues, managed to assemble, it was almost too late. Israeli efforts to dislodge the Egyptians by armoured counter attacks and near suicidal air strikes failed, due in part to the Egyptians' superb handling of modern missiles, which caused severe casualties to the Israeli soldiers.

What follows is a little-known story illustrating the dedication and courage of a company of Israeli tank crews who tried to stem the onrush of an entire Egyptian marine brigade which had crossed the Canal and was now trying to break through to the strategic mountain passes of Gidi and Mitla, both of them only lightly defended at that time.

The Egyptian 130th Amphibious Brigade, commanded by Colonel Mahmoud Shoeib, was considered a crack unit. Its 1,000 men were a selected and highly trained group, well-motivated, and longing to strike a serious blow at their Israeli enemies. Organised into two reinforced commando battalion groups equipped with Soviet PT76 light amphibious tanks, BTR50 or OT62 armoured troop carriers, Sagger-mount BRDM and supporting artillery and mortar carriers, the brigade crossed the Great Bitter Lake at 0155 on 6 October. They landed approximately seven kilometres north of an Israeli stronghold codenamed 'Lituf' where the occupants, reserve soldiers of the Jerusalem Brigade, were praying. The Egyptian attack came as a great surprise. Although some warnings had been issued of Egyptian troop concentrations, the sector commander had thought that the Egyptians would content themselves with a fire assault, such as occasionally occurred during periods of high tension in that area.

As soon as the 130th came ashore on the eastern bank, Battalion Group B led by Major Abdul Azziz immediately moved to secure an important junction, known as 'Lexicon', on the coastal road, with the task of blocking the Israeli reinforcements who, it was expected, would soon come rushing down. Situated on that junction, which led towards the Gidi Pass, was a small Israeli position, codenamed 'Mitzva' (good deed). Although in no position to stop an armoured onslaught, its mission was to delay and hold until a troop of tanks could reach it.

Major Azziz was scanning the desert for the dust clouds which would announce the approach of Israeli tanks, when he saw the telltale signs coming right at him. Setting up an anti-tank missile barrier behind a sand dune just off the junction, he sent one of his forces south to make contact with the Israelis' 'Lituf' stronghold on the lake side.

Colonel Amnon Reshef, head of the Israeli 14th Armoured Brigade, in charge of defending the sector, had received news of the attack and, although it was still scanty, had alerted Captain Boaz Amir's tank company and sent him off to the junction to engage the enemy. Neither Amir nor the colonel could imagine the scope of the enemy attack, but there were in any case no larger forces that could be spared, as Reshef's small brigade was already heavily engaged all over the Canal front, numerous crises having broken out which he had to deal with simultaneously. Captain Amir's company consisted of eleven M48A5 Patton tanks armed with the 105mm tank gun.

The tanks did not have far to go – they were soon in battle with Major Azziz's Battalion Group B placed on the junction. Amir was young, but he was a well-trained tank officer, and he approached carefully, setting up a good position behind a small sand ridge east of 'Lexicon'. Looking through his binoculars he could see the Egyptian force deploying on the junction, under small arms and mortar fire from the nearby 'Mitzva' position, while another force was seen going south towards 'Lituf'. Amir decided to wait until the enemy force came into minimum range, where every shot would be a certain kill. Most of his men had not fired against a moving enemy target in anger, and Amir wanted to ensure that their first firefight would be a success and boost their morale.

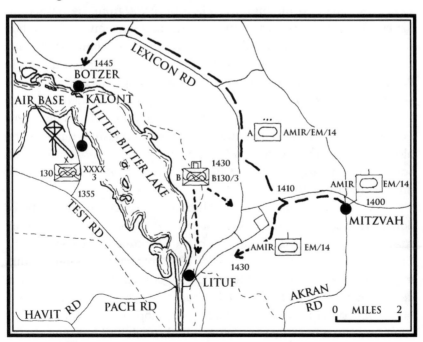

215

Although Major Azziz had seen the dust cloud raised by the Israeli tanks, he had missed their actual approach due to a dip in the ground, so he decided to push on to a ridge he could see ahead of him, unaware that that was exactly where Captain Amir had set up his own tanks in hull down position, ready to fire. Battalion Group B, therefore, advanced in battle formation to a mere 40 metres, when the Pattons opened up with deadly point blank fire, penetrating the lightly armoured PT-76s and APCs. Within seconds Azziz's force lost some 25 vehicles, some of his men burned to death inside their flaming coffins, others rushing wildly for cover. Two Pattons were hit by Saggers from the Battalion's anti-tank barrier, but these in turn came under light mortar fire from soldiers at 'Mitzva' in the flank. Major Azziz was in a crisis and informed his colonel of his plight. He was ordered to withdraw to the water line where the first elements of Brigadier Ahmad Badawi's 8th Mechanised Infantry Brigade was coming into the bridgehead. This left 'Lituf' still under threat from the force sent earlier, which had not encountered any serious opposition on its way south.

While Azziz was engaged at the 'Lexicon' crossroads, Battalion Group A, commanded by Major Ibrahim Salem, bypassed the dangerous area and started to advance towards the Gidi and Mitla Passes. With Group B evidently stalled, it would now be up to the young major to get the forces on the move. Leading from the front, he pushed his forces on – until they reached the eastern road junction, where he had to make an important decision: to move ahead straight for the Gidi Pass, or to turn south and head for the much more important Mitla Pass, known to contain the underground headquarters of the Israeli Southern Command. Salem went for the big prize, and ordered his men to turn south-east – a decision which he would rue before long. However, at 1600 hours, sitting on top of his command vehicle and bowling along towards Mitla, with the wind blowing in his face, Major Ibrahim Salem was a happy man, confident that his force could beat any enemy put up against them.

At the same time, nine Centurions of 'C' Company lumbered down the desert road towards the Suez Canal. Their aim: to join their comrades, beleaguered in outposts along the canal. The crews of the Centurions were mostly eighteen-year-olds, only two weeks out of training; they listened attentively to the orders of their company commander, a 'veteran' – a lieutenant all of twenty-one years old, named Gadi.

Directing his tanks over the radio to stop engines, the company commander scanned the area before him through his binoculars. In the rapidly fading light, the setting sun in his eyes, he could just about see the thin line of the canal in the hazy distance, a dark stripe running through the sand-coloured immensity of the desert. Lieutenant Gadi had spent most of his three years in the army in Sinai and knew the terrain by heart. Now, the first time he was to be in a real fight after years of training, he was raring to go into action. 'Stations Gadi – start engines and follow me', he said into his microphone and, standing erect in his turret, waved his arm.

The tanks trundled off again, raising clouds of dust as they moved along. As they reached the familiar pass, darkness was almost complete, the fiery sun having long since set in the west over Africa; only a glimmer of blue light remaining in the evening sky. A few minutes after clearing the defile which towered over the tanks on both sides, Yefim, the Yemenite gunner of the second tank, squinted through his periscope at an amazing sight. The dark blue sky was streaked with orange and red – an awesome display of fireworks. Although he could not hear the noise of battle over the throbbing roar of the tank's engine, Yefim gazed in fascination at the lit-up sky, entranced by the sheer beauty as the shells, rockets and Katyushas crisscrossed his field of vision. Then, coming back to earth, he checked out his own equipment as the tank sped forward to join the battle.

At approximately 1700, with darkness already setting in, Major Salem stopped to survey the scene ahead. Before him he could just make out in the distance the mountain ridge of the Mitla Pass, and his excitement rose as he scanned the region through his night glasses. But suddenly he saw a cloud of dust, a few kilometres away – it must be the Israeli reinforcements driving straight at him! In fact, shortly before, Israeli observation posts established on the mountain had detected Salem's advance and had switched onto Lieutenant Gadi's radio channel, urging him to take care, as his present route would take him right up to a still unidentified enemy force.

Battalion Group A was now about fourteen kilometres from the shore of the lake, as the major saw by shining his hooded torch on his map and he waited, excited but confident, for the Israelis to come. Now they would get some of their own medicine!

Company 'C' was charging along the desert road in the darkness. Gadi, who had led his Centurions many times over this ground, knew every copse and rock as he passed the familiar signs. But just as he was rounding a bend in the road, it happened...

Suddenly, without warning, the darkness exploded around them. The Egyptians had fired parachute flares, illuminating the oncoming Centurions which they had located with the aid of night vision equipment. The Israeli tanks stood out clearly in the bright light which engulfed them. Reacting swiftly, Gadi ordered his tanks to spread out and take cover behind the sand dunes. He scanned the front, searching for enemy positions ahead. Satisfied that all was still clear he ordered his tanks to advance again, though cautioning the commanders to remain on full alert.

The company rolled on; the long drive, added to the monotony of the noise, heat and dust, lulled the senses of the young crewmen. Suddenly the voice of their company commander roused them from their half doze: 'Alert! Fire coaxial machine guns to the right – bazooka teams sighted!' Nine tank turrets traversed immediately; eighteen pairs of eyes locked onto the sights, as commanders and gunners scanned the night. Company 'C' had gone to war!

The loader of the second tank was named Chuck, a fairly unusual name for an Israeli, but he had been born in America and had only recently come to Israel. Slamming a 105mm round into the chamber, he waited until the breech slammed closed then, as he heard the clang, he tapped Yefim's shoulder, signalling that the round was loaded. Next he checked the long cartridge belts of the machine guns, making sure that the guns were loaded and secured. Satisfied that all was in order, Chuck waited for Yefim to fire. Seconds later a deafening noise, a suffocating stench of cordite and a painfully bright flash assailed the crew's senses as the HESH round left Yefim's large gun barrel to smash into an Egyptian tank killer team huddling behind a sand dune not far away.

Major Salem tried to direct his men, dispersed over the rocky ground attempting to find some cover from the Israeli fire. His Sagger crews were doing well, he thought, better than he had expected. But through the roar of battle the anguished cries of wounded men could be heard, and there was little that he could do – his medical teams were far behind and he hesitated to call them forward into this cauldron of fire.

Lieutenant Gadi had not realised how big the force was that he was facing until the clash began, but had he known that he was facing the forward elements of an entire Egyptian battalion, he would have pressed on anyway. His training had made him confident, in fact quite cockily sure that he and his tank crews could take on anything. He was itching to move on and push through the opposition, whatever the cost.

Major Salem had now managed to establish contact with his rear elements and called for artillery to harass the enemy position behind the dune. The call was acknowledged, and the captain in charge of the mortar section radioed that the first rounds were on their way...

Once more the order was given for the Israeli tanks to follow their leader and the tanks, engines roaring, set out along the dusty road. Minutes later a sudden shriek and thunder heralded heavy artillery coming in. The tank commanders scrambled down from their open hatch positions into the turrets, slamming the steel covers shut, and squinted through the narrow slits of the periscopes. It was claustrophobic for the tank commanders working with closed hatches, and it also impeded their vision, but many casualties had been suffered in previous wars by crew members working with open hatches, and strict orders had been issued to fight with hatches closed under artillery fire.

The Egyptian artillery, accurately directed by concealed forward observers, quickly found the correct range to the Israeli tanks and pounded them with hundreds of shells, whose explosion added to the din. 'Keep moving!' shouted the company commander over the radio, knowing that a stationary tank was a dead tank and only mobility could save them by making them a more difficult target. The inexperienced, frightened crewmen gained confidence from the calm voice of their commander, rallied, and took up their task with renewed courage.

As the evening progressed Colonel Shoeib, commander of the 130th, became more and more concerned. His brigade was widely deployed and fully engaged on two separate fronts, and he mistakenly assumed that Major Salem's force was fighting against vastly superior forces. He contacted Salem over the radio – although communications were difficult – and tried to tell him that he was too far east and in danger of being cut off from the rear. What neither the colonel nor Salem knew was that the main force was still bogged down far back, with only a small element which included the supporting artillery anywhere within striking range of his forward position. Salem, listening to his colonel's voice rising and fading over the static, became extremely concerned. He did not know that he was actually engaged by a mere company-sized force, and Lieutenant Gadi, who was firing continuous gun salvoes from his tanks, did not make it any easier for the Egyptian officer to understand.

A little later Colonel Shoeib became even more concerned about his brigade's situation. Frantic calls were coming in from Major Azziz's Battalion Group, hotly engaged with Amir's Pattons, which had now been reinforced from the rear and were pushing the Egyptians back towards the lake. The forces confronting the Israeli positions at 'Mitzva' and 'Lituf' were also hard pressed, and the colonel ordered a withdrawal to the bridgehead on the lakeside, where he hoped his rear headquarters staff would by now have arranged for resupply, especially of fuel and ammunition, which were now running dangerously low. The fuel situation was very bad: many vehicles had spent their reserves in crossing the water and ever since had been unable to shut down their engines even when stationary. During the withdrawal, lack of fuel forced several tank and APC crews to abandon their vehicles still intact!

Major Salem also decided to disengage. He ordered his artillery to send one final barrage onto the Israelis, and withdrew. The drivers made their way back to the bridgehead, where guides waited to signal them onto the lateral road. So far, so good, but the silence was short-lived.

By midnight the shelling had died down somewhat and the Centurion crews, now familiar with the noise of battle, began to relax. The tank commanders, cautiously opening their hatches, peered out and realised that they had actually reached the canal. On the company commander's orders the nine tanks climbed to hull-down positions, prior to shooting at the Egyptians on the far side of the waterway. As Yefim caught the first glimpse of the view in his sight, he shouted 'Stop!' and Boaz, the driver, slammed on the brakes, enabling Yefim to open fire from the lowest position possible, while still giving the tank maximum cover by presenting the lowest profile to the Egyptian tank crews positioned on the far side on elevated ramps. Sergeant Yaron, the tank commander, traversed the gunsight with his dual control lever, then ordered Yefim to fire an armour piercing round on a tank which was just visible on the brightly illuminated sand dune some 400 metres away. With split second precision, Chuck loaded the gun, the breech clanged shut and Yefim pressed the firing pedal, sending the high velocity round on its way. A second later an Egyptian tank was set ablaze, the flames shooting up into the night sky.

The situation of 130th Amphibious Brigade was getting more and more serious as the night went on. Colonel Shoeib had several problems to solve at once as he deployed the dwindling forces at his disposal which had come into the bridgehead. He had no contact with any other Egyptian forces either to the north or south, his position alongside the lake being extremely isolated. He was completely alone. Sporadic fire was coming from all directions and radio contact with his logistical base on the western shore was erratic at best. Only a few boats came in, one at a time, with supplies which were insufficient for his needs. But he was determined to hold on and fight off the Israeli counter attack, which he was sure would come – and soon!

Soon after midnight a sharp battle began to rage as his forward elements fought off what seemed to him a determined tank attack from the Mitla road. The colonel's orders were swift and clear: fire with all available weapons... The Egyptians acted fast and decisively. Infantry tank killer teams were hiding out in the sand dunes. One of these, carrying Sagger anti-tank missiles, approached, unseen as they crept behind the elevated ramparts. The Israelis' attention was elsewhere – the enemy artillery had started its barrage again, sending the tank commanders into their turrets; two Israeli tanks were hit by exploding shells, but only minor damage occurred. But all the while the Egyptian Sagger team was setting up its deadly weapons, under cover behind a small copse which hid them from view. Their operator launched his first missile from about 1,000 metres, and Yaron's tank was hit below the turret ring. Flames started blazing from the rear deck. Calmly, the Israeli tank commander told the driver to stop and carry out fire extinguishing drill, as in training, but despite the drill the fire took hold and soon got out of control. The damaged tank was now a sitting duck, clearly visible, and the Egyptian gunners began to direct tremendous fire at it. The crew bailed out, one man being slightly hit by a stray bullet as he clambered out over the hull. A passing tank stopped and picked them up and, as the men crowded into the already packed interior of the fighting compartment, they did their best to stay out of the way of their 'hosts', who went on with their tasks of driving and firing. The stench became almost unbearable – the cordite fumes nearly suffocating the men in their cramped surroundings. They were getting very tired now, and the tank commander, in spite of the risk, opened his upper hatch to let in some welcome fresh air.

Suddenly a flash of blood red light enveloped the tank next to them. The whole front of the turret seemed to melt in a reddish mass of molten steel. As the eight men huddled inside the rescuing tank watched in horror, a blazing shape thrust itself out of the commander's hatch and jumped to the ground. Engulfed in flames, he rolled himself over and over in the sand trying to extinguish the flaming overalls he wore. A crewman, the driver, jumped free of the tank; the other two crew members did not emerge from the blazing steel hull. Then, with a fearsome roar, the tank exploded, flying fragments striking the commander and driver on the ground, killing them outright.

There was a sudden hush. Then Lieutenant Gadi's voice came over the radio. Did the commander's voice tremble? No one was sure. 'Prepare to move and follow me'. The seven remaining tanks left the killing ground, studded with dozens of Egyptian casualties, which lay all over the sand, mingled with the charred bodies of their comrades. Company 'C' drove on into the night and into the first light of dawn. Another day of battle was ahead, and for many it would be their last.

CHAPTER TWENTY-THREE

THE DRAMA AT CAMP NAFAKH

The Golan Heights are an escarpment rising to 800 metres above the Sea of Galilee and the Jordan Valley. They rise gradually from south to north, their peaks – created by volcanic activity – towering over the Rift Valley to the west and south. Mount Hermon, a multi-peak mountain, completely dominates the scene and on a clear day its snow-covered peaks can be seen all over northern Israel. A maze of ridges and lava-covered patterns cover most of the Golan area, making it impassable for most vehicles; even tanks have to manoeuvre carefully in some places to negotiate the steep slopes. Major roads and tracks are therefore an important factor in military action here.

On 6 October 1973 the Golan Heights were defended by a meagre Israeli force – just two small brigades of tanks and a battalion of infantry manning the borderline outposts. On the Syrian side, over three mechanised and two armoured divisions stood poised to attack.

They struck just after midday, preceded by a tremendous artillery barrage which took the Israelis completely by surprise, while scores of fighter-bombers attacked command posts and rear installations.

In the middle of the Golan stood Nafakh camp, the Israeli command and communications centre, located near an important crossroads. Brigadier General Rafael Eitan, a burly paratrooper known to every Israeli as 'Raful', was commanding the Golan sector. Raful was a legendary paratroop commander, one of the heroes of General Israel Tal's armoured division storming Rafa junction in 1967. A taciturn, somewhat gloomy character, he was one of the most courageous combat leaders in the Israeli Army. At noon Lieutenant Colonel Avigdor Kahalani, senior battalion commander of the crack 7th Armoured Brigade, had arrived at Nafakh for an order group meeting, together with other commanders who had assembled; they had just begun to listen to the lanky, 38-year-old brigade commander, Colonel Yanush Ben-Gal, when low-flying aircraft flew overhead at near zero level. The officers were surprised – it was Yom Kippur, the holiest day of the Jewish year; normally no flying was allowed on that day. But the riddle was cleared up within seconds when bombs and bullets began to rain down on the camp, sending officers and men running for cover. Vehicles exploded, buildings were engulfed in flames, the wounded shouted for help. It was a scene of utter chaos. Suddenly the tall figure of Ben-Gal emerged from one of the buildings and shouted to the men above the din: it was time to man the vehicles, switch on radios, and go to war! Kahalani rushed to his waiting radio jeep. The driver had already started the engine and switched on the radio. The jeep raced for the main gate, evading a burning lorry and, once out on the open road, Kahalani grabbed his microphone and ordered his battalion to move out. By now a terrific artillery barrage was whistling down onto the road. Shells were crashing down, and the jeep twisted and turned to avoid them in a horrifying parody of a slalom run.

Not far away, his battalion was already poised in perfect battle order, ready to move. The colonel quickly scrambled onto his tank and, sticking his combat map to the holder in front of him, gave the signal and led his battalion into battle. For the next 24 hours it would be fighting against horrendous odds in a desperate effort to stop the Syrian onslaught. It would be 7th Armoured Brigade's finest hour.

On the Syrian side, Major Abdullah Qablan was leading a battalion of T-55 tanks into battle. An immense wall of steel, they were grinding forward under cover of a barrage of shells which crept forward metre by metre, combing the ground with tons of steel. All around him the ground seemed to be exploding, terrifying volcanoes of earth and stones erupting as each shell struck. Qablan was filled with confidence by this tremendous show of force. The advancing juggernaut of which he was a part seemed to him to be totally invincible.

All over the front line similar phalanxes of Syrian armour were advancing into the Golan Heights. The Israelis, hugging their sandbagged trenches, were overwhelmed by the noise and dust; watching the steel monsters advancing right on to them, there seemed little they could do to stop them.

By mid-afternoon of the first day of what came to be known as the Yom Kippur War, the Israelis were in a serious crisis. Desperate efforts by the air force to stop the advance failed, as aircraft were being hit in the sky by air defence missiles before they could even get to the Syrian armour. In the north Kahalani's men were fighting the Syrian tanks trying to breach the anti-tank obstacles, while in the south Colonel Itzik Ben-Shoham, commander of the 188th Barak Brigade, was fighting a losing battle against vastly superior odds, as an entire Syrian division was breaking through the thin Israeli lines.

While Major Qablan's force came under heavy fire in front of the anti-tank barrier, his mineclearing and bridgelaying tanks being decimated by Kahalani's gunners poised on their firing ramps, the Syrian southern prong was racing through Ben-Shoham's tank crews, who were losing ground at an alarming rate. The main threat was that coming along the Tapline route right towards Raful Eitan's headquarters at Camp Nafakh. This route accompanied the world's longest oil pipeline, which starts its journey in Bahrein in the Persian Gulf and reaches Lebanon after nearly 3,000 kilometres. It was to become a tremendous battleground here on the Golan, but, strange as it might seem, the precious oil kept flowing silently through the underground pipes all the time the battle raged overhead!

As night fell, the situation seemed catastrophic. It seemed that nothing could stop the Syrians from getting as far as the Sea of Galilee, which would mean disaster for Israel.

It was then that a few resourceful young Israelis began what was to become a saga of courage and determination. At about 2120 Captain Zvika Greengold, commanding a makeshift company which he had hastily assembled at Nafakh camp earlier in the evening, spotted a solitary Syrian tank on the road, about four kilometres from the camp. He tapped his gunner on the shoulder to alert him; the gunner fired and the Syrian tank, by then only ten metres away, burst into flames. Zvika ordered his driver to back up fast to avoid the force of the explosion but his antennae was blown off by the blast and he lost communication with the rest of his tanks, so he jumped down, raced along the road, climbed into another tank, and drove on. Soon he spotted another column of Syrian tanks which drove along with headlights blazing, presenting a perfect target for his gunner, who immediately sent two quick shots into the leading Syrian tank. This company belonged to the 51st Independent Tank Brigade which was preceding the Syrian assault to exploit the breakthrough in the south. Greengold's tank was now alone

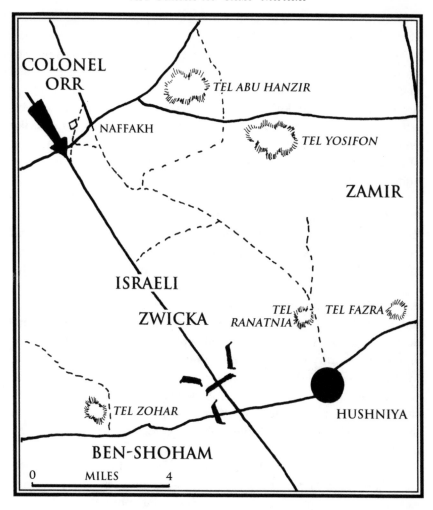

in the dark, the rest of the company somewhere behind. He pulled over behind a tiny hummock in hull-down position and peered into the darkness ahead[*].

Zvika did not have long to wait: soon the main body of Major Farouk Ismail's 452nd Battalion came into view, driving in perfect order, spaced out along the road as if on parade. The captain waited until the lead tank was only twenty metres away, and then opened fire, stopping the tank and thus stalling the entire column. The Syrians were bewildered – they had expected no opposition on that road. Some of them switched on searchlights, but this only made them better targets,

---

[*] For details see *Daring to Win,* by the same author.

and soon ten tanks were blazing away. The rest, including that of Major Ismail, turned tail and withdrew.

The rest of Zvika's tanks had now come up but, as one was manoeuvring into position, it was suddenly hit by a rocket propelled grenade, then another was hit. Some Syrian tank-killer teams had crept up undetected in the dark to fire their deadly weapons. Next to be hit was the captain's own tank. The gunner was injured, and Zvika dragged him clear, only to feel a searing pain as he pulled himself out of the turret. But the delay had convinced the Syrians to wait until daylight to resume their attack.

While Zvika Greengold's force was fighting, and rapidly losing, its battle on the Tapline Road, another drama was unfolding further to the east. Colonel Ben-Gal had kept back a small force of tanks as a kind of unofficial reserve, while Kahalani's tank crews were hotly engaging Major Qablan's battalion to the north. This was a company of Centurion tanks commanded by Captain Meir Zamir of the 82nd Tank Battalion, the senior unit of the crack 7th Armoured Brigade. Because of its radio code being 'Tiger', Zamir's force was called Tiger Force for identification purposes. Captain Zamir had deployed two of his tanks abreast one of the infantry held bunkers on the demarcation line, and the rest in well-chosen, hull-down positions to confront any infiltrating armour coming west. It was an excellent ambush position, and all he had to do was wait. It was now totally dark and Zamir ordered all his crews to shut down and wait in total silence for the enemy armour to come into range...

The Syrian commander leading the vanguard was totally oblivious of the waiting Israeli tanks, and they were advancing in a column, as if on a parade ground, along the road. Lieutenant Mayer, Zamir's deputy, was stationed ahead, about 2,000 metres in front, acting as look-out and in position to ward off the Syrians if they should try to turn around and escape the ambush. As the leading Syrian tanks approached, Mayer let them pass into the killing zone, remaining quiet, hull-down. Captain Zamir was known for his laid-back, relaxed approach, but he had nerves of steel when the occasion demanded – and today was just such an occasion. He let the Syrian tanks close in, keeping his men on a tight leash. The tank gunners, seeing the enemy tanks bulk alarmingly larger and larger in their sights, grew more and more tense, but the captain was adamant, disregarding all their pleas. The first Syrian tanks were now right on top of the ambush, their steel hulks looming like Behemoths in the dark, their exhausts throwing red sparks up into the night. Only when the tanks were within 300 metres range did the captain order his gunner to snap on the searchlight – and the bark of tank guns followed instantaneously, hammering into the hapless Syrian T-55s whose commanders and gunners were blinded by the glare. The Israeli gunners were superb marksmen; each round found its mark and, within seconds, the leading Syrian tanks were exploding, flames belching around them. Every Israeli gunner tracked his target individually, the well-drilled loaders ramming rounds into the breeches, panting with the effort as they manhandled the heavy shells at top speed. The turrets of the Centurions were filling with evil-smelling cordite fumes, but the crews were too busy to notice as they peered into the sights searching for enemy targets.

Some of the Syrians, recovering from their initial shock, were now returning fire, but Zamir had chosen his positions to perfection and the Syrians could not pinpoint their targets except for the fleeting seconds when the guns flashed, so all their shots went wide. The only target which did draw accurate fire was the searchlight, and Zamir ordered it shut down – there was sufficient light by now from the blazing hulks of the Syrian tanks.

The battle raged for only a short time, but 25 Syrian tanks were hit and in flames, while Zamir's force was intact. The Syrian survivors panicked and tried to turn round, only to crash into each other as they raced for cover from guns which they could not even see. In the pande-monium which followed, some did manage to retreat – only to drive right into Lieutenant Mayer's look-out position, where they were destroyed. The young Israeli captain and his crews had ambushed and totally destroyed an entire Syrian tank battalion, and entirely on their own, without any support.

Just before dawn on 7 October Colonel Tewfiq Jehani organised his 1st Tank Division to attack together with the infantry brigades which had broken through the Israeli lines. Jehani had a fresh division, equipped with the best tanks the Syrian army could field – brand new T-62s, mounting high velocity guns that could outshoot anything that the Israelis, even with their better gunnery technique, could field. The lead-ing battalion, commanded by Colonel Shafiq Fiyad, smashed into the Golan and raced for Hushniya camp, reaching the outer fence by 0900. Despite repeated efforts by Israeli fighter-bombers, the battalion lost none of its momentum, and now turned towards Nafakh. Its aim was to take that camp in a combined attack with the remainder of that same tank brigade which had engaged the Israeli stragglers during the night.

Colonel Ben-Shoham had spotted Fiyad's armoured column from his position on the edge of the escarpment, but he had with him only his command group and three tanks, a force which stood no chance against such a superior force. Reports were coming in, however, that Colonel Ori Orr's reserve brigade was on its way and would arrive at the front within an hour or so. Encouraged, Ben-Shoham decided to round up as many of his tanks as were still running and delay the enemy columns as best he could in an attempt to block them from reaching Nafakh camp and its nearby road junction.

Meanwhile, inside the camp, Raful Eitan had begun to organise a perimeter defence, rounding up anyone who could fight, and ordering Lieutenant Colonel Menachem Cooperman to take command. Cooperman, a staff officer and formerly a field commander in the crack Golani infantry brigade, was just the man for the job; he immediately began to scour the camp for possible fighters, handing out infantry weapons and bazookas.

The first brigade of Jehani's division reached the road to Nafakh at mid-morning, linking up with the exhausted men of Colonel Hassan Tourkmanni's badly mauled brigade. Ben-Shoham was aware of this new threat on his left flank, but there was little he could do with the tiny force he had left. Then suddenly a welcome sight came into view: two platoons of tanks led by Major Dan Pessach – the vanguard of Ori Orr's brigade. His left flank now covered, Ben-Shoham quickly briefed the reserve officer and the combined Israeli force went into action. Ten Syrian tanks were soon destroyed on their exposed flank by accurate gunfire, but they responded fast and several Israeli tanks were also hit. Colonel Ben-Shoham's forces were in a precarious position, dwindling fast while the Syrians continued to receive reinforcements all the time. But determinedly he stayed on the Nafakh road to stem the Syrian advance until Colonel Orr's reservists could reach the battleground.

Brigadier Eitan now received word that Nafakh was about to be attacked, and radioed Ben-Shoham to withdraw and form a last defence near the camp itself. The colonel complied, although he must have realised that the order would sap the last remaining strength from his command. Taking the lead, he raced his small force up the Tapline road to the besieged camp. Lieutenant Colonel David Yisraeli, Ben-Shoham's deputy, was in the second tank behind his leader. En route, empty of ammunition, they stopped to take some from a derelict truck which stood by the roadside; seconds later Yisraeli's tank came under fire from a Syrian T-62. With no ammunition yet loaded, the commander ordered the driver to charge the Syrian tank which stood only metres away and, coaxial machine gun firing, the Israeli tank smashed into the Syrian one, whose bewildered crew abandoned it and fled. But, in a tragic mishap, Ben-Shoham's gunner fired and set the abandoned tank on fire. Yisraeli's crew, shaken from the blast, could not back off in time. Their tank, too, exploded. No one bailed out. The colonel was dead.

Colonel Ben-Shoham watched in grim silence as his deputy died. Then he rallied and, at the head of his small column, continued to relay orders to form a last stand against the Syrian armoured brigade which was now pushing forward at full speed. After warning Eitan that he could not hold out much longer, Ben-Shoham switched frequencies to call in some last resort air support. Some fighter bombers came in almost immediately and managed to stall some of the Syrian tanks; but not for long: as the jets left, the Syrian tanks closed in once more on Ben-Shoham's pitiful force.

The colonel had now withdrawn to almost 300 metres from the camp fence. His tall figure could clearly be seen, standing erect in his turret, scanning the front with his binoculars. Suddenly some Syrian infantrymen appeared, running through a shallow ditch nearby. Ben-Shoham cut loose with his turret machine gun and sent them bowling over. But from the other side a Syrian tank approached and fired straight at the brigade commander's tank. Colonel Ben-Shoham slumped back into his turret, killed outright. With him died his loyal operations officer, Major Benny Katzin, who had been at his commander's side from the start. The Centurion turned over in a ditch.

Now there was nothing left to stop the Syrian advance into Nafakh camp. Lieutenant Colonel Cooperman looked out at the oncoming tanks and prepared himself to die. But he decided to take with him as many of the enemy as he could – and set up some of his anti-tank weapons. As the first Syrian tank broke over the outer fence Cooperman fired his bazooka and knocked it out. Nearby a young officer who had never fired a bazooka before now shouldered the weapon and fired at another tank, but missed. Cooperman saw what had happened, ran over, took the weapon, rammed in another round and charged towards the Syrian tank, dodging bullets as he ran. The rocket streamed right into the driver's aperture, stopping the tank on the fence; the Syrian crewmen scrambled out in a hurry while the tank exploded.

Even the brigadier joined in the fray. Emerging from the command bunker he saw a Syrian tank approaching. Grabbing a bazooka from a bewildered cook, who had been given, but did not quite know what to do with it, Eitan fired and stopped the tank in its tracks. But now enemy tanks were looming up from all directions and, even though some were hit and many explosions were heard, all seemed lost when, suddenly, Colonel Ori Orr's reservists appeared coming from the Jordan Valley, a welcome sight with their brand new Centurions.

Deploying quickly into battle formation, Orr's tank crews surged forward and took on the Syrians, who reeled from the shock. Colonel Tewfiq Jehani was stunned; with Nafakh almost in his hands, he was now facing a massive onslaught from a fresh armoured brigade with tank crews raring to go into battle. Although in firm control of the two roads leading to the camp, he was now being outflanked and if he did not extricate himself quickly his proud formation would be decimated by the oncoming Israeli armour.

Nafakh camp was the scene of total confusion. Men rushed from one end to the other without knowing why, while new soldiers arrived out of nowhere, only to be swept up into the whirlpool of chaos. Captain Zvika Greengold arrived there, too. He had survived the desperate battle during the night against the Syrian armoured onslaught; now he raced his remaining Centurion through the camp fence, right into the turmoil. His tank was stopped, but the gunner continued to fire, sniping at the Syrian tanks as they came into view over the outer fence. Suddenly Greengold's driver stood up in his hatch, gazed at his commander wildly and, before he could be stopped, jumped out of the tank, rushed up to a nearby halftrack, and drove through the gate at top speed. Clearly the terror of the night had deranged him; he could no longer take the strain. Greengold dropped from his turret to the ground and strolled over to one of the platoon leaders of Colonel Orr's brigade, who was stunned by his appearance, wounded, covered in mud and dust, and staggering with fatigue from the many hours he had fought facing certain death. But Zvika was not finished yet! Commandeering a new tank, he went back into the fight, which was still far from over.

Another unit was now entering the battered camp. Major Yoni Netanyahu led two companies of his crack paratroopers in a convoy of halftracks into the wreckage of Nafakh. Their arrival was a welcome boost to the sagging morale of the survivors and they could not have arrived at a better time. The view which met their eyes was terrifying! Blackened Syrian and Israeli tanks were strewn around the camp, trucks and jeeps turned over in heaps, huts blown apart, the ground festooned with torn telephone cables and broken pipes. After conferring with one of the commanders on the spot, Yoni led his men to deploy in all round defence, to await the new Syrian attack which was expected any moment.

And soon the Syrians came again along the Tapline road, which was almost covered with smouldering wrecks. The enemy shelling began to crash relentlessly into the camp again, and Major Yoni rushed from foxhole to foxhole reassuring his men, who adored him. Since not many of the radios were still working, there was much confusion as to where the action really was, and the operations officer in charge ordered Yoni to send one of his jeeps along the Tapline road and see if he could pinpoint the Syrian advance. It was a suicide mission, and the men knew it, but two of them volunteered anyway, and drove the jeep out through a hole in the fence. In the bright moonlight, which illuminated the terrible carnage which had taken place along the battered road, the jeep soon came under withering fire from a column of Syrian tanks. The flash and roar of a tank gun – and the driver wrenched the vehicle virtually full circle, making a full turn on the narrow road, and zig-zagged back as fast as the jeep would take them, and made it back through the fence.

At first light three big Ilyushin troop-carrying helicopters skimmed low over a ridge to the north. The Israeli tank crews were on the alert and blazed away with their guns at the choppers which were sitting ducks against the rapid-firing, high-velocity guns, and soon two dipped over and crashed, spilling their loads of men. Yoni, rushing to his halftracks with some of his men, set off on the chase and was soon mopping up the survivors. Some of the Syrians, well-trained, courageous troops, took up the battle against Yoni's men, but they had come up against the best infantry that the Israelis had in the field and, after a sharp fight during which two of his men were killed, Yoni and his paratroops eliminated the Syrian commandos.

After this, the Syrian onslaught on Camp Nafakh seemed to peter out and, under a last heavy artillery barrage, Tewfiq Jehani's armour began to withdraw. Nafakh was saved; within hours more and more reserves started arriving, pushing the Syrians back towards the border line. An invigorated Israeli Air Force swooped in to strafe the withdrawing Syrian columns, wreaking havoc on the stragglers. Relief also came to the battered remnants of Colonel Kahalani's tank crews, who had fought a magnificent battle stemming the Syrian onslaught in the northern sector.

As the Syrians retreated in disorder, the Israelis reorganised and a massive counter attack brought them within artillery range of

Damascus. The Golan Heights were safe once more, but the battle-field was strewn with thousands of tanks and vehicles – grim reminders of the furious battles which had raged over four bloody days.

Captain Zvika Greengold was awarded the highest Israeli order for bravery for his part in this battle. The young kibbutz member had fought almost single handed for nearly 48 hours, having had six tanks shot out from under him, but survived, although badly wounded, by a sheer miracle.

Brigadier Raful Eitan later became Chief of Staff. Major Yoni Netanyahu was to gain world-wide fame as the saviour of Entebbe*, but sadly was killed during this daring rescue action.

---

* For details, see *Daring to Win*, by the same author.

INDEX